Manscapes:
An American Journey

Colin Henfrey

MANSCAPES:

An American Journey

ANDRE DEUTSCH

First published 1973 by
André Deutsch Limited
105 Great Russell Street London WCI

Copyright © 1973 by Colin Henfrey

Printed in Great Britain by
Ebenezer Baylis and Son Ltd
The Trinity Press, Worcester, and London

ISBN 0 233 96054 6

50 p

CONTENTS

NOTE

At one point, in writing this, I included an introductory note longer than the present one, to explain its origin and why it doesn't include this or that. ('How about someone in the Pentagon?' one person had commented.) But I think it's better left to explain, or fail to explain, itself. I'll only say that it began as a diary rather than a book, so it makes no pretence to be 'an account of the USA.' It's simply an experience of it – most of it shared with June, my wife, and sometimes we had friends with us – at particular places and times. (Such topical references as occur, mainly in the closing chapters, are to late 1968.) But I think I was guided even then – not just now as a rationalization of what is included here – by the premise that what seem to be the edges of a society aren't necessarily so. Especially in the USA, it all depends on where you look from, and maybe, how far ahead, which looking back in time can help with.

I'm still not sure what order to put 'The Men, the Women' in, so they needn't be read as they occur. The opposite order may be better; or together rather than at intervals. Or any of them at any point. Please yourself.

Amongst the many friendly people who enlightened, fed and sheltered us I should particularly thank those in the Harkness Foundation for their support and encouragement. They are blameless for the result, I should add.

C. H., LIVERPOOL, 1971

FROM AGEE

'All that each person is, and experiences, and shall ever experience, in body and mind, all these things are differing expressions of himself and of one root, and are identical: and not one of these things nor one of these persons is ever quite to be duplicated, nor replaced, nor has it ever quite had precedent, but each is a new and incommunicably tender life, wounded in every breath, and almost as hardly killed as easily wounded: sustaining, for a while, without defence, the enormous assaults of the universe. . . .

'If I could do it, I'd do no writing here at all. It would be photographs; the rest would be fragments of cloth, bits of cotton, lumps of earth, records of speech, pieces of wood and iron, phials of odors, plates of food and of excrement. Booksellers would consider it quite a novelty; critics would murmur "Yes, but is it art?" And I could trust a majority of you to use it as you would a parlor game.

'A piece of the body torn out by the roots might be more to the point.

'As it is, though, I'll do what little I can in writing. Only it will be very little.'

(From *Let Us Now Praise Famous Men*, a study of tenant farmers in Alabama in 1936, by James Agee and Walker Evans.)

'And it shall come to pass afterward that . . . your old men shall dream dreams, your young men shall see visions.'
(*Joel* 2:28)

CHAPTER 1

QUESTION:
Manhattan and Cornell

Manhattan Atlantis-like out of the sea (like a Pan-Am commercial, you'll say, but that's it, the first test in the USA, can it be sensed, can I sense it after the onslaught of the image and Europe's anti-Yankee clichés?), pearly toyland in dawnfire, steeples of sunlight and glass glitter, a galaxy fallen down in the darkness ejaculating its streamers of light, whorls pillars banners of light that blacken the nightbelly around. And realize: yes, it is, of men and stone, men thought it, made it, they were here, Ellis Island's immigrant faces of two and three generations ago, it was their grandchildren on the plane like no other nation returning home, heads popping up and pointing it all out to each other as if they'd never seen it before.

(Besides it was here in Manhattan, remember, that glance from the customs officer which was the very first to tell us with those particular new meanings that June is now black – though brown in fact – and I white: our brief Ellis Island in his eyes. He being black, careful, cheery. In a flash, just something like: know where you are from now on? Okay, learn to cool and forget it and good luck. 'Okay, have a nice visit, next please.' As in its way was said again from Harlem to Los Angeles, but this first time uniquely alerting, baptismal. Forget it.)

Movement is its essence, not height, the cabby's patter, the pizza-twirlers, the Coca-Cola galaxy, the cranes, cop cars, helicopters, not Europe's stylized wending down the dolphin tracks of the past but feel man in their making movements, new reaches for the mind to soar –

Soar or drown in, in the everlastingness and sheerness of its energy? And what's the link between them, those immigrant faces and today's? Or between the new dawn's contradictions after plate-glass novelty? The skyscrapers and tenements, super-coordination and chaos (a dog loose on Brooklyn Bridge and the morning traffic clots) Tiffany glitter and Bowery doorways (Dow Jones average up two points and the old man – old? – with the crunched up face darts out at the intersection dabs the windscreen with his rag, give us a quarter, no nor a glance, kicks the fender) jostling and loneness, slick-thighed Greenwich Village girls chrome surge and Harlemslow figures. How do all of these relate to that old Ellis Island vision recorded by the camera's eye of a new world within reach at last beyond Manhattan's arrival movement?

In Ithaca upstate New York, with its Ivy League Cornell, no answer. Few signs as yet of the break soon due with massive anti-war protests and blacks holding the students' union; just the antithesis to provoke it of Babbitt seemingly supreme and power unable to question itself ('Hello there, another good morning from your Cornell radio station and we've a lot of messages for you, big bargains at Montgomery Ward, a lecture by Professor Grunch on investment prospects in Peru and now a word from your Chevrolet dealer'), as if Utopia achieved has relegated Ellis Island's hopeful human tenderness to a fading photographic dream.

Silence on Stewart Avenue as soon as five-to-nine is gone; and silence on the campus by nine, where all the world's a questionnaire that binarises humanity in fifty yes/no items. Including us: culture shock, yes. So try again, the registration forms, the tests, the Ithaca Jaycees' Goodwill Trip introducing Ithaca, cost price to foreign students. Same again: A & P supermarket, plastic orange bowling alley, little speech on Education and the Free World Today and the delegation discreetly assigned to tell the lonely Indian student that Ithaca Doesn't Spit on its Sidewalks. 'Bye now, enjoy yourselves.'

Is it just to our European eyes, this lack of the uniqueness we expected, not least of Cornell, once a conscious breakaway from intellectual convention, a new university to express a new society? Seems just like a Feiffer cartoon: the sweat shirts with Cornell U, the professors like an officer corps, with their weekend flips to Peru to advise on poverty (one wears a poncho over his suit, pinned with a Phi Beta Kappa emblem), the eighty out of a hundred marks that take you to a Ph.D.. Cornell is better than better than best and the girls in the students' union wow but what do their banners say?

SERVE CORNELL
Enlist here for
Reserve Officer Training Corps

They do.

It must be a hoax. Yet on it goes, like *Catch-22*, please Professor Major Major, no, bang, dead, no Ph.D. When Ellen's been home for her brother's funeral, missing a week of the semester, Professor Major Major makes no comment as she explains. And fails her for not attending her courses. That's why she misses her fellowship. Even Momma's in on it. When we visit Kathy in the sanatorium just before exam week, it's full of students who've cracked at the strain. The 'phone by her door is going all evening, parents ringing up their kids. And time and again it's the same. 'Sure, Momma, I'll be there, I'll make ninety, that's a promise.' It's been like that for days, she says. Apparently they aren't ringing up to see how the kids are so much as to check that they'll do their exams.

Thing power: must all compete to be the thingest people, from hip to Phi Beta Kappa thing. Including those Peruvians, if Professor Major Major and the social sciences (which is why I'm here) are to be believed: not about being, but ought-to-and-will-be-the-ultimate-worldwide-modernized-thing by means of entrepreneurship and the Organization of American States. Even some of the black students (professors tell you with lowered voices how many we've got here now) still play at the black thing in the language you sometimes feel they've learnt on a hip language course, complete with admirers. Though we sense why. Because category brother we're thingy too, not she and I, notable for this and that respectively, but as a mixed couple thing (one brown, sorry black, one white, Guess Who's Coming to Cornell Tonight). Not that folks aren't nice about it, they're as nice as thing could be, why, as soon as we're introduced to Professor Major Minor he asks us about the problem in England. ('The problem'? Politics, we each assume, but: 'No, the race problem over there.') Then he invites us down to New York to attend his impending lecture; it's on inter-racial marriage, he explains. In fact baby we're the thingiest, we read novels, it gets us a reputation; after which some people among the more serious Ph.D. students do get a little funny about us. ('You must be majoring in literature,' Mrs Major Minor observes. 'No? So how did you get to read Dos Passos?')

Nor is this system of thing before self and self before man just a campus one; it's processed the outside world as well, such echoes of it as we catch. Ithaca certainly isn't that different, blank-faced little upstate town, Cornell its major industry, followed by the gun factory, Montgomery Ward, Woolworths, and Hollywood musical movie theatres stretching down to the railroad junction and grey shores of Lake Cayuga underneath Cayuga Heights, professorial suburbia with a preference for imitation Tudor (building concessions limited to investors of $30,000 and over). End of town is a mile or two of supermarkets and wrecking yards. And then old upstate farming country, moving in a mournful way: gorges with clattering waterfalls and slow-walking rivers with musical names, the only memento of the Indians who now live off social welfare and anthropologists' research in shacks on upstate reservations. Lonely farms foot the snow-line, bone-bare trees spill down the gullies. Yet for Cornell it might not be there, this continent criss-crossed by dreams.

The Wobblies might never have organized, the Okies might never have moved and newer protest is still sung low. Its only intimations come from our similarly schizoid friends – Mark's East Side childhood in a vanished tenement, Pat's descriptions of Mississippi during 1964, Saul's voice as he talks of nights camping in New England woods. And old Man Thomasson, our landlord and South Dakota sharecropper's son, with tales of his harvest days: 'Every summer we'd go working on that old style harvest combine, start down California way and work right up to Wyoming, Montana, and into Alberta, Canada, following that summer harvest. Oh boy, them Scandinavian meals, ham, eggs, and fresh cream and you lay down to sleep in the barn, nothin' like hay for a real sleep, I was young then of course.'

Ithaca's only hint of it, this man-and-continent's interweaving, is down by the railroad junction haunted with a one-time vision of the nearby Finger Lakes as the gateway to Canada. Now there's no passenger service even: only the battered freight cars of the New York Central line pelting through the naked landscape, the long bare corner bars where they're surprised to meet a student and the peeling wooden houses with their broken balconies. (One, with a lop-sided notice, D A V E ' S, is said to have been a favourite clip-joint with the passing freight car jumpers in the big railroad days. Closed now and mocking silent.) Only these echo a people, along with the nearby black section where even if Ithaca's best offer is to be campus janitor, there's at least a feeling of life, washing hung behind the fences, gardens visible, crowds at the bus stops, kids not cloistered, all their playground: some even say hello to strangers.

There's just one trace of it closer by, in the backyard below our window. An Italian-speaking family with a bronze-coloured Cadillac; got it just after we arrived and polished it worshipfully every day until the fender was bashed in. Life still revolves around her, sleek New World goddess revving up beside the garbage but always stuck in the backyard mud, tyres howling and engine roaring to screams of Neapolitan abuse. No curtains in the window; we see their little boy every evening doing his homework at the table and wonder what he makes of it, the campus life outside the door, and what it is he's thinking of as he looks up from his exercise book.

Spring: the land seems closer. Snow drifts narrow and farms reappear, maple leaves burst into green and finally the black swifts return, soaring scissor wings filling the sky with their exulting freedom of flight. Feel the land stirring again like a hibernating giant from California across to Maine as the pleasure steamers on the lake sound their first summer horns, muffled by the sleep of winter. Four months to travel, plus Chevrolet. Just savouring the names (Kansas City, Walla Walla) is an end to confinement. And saying goodbye is the first moment of what the big land's about, its movements, partings – Michael and Sylvia, see you in Israel, four or five years' time maybe; Max and Diane, Mexico City, in September; Saul and Judy in Boston; Pete and Ditas some time, somewhere.

Something past nine of a summer morning. Stewart Avenue duly deserted except for old man Thomasson taking in his empty trash cans. Down through sultry small town silence, black sector's brief vibration, kids play in a wooden cart, over rusty railroad tracks and the last of Ithaca is the old man who sweeps the leaves, always there, sweeping the leaves.

(And old man Thomasson's farewell after those mellow evenings together? Charged us twenty dollars for leaving a trunk in his empty attic, although we were still paying him rent – 'less than them storage companies,' he said.)

Road bowls up into the barescape.

Jacob Slotnik, 81

SLOTNIK, *Jacob, 81.* b. *Mogalov, Russia. Immigrated in his early twenties and has lived ever since in Worcester, small New England industrial town. Widower, with apartment in a slightly faded sector, maples and three-decker wooden houses. Runs a one-man tailor's shop. Problems, e.g. when steps are icy, but still goes to work each day.*

They say I'm stubborn. That's right – some days I tried staying home and I get crazy like a tiger, walking here, walking there, I didn't know what to do with myself. So I go back to work. That's the way I lived, you know—don't make no fortunes but I see the customers, talk to them, and I cover expenses, rent, electrical, gas bill, I'm satisfied – don't have to ask for anything.

(*Five feet tall, Yiddish accent like a parody of itself. Face a little moon-shaped; wears no mask, lighting up and fading and lighting with the emotions of what he's saying.*) I don't remember everything – some bits like it was yesterday – in Mogalov – hard for Jewish people – in the big cities the Cossacks, they kill a Jew and nobody worry – night time – had to be in the ghetto – gangs, *katzapes,* you know, the 'tough babies', they beat the Jews. They see anyone run, they beat him, nobody ever stop them, the government let them do all they want – Jewish children wasn't allowed to go to school – mainly my mother taught me – now it's better – no future then for a Jewish boy or girl – couldn't understand why people would do these things, you know, so cruel. I was a child.

(*Youngest in the family, father died when he was five. At twelve was an apprentice tailor.*) My mother was smart, she arranged for me to learn tailoring. Then it was pretty bad, you know, 1905,

1906, 1907 they had the pogroms – meetings against the government, in stables and cellars – I went to some – they send Cossacks, you know the Cossacks, the real babies, where they went was all blood – how they make that revolution I don't know, it's a miracle they did it, everywhere was spies and police – in Mogalov the Cossacks kill some Jewish people – just ride past and bang, or they chop them – it was terrible, terrible. People hide. Others leave.

(*1907, after mother's death, followed his elder brother and sister to the USA, leaving only one other sister, later died in nazi camp.*) I took the boat, immigrant boat, from Rotterdam. The *Statendam* – ten days to come over – a Saturday and we sat on deck and the weather so nice, I feel so free. Then on the third day – so bad, I got sick, I thought I was dying – food for pigs – mostly from Russia, from different cities, different states, most were young people running away. There was nothing for them in Russia – New York – strange – feel now we're free, but the first thing, they keep us in Ellis Island, wouldn't let us touch anything. It was like a jail, a cage – nobody had food, no money – some of the women and little children were going crazy, they were so hungry – only when the Jewish committees came to help us, then we had food, sandwiches – New York – I thought this is a crazy city, you know, everybody running – all running to make a dollar.

(*Two days later with his brother in Worcester. Never left again for more than a few weeks at a time. With a trade and a brother to advise him, was well off as immigrants went.*) First couple of years was hard, unemployment – I was still a greenhorn – still learning English, I learn it at night school – took a time, a couple of years, before I start to make a dollar. First I was helping my brother, painting. Then I find work in a shop, as a tailor. To find it in those days was hard, especially for the immigrants. Every day it was ships coming, ships loaded with immigrants, so the manufacturers had an advantage – three dollars a week to the girls, in the garment factories – just had to buy a loaf of bread and something else, a pickled herring, that's the way we all lived – slavery – no union – too many people – 'You wanna work, I pay you one dollar, no, next feller, you want it?' And the next feller has to take it because he's crazy, his children are hungry – 1910 the union started – New York, the Ladies' Garment Workers' Union – hard time – manufacturers had tough gangs to beat them up – like Russia, the beatings. Same with the Amalgamated, the Men's Clothing Workers' Union, the gangsters beat them – now the unions are strong.

(*Met future wife here in Worcester. Also an immigrant, from Lithuania, in the States since she was five, more schooling than him. In this and every other way the prop of his life. N.B. the starkness of its themes – survival, work, growing family. For a while lived with her parents in what might still have been a Jewish home Central/Eastern Europe, all Yiddish-speaking with big family gatherings for Jewish festivals. Not that particularly isolationist: Brown Street area an immigrant rather than ethnic community, Irish, French-Canadians, Jews. Got on well, common business of survival. If life relatively unvaried, largely for this reason: six-day week of ten/twelve hours a day, little time for anything outside the family. Things improving gradually, deposit for small house etc, but slow process. 1917: two small children, mortgage, tight-fisted employers still living in early immigrant days, banning union, refusing raises. He and others began to lose patience.*)

The war – employers were making big money – cost of living – wouldn't give us a raise. One feller cut his finger, so he stop to bind it up – the boss: 'You bums don't wanna work, you get the hell outa here.' And he fire the feller. So we strike – seven weeks – getting hungry, I tell you – so we quit. Me and I guess four or five others, we decide to go to New York for work – the boss there: 'Okay, forty dollars a week.' Here in Worcester was seventeen. I stay a whole season. But I was lonesome and you know she was lonesome, the family was here, I was there. So we came back, me and two of the other fellers. And we opened a store of our own, just four of us, on Chandler Street. Then the Depression – no more credit. And four together was a hard thing, you know, one say this, one say that. I think because of the way we began, all of us were immigrants, that was so hard for everybody, you could hardly help another – friends yes, but everybody was fighting, just fighting to keep alive. So it was hard to work together. We stayed friends but after a couple of years we break up. Since then, 1922, I had my own store, just me – hard work – eight every morning, work till six o'clock at night, six days – Sunday morning I used to go in and do the cutting, prepare everything –

the children grew up, they get good schooling – good times with this big family, we never could buy a machine, a car, but we didn't need such things – believe me, I had a wonderful life with her, we were married fifty-four years, never had an argument – used to bring up the children so nice – we were happy. I kept a yard, a little garden, I planted two pear trees and she used to can, one fall she canned sixty quarts of pears – the children help, we make it together, I used to love that kind of work. And grape-vines, I used to make jelly and grape juice. And sometimes a little wine, and chickens, I used to raise a few, I was a crazy feller then. You know in the old country we used to plant everything, flowers, everything. When I went to Israel on the tour, that's what I like, I was crazy to see it, the trees and how everything is growing, the oranges, I like it so much. That's why I kept the little garden –

the Jewish holidays – all the families – Passover, the bar-mitzvahs – dinner for the whole family – after our children marry, same thing, they used to bring their children, sometimes there was twenty-five, thirty people here together – nowadays they make a big show, caterers – those days it would just be a meal and a jigger of whiskey, pickled herrings – that way was good, made you feel joyful.

(*But ties weakened. Ethnic and neighbourhood ones as people got wealthier and moved away. Family ones with World War II; his brother to New York, one daughter to Tennessee, another to Washington, son to Boston. None of them orthodox Jews as he is, and visits rarer now and less festive. East Worcester changed too; old houses converted to apartments, transitory faces. Too settled, though, to opt for suburbia. And never had car.*)

The family's spread out and I'm alone here – don't do what we used to do. What it was and now are two different things – got to take it how it comes – my home, make a few dollars –

good children – what could I expect better? I don't complain – sometimes I see my son from Boston, he drives over or I take the bus. Or I go down to my daughter in Washington or Tennessee. Last summer I was there – and sometimes like Passover there's a little coming together – just sometimes I see them all, maybe a funeral or a wedding – fifteen grandchildren now and four great-grandchildren – don't see them so much, but they grow up all right, what more can you ask? One of my grandsons put his pictures in a gallery in New York, right away he sell fourteen – walks around with this long hair – and the girls, you know, with the skirt so short – they come in the store: 'Mr Slotnik, I want you to shorten it.' So I always say: 'You ask your Momma?' But they got their own way, that's right, we had our ways – four great-grandchildren now, this new one in Texas, he makes four, the baby boy, I'd love to see him. But Texas –

that's how my life is. Sometimes – lonesome in the house – during the week I don't mind, I go to the store. But Sunday – and now I can't work how I used to – arthritis, sometimes I can't keep the thimble there – but I can't stay home, you know, I get crazy. Lots of people, they get sixty-five, they give up – walk about like dead people – thank God I got a trade, I don't have to go to my children and ask them for a few dollars. That's lucky. And down in the store the customers come, we talk a little, this one comes and that one, I see people, the day goes by –

CHAPTER 2

DREAMS:
Upstate New York

Beyond Ithaca's lake-shore suburbia, farms ride the hills like ghosts, their buildings warped and flayed by the wind. Below, in the long open valleys, you sense that it's old Indian country: pebbled, shallow-flowing rivers wooded to the water's edge and once the surprised glance of a deer, as if it's unused to the sound of an engine. Houses grow further and further apart. Gusts of rain whip the fields that still carry the blankness of winter: a lone tractor scars the soil, gulls floating over it, the only visible signs of life. As soon as we stop its remoteness envelops us. Bird-song makes an unanswered enquiry that drowns in the languid emptiness. The slowly fading buzz of a truck deepens instead of relieving it. A feeling that almost always hits you on leaving a town in the USA, the all-engulfing space and freedom, the silence between the passing cars, the distance between the farms, the occasional houses so daunted by it that their land is stripped of trees as if to give them a grip on it, anchor them against its vastness. It's like the farewells, the fragility of farms and friendships subject to that same big limbo, a land on the move, uprooting, questing.

It's here in upstate New York that this fragility's acutest. Without the desert's austerity or a mellow past to underwrite it, its vacancy suggests an abandoned rather than a completed journey. Perhaps it's partly the name New York with its mocking note of glitter and verve: but mainly it's the land itself, the last stage of Appalachia running through the eastern hills with its gutted coalmines further south and fanning out here into the farms long beaten by a new world to the west. Already in the scant figures (peaked caps, green denims and hardly ever a jaunty movement) and the two awkward girls at the corner, slow walk and staring after us, even Ithaca seems like a Mecca, ten or twelve miles away and visited once or twice a year for a Christmas outing or family shopping. The farmyards re-echo this desultoriness; battered farmhouses stand half empty with only old people about and one end now a stable or stall to replace the decaying barn with its Dutch bonnet roof and silo, like a tottering lookout post from the battle that ended in this deadlock. And sometimes in complete defeat, leaving just the stone foundation and maybe a chimney breast pointing gauntly at the sky through a tangle of vegetation. (Reminders of that story of Max's: 'We were out walking once, it wasn't too far from Ithaca, and we came across this deserted farm – least there wasn't anyone there, but there were still some animals tied up, some dead and the others starving. We enquired at the next farm and it turned out that the tenant had quit without telling anyone – couldn't make it pay any more, had a pile of debts, so he just vanished.')

Others look on the edge of collapse, with thin-faced, even barefoot children staring surprisedly after us, their playground a weed-patch and the hulk of an abandoned car; and it's not the poverty of the South, no ambivalence, no idiom to it – just the drabness of having lost out. Many of the villages echo it, eight or ten houses, some boarded up, their derivative names accentuating the atmosphere of concluded briefness. In one of them, Venice, a little notice: 'First cabin built here by Samuel Wycott, 1825.' Third-class post office. No store. Just one or two middle-aged people in sight, slow-moving, as if they're unsure of their purpose. We stop for a coffee and in the diner the reactions are close and suspicious. Our accents check the subdued conversation; not that they identify them, but their strangeness alone is intrusive and almost suggests that we share the blame for this stagnation. New York City or London, it's all the same; both cities, far away, domineering. The worn, give-away-nothing faces seem to be willing us to leave. The landscape's only features with a look of permanence are the lonely roadside graveyards, fenced and conclusively full of headstones; and although the bigger towns have an air of remembered glory, there's still the same damp vacancy, as if

nothing's happened for generations, since they built the brownstone courthouse, say, or the wooden hotel, dark and warped,
with magnificent balconies ambling round its three floors and
its clock stopped at five to seven. The one by the green says
five past two; the one in the grocery ten fifteen. Carthage,
New York, at four o'clock in the afternoon.

It's only when the foot-hills of the Adirondack Mountains
appear that the landscape takes on a vitality, with the road
riding up at pine-topped bluffs between maple green and silver
birch. There's a self-sufficient neatness about it, the begininng
of New England in the first small lumber towns with their
pulp and paper mills crowding up to cold black rivers pitched
down from the sharp hills. Houses are trim clapboard white and
even the timber trucks aren't much newer than the ancient
Model A Fords maintained with spotless, shining pride in a
number of front yards. Another USA of the past, but here it's
one that seems fulfilled, a wry spectator of the present rather
than its sullen victim. The faces are more alive, still oldish, but
sharper, woodsmen, and self-possessed. This time in the diner
there's just easy curiosity – the proprietor asks where we're
from and heading and there's nobody who doesn't have his
own idea of the best route to take.

Alongside Lake Champlain, border between New York State
and Vermont, the towns look more prosperous: big-balconied
old houses must have watched the steamers pass when it was
the main route from the Hudson River to Canada. On the ferry
the teenager collecting the fares stops to chat, his accent near-
English, wide-eyed in surprise when he learns where we're from
and – in so far as we know – where we're heading. 'Gee, you got
room in that trunk? I'm about ready to move out.' For a
moment he looks serious, the sense of the big land in his eyes as
if he'd come straight off the boat with us. 'Furthest I ever been
was Boston and that was when I was just a kid. Won't be here
in a couple of years – maybe I'll catch up with you.' The boss
sees him talking and beckons him on, but when we reach the far
side he waves goodbye and raises a thumb as if he's joined us in
spirit at least.

Lights flick on in the farmhouses underneath the Green

Mountains. The man at a gas station recommends a nearby camp-ground beside the lake. The old caretaker looks surprised. 'Pretty early to be camping, didn't expect you tonight, no sir, take any spot you fancy.' Spells out our names painfully onto a registration card. Gets the address wrong, but shrugs. 'I'll jest put New York City, guess that'll be near enough. Never did get there meself.' Jagged face, old cloth cap and threadbare woollen overshirt. Fumbles with the receipting machine. 'Sorry, folks. I'm new here, see. Told me I was gettin too old for the saw-mill down there. Fifty years as a lumberman and I end up with this goddam machine. Bah.' He writes the receipt instead. 'Find any place that suits you now. Build up a fire, keep yourselves cosy.'

We go back and talk to him later on in his wooden shack lit by a single lamp. 'It's a lonely job, but I reckon I'm lucky to get her. Not much else I could do now, not around here, you know. My wife, she's gone a few years back and both the boys some place out west. One of them don't scarcely write and the other, I don't know where he is, never did write since he's gone. Three years back, that was. That's how it goes – my father, he was the same way. Come down from Canada when he was young feller and his folks never did know what come of him. That's how it is. Got to be thankful for what keeps you going.'

The polished blackness of the lake, soft enquiries of an owl and dawn filtering through the trees have a stillness and permanence, a rock-deep continuity; one that sets off the shifting lives, broken farms and migrant dreams, (Agee: '*All that each person is and experiences ... not ever quite to be duplicated ... each is a new and incommunicably tender life, wounded in every breath*') lives whose sound echoes through the cold night earth as the trucks go by ('*and almost as hardly killed as easily wounded: sustaining for a while, without defence, the enormous assaults of the universe*') so that those two faces, caretaker and teenager, become a single image of this first relinquished corner of the man-consuming land.

Down in Bristol, a bustling mill town, morning chimes are muffled discreetly by the leaves of the village green. They echo that New England feeling of being on the edge of things; and yet the town has a style of its own, at peace with itself, an independence shaped by its physical surroundings, mountains, woods and quick-running river. Pick-ups line the casual streets regardless of the parking meters; the farmers and lumbermen in the restaurant (maple syrup sold by the gallon) sit chatting all on Christian name terms, a world away from the hunched silence of most early morning diners. They don't seem in a hurry to leave. As we pay our breakfast bill of two dollars and some cents, the proprietor tells us to make it two dollars – the first time we recall that happening since we've been in the USA. The clatter of looms from the garment factory round the corner is unobtrusive. We catch the women workers' glances through the doorway as we pass and their talk and even snatches of song follow us down the shadowed sidewalk.

The narrow valley farms further east have the same intimation of lives interwoven with their setting, with the small, clear-running streams and quick stony slope of the hills. A single figure moves backwards and forwards, ploughing with a pair of work-horses, ascetic and changeless against the bare soil. There's a Welshness about it, tough and remote; not depressed, like upstate New York, but sinewy, just enough to live by and that carved out meticulously and clung to for generations. A lot of their ancestors came from Wales a couple of centuries ago, slate-workers in nearby Barre. Strange this, how people seem drawn to a familiar landscape. Either that or they're able to fashion it to their particular imagery, recreating the Welsh solitude of the hills behind St David's.

Unlike almost anywhere outside New England's boundaries, it feels like a pre-urban world, miniature now that we've got used to the scale of another USA. Quite viable, though: the old covered bridges over the streams still look in keeping with the rest and the farms cheerfully self-sufficient. Big old barns with double dovecotes are painted a friendly red and blue, rambling and individual, as if they've grown out of the soil; added to at odd points, they're joined up with the farmhouses to give access to the livestock during the deep New England winter. Even in the villages many houses are built in this style of casual continuity. Their harlequin sections run into each other as if the owners have preferred to add a new one for each generation, on top, at the side, at the back, rather than build a new home.

Across the slight Connecticut River, gateway to New Hampshire with none of the claims and epigrams that festoon most state lines, it's into lake and pine country, brittle fresh and growing wilder, unpeopled rather than deserted, a few spindly side roads and villages further and further apart. Savage line of the White Mountains pokes up at a racing sky; the river breaks up into long rapids. Clouds reach down the foot-hills and round the spruce tops and narrow road as it still twists upward. No more farms, just logging lines. Even here in its oldest and smallest corner, this continent can still feel untapped. Colebrooke, a mountain lumber town, has a breezy frontier look. Wooden false-fronted buildings in Main Street lend a swaggering Western note. Pistols and ammunition are for sale in what solemnly calls itself the Colebrooke Jewelry Store. Denim figures on the corners have a lean, sharp look, many of them French Canadians with their hair in heavy sideburns.

Round the corner from Main Street is a yard stacked with ancient ironwork; behind it a shed with a faded notice, HENRY HUGHES – HORSESHOEING – JOBBING. An immense figure stands in the doorway, king of a world of old truck bodies, winches and horseshoes on the wall. He watches us. 'Sure, go right ahead, take a picture.' Two less conspicuous figures behind him fade away into the shed. 'Where you folks from, anyways? England – Jeez.' Pushes his cap right back and replaces it contentedly, as if everything's all right with the world but a novelty like ourselves requires some gesture of recognition. 'Guess you must be pretty thirsty, seein you've come right from England – come on in, take a drink.'

He leads us into the dark shed where the other two men, near identical, are sitting silently in the shadows. A bottle of vodka on the work bench and a single paper cup. A sudden touch of big boyish shyness on the part of Henry Hughes. 'I guess you'll have to use the bottle, I been using that cup meself.' He's surprised when we don't mind sharing it. 'Well, some folks, y'know, city folks, they wouldn't like it.' Sits us down on the wooden

bench and waves a hand at the other two and an old man with
a grizzled face who's seated himself on the scrap outside. 'Don't
you worry about them fellers – they're kind of quiet, lumber-
men, takes around ten, fifteen years before they says anythin'
to you. Don't get much to talk about in them logging lines,
right grandpa?' The old man ignores him, though the other two
laugh in assent, courtiers in Henry Hughes's domain. 'I was up
there a little time meself but I didn't fancy it, guess I like to
talk too much,' and he gets up and goes back to the doorway
to survey the world outside, as if loath to miss a passing detail.
'Mind you, it's the same down in Boston, I was workin down
there for a time, but city folks' – shakes his head – 'Jeez, did
I hate that place – I was living in this apartment, never even
got a "hi" from the folks next door till the day I was leaving.
That's why I like it up here – good folks. Take their time, but
they're friendly.'

A girl goes by at the end of the lane. He waves at her. 'Hi.
Janie, you want it today?'

The answer comes back cool and cheery. 'Not today, thanks,
Henry.'

He grins and pushes his cap back, pleased at this little
repartee, a part of the world's revolving round him. 'Knew
her since she was a kid, she never did tell me yes yet. Well, if
you can't joke a little – Jeez, I been joking for fifty years and
it don't do a feller no harm. Take another' – he opens a fresh
bottle of vodka, pitching the empty into the shadows.

One of the pair at the back grins. 'That's Henry.' Slurred,
clipped speech. Henry turns round 'You talking already?
That's mighty chatty for lumber-men.' Turns to us. 'You might
be here a couple more years and that's the longest speech you'd
hear from em. Twins, them two. No end of trouble. One of em
borrows a buck off you, next day you ask for it back and he
tells you: Hell no, that was my brother! Rebounds on em,
though. Jim here, he was drunk on the streets just a couple of
days back' – Jim grins sheepishly, but obviously flattered at
Henry's attention – 'so they throw him into gaol. Then the
officer's back on the street and hell – he sees Jim again, standing right on the same spot. Arrests him again. Hollered his

head off. Weren't until the next morning they found out it really
was Jerry. Cold sober he was, first time ever.' He laughs
his big belly-laugh.

The old man sitting outside mumbles quietly to himself.
Keeps his face turned away shyly when we ask him what does.
'I take care of horses – waiting for Dupont right now, he's the
feller I'm working for.' But he slowly warms up and concedes
a smile. 'My folks, they come from England – some of em, anyways. England, Ireland, France too. My mother, she was a real
lady, come right from England to Canada.' He jumps at the
cigarette I offer and knocks back a drink in a hungry gulp.

'You have any folks over here?' He spits. 'Nope.' And goes
back to his silence. Henry watches him, amused. 'Stubborn old
bastard, he is, worse than them two in there – old lumber-men,
they're all the same.'

A little boy comes round the corner, tearful, his scooter
broken. Henry fixes it in a flash and watches, pleased, as he
pedals off. Another figure passes by, a young man wearing a
suit. Henry: 'Hi, little girl.' Laughs. 'He was a pretty nice kid,
wild like the rest of em. But you wouldn't know him now,
works in the city, down in Concord, just comes back for weekends and he don't like to talk no more. Used to be in and out
of here – well, that's the city for you. I get city folks stops here
sometimes, they come pokin around in here and offer me crazy
city prices for things I've got lying around. But I don't let em
have em. Hell – if they're worth that to them, they're worth it
to me. I just like to have em around.'

'Do you get much work here still?'

Tilts his head. 'I get enough. Enough to run my own place and
keep myself from gettin thirsty. Mind you, it's different work.
When I was a young feller it was mostly shoein horses – but
now there's only one old feller still runs a buggy, up in the
valley. Can't see a goddam thing, but he still comes in here
every day, never missed a day yet and the traffic has to stop
for him. Now it's mostly trucks and tractors, but even that's
not much work. This could've been a different place – but it's
pretty Yankee, the city fathers didn't want a mill town and
they're still the bosses here. Yes sir, old times this little town

was real Yankee. Them French Canadians, lumber-men, the
bosses used to treat em like nothin, worse than they treat the
blackies down South. Still, it's different now, things has changed,
there's pretty fine folks livin here. I wouldn't go no place else.'
    The old man gets up and shuffles off, followed by the other
two as Henry closes his workshop door. He shakes his head.
'Lumber-men – good folks, but slow talkers. I sure do love some
talkin'. So long now, take care of yourselves.'
    Back on Main Street half an hour later Jim and Jerry are on
the corner, rocking gently on their heels, with a back-slap and a
loud greeting from almost everyone who goes by. They beckon
to us. Jim is less bashful this time: 'Just headin back to the
cabin,' he says, as if strangers involve some apology for in-
activity, however obviously untrue. 'Like to give us your
address? Never did meet folks from England.' When he writes
theirs down in return, it's slowly and painfully, in a barely
literate hand. And an hour later they're still there and wave as
we drive out of town.
    Southward through the mountains rock pinnacles steeple
down in an old Norse saga landscape: crystal lakes, brisk rivers
and the silvery bell-like song of some bird, an invisible northern
sprite, that follows us from dawn to dusk through the narrow
lumber towns, shingle roofs and belching mills, spruce, birch
and black-watered rivers, star-like flowers on the slopes,
Mount Washington with mist and sun bowling over its gaunt
shoulders, until slowly the pine stands recede. As the White
Mountains level out, delicate wooden spires appear through the
lighter summer green. The magic of the North has vanished in
this older, more mellow New England, but the faces are still
shrewd and independent. Greetings are polite and brief and
few advertisements in sight, as if local minds are unalterable;
just the odd hand-written notice for maple fudge or maple
syrup posted casually on a gate.
    It's the handful of early out-of-state tourists who highlight
this law-to-themselves flavour of the New Englanders around
them. They're the only people in the diners and tourist sites
who give us that standard unflickering stare (charge: deviation
– verdict: guilty) which is one of the national hazards of mis-

cegenation, beardedness or, perhaps most of all, just being un-placeable. Once, a cigar-chomping man from Ohio, according to his licence plate, points us out to his blonde wife, who points us out to their four blonde children. Whereupon the smallest – each has a little camera – raises his viewfinder towards us. Apparently he took her to mean that we're another curiosity for the folks back home to see; but she slaps his hand hurriedly, so that he howls in bewilderment. More chastisement, until they abandon the view below and retreat to the family Pontiac. It's surrealistic at first, this naked statement from total strangers, so far from your sidelong English glances, as if they're formally defying you to question their right to question you; you feel you've made a strange mistake, dream-type, like for-getting your clothes, and want to wake up to escape, but can't. A common enough experience, but absent from the past few days, as if New England's still further removed from these other Americans than from us.

In other ways the intonations of the phrase 'New England' are clearer. A summer evening's tenderness in silent Canterbury Village. A slim white clapboard church presides, its neatness echoed by the turf and the town hall next to it, 1785 above the ascetic frame doorway. The neighbouring house is marked 'town clerk'; chairs on its lawn have the look of still longer evenings. Old fence leans at an angle under the heavy horse-chestnut blossom, the gravestones behind it nameless with time, A mysterious notice points up a lane: 'Shaker Village, 2 miles'. Town meetings and astringent minds, Thoreau's pastoralism and Robert Frost's vision in a world where the state legislature still has a member for every community, from Concord, 30,000 people, to Canterbury, less than a hundred. First and maybe the truest in the long chain of myths that compose the idea of the USA. Yet it's no longer American: a bystander, watching new myths unfold. And not a little sceptically.

It's a week now since Memorial Day, but the village flag is being lowered in front of Canterbury's combination gas station, store and post office. Son takes care of the groceries while father looks after the gas and mail, he tells us, as he fills our tank. There's a self-assurance in his informality: a modest version of Henry Hughes's immunity to the vanities of the wider world. 'We don't get many folks around here filling a big tank these days – mostly a dollar's worth a time in the old pick-ups. Burn a good bit of oil, mind you, the old fellers round here.'

We ask him about the signpost to 'Shaker Village'. 'That's dying out now, you heard about it? Folks up there had their own religion, special services, shaking and trembling. Kind of communal living they had, quite a big thing it was one time. But they didn't see fit to marry, I guess that's why they started dwindling. There's only a few of them left, the real Shakers. You could go up there and take a good look. Nice little museum they've got.'

The evening sun drops splinters of light on the overgrown road, hardly more than a lane. Another cluster of clapboard white on a knoll overlooking a gentle slope; the buildings are all in colonial style, tall façades and elegant shutters. A long maple avenue leads up to the main house. We ring the bell, slightly ashamed of its intrusion on the calm. A tiny old lady appears, pink dress down to her ankles, and a delicate white bonnet above her startlingly lively eyes. 'You should have been here sooner. You see, we have to be on our own now. Alone with our thoughts. Peace is so rare' – she smiles demurely as if to soften this mild rebuke – 'we have to get what we can. But if you come along in the morning you can see our community and some of the things we Shakers have made since we came here in 1792. I'll tell you what we can do' – she retreats and returns with a couple of booklets – 'you take these away and read them before you come back tomorrow, they tell you all about the Shakers. Imagine – at one time there were four hundred people living here.'

She looks across at the maples and the blue fields beyond them. 'Those trees – you know how they came to be there? Well, the Shaker community used to adopt a lot of children and we felt it would help them, make them feel more secure, if they each had something of their own. So each child used to plant a maple until they had a whole avenue of them. Every child knew his tree and watched it grow up beside the others.

I always like to think of that. It's a very different life from the
one you young folks have out there. But it's wonderful. I came
here when I was eighteen and if I could live it over again I
wouldn't change one day of it.'

Even dusk is green here: the rest of the world might not exist.
Though it isn't far away. In the nearby State Park the solitude
of previous camp grounds gives way to a weekend exodus from
the neighbouring towns. Radios blare and family trailers jostle
for a parking spot. Our neighbours sit in a solemn circle round
a portable television. The chipmunks join them. (We wonder
what they do in the winter when they're without Perry Mason,
Thoreau's heir to the landscaped woods with their hot and
cold water and flush toilets.)

Back at Shaker Village next morning another bonneted old lady
is working industriously in the garden: half an hour, she tells us
firmly, then you can come right in. The tall maples drop welcome shadows: the honey-warm scent and hum of summer,
the song of a bird in flight overhead and old stone walls bound-
ing the fields that slope down to the soft grey valley. Its
intimacy is as deep as Vermont's, that long intertwining of
landscape and man, but mellower here. And still as a pool.
Perhaps because of the contrast with the world so close to it,
it's hard to imagine a deeper stillness.

Yet the Shakers' story is a very American one, expressing
something much more central than the apparent exoticism of a
vanishing mystical sect. It can be surprising when Americans
suggest that their past is less pervasive than Europe's. Often its
presence is more intense, certainly more tangible, partly because
it's closer in time, but also because its materials are different.
Human rather than political; in place of Europe's monarchies a
flood of raw humanity, epic in a bigger way, less coherent but
more vital, a chaos of themes and variations recurring in the
still-raging storm of creating a self without precedent or definable end. Life choices and symbols renewing themselves at every
turn – Yiddish accent in father and American accent in son;
the political boss, from Irish Curley to Clayton Powell, answers
to Horatio Alger; the Pennsylvania Amish with bushy beards,

2

black-rimmed hats and nasal German dialect asserting the
integrity of their medieval virtues; the layout of modern Midwestern towns, reflecting their birth as railroad halts; Holy
Roller sermons which echo the Kentucky Revival in the latter
day nativism of the oil kings who finance them; Mexican
migrant workers as the new Ellis Islanders; trailer living like
the movement of the old covered wagons. Even the Kafkaesque
experience of leaving any large city through a circus of coloured
lights, price wars and plastic façades can seem like just another
answer to that old, primal search for an unprecedented lifescape
– as if some breakaway Pilgrim father might have put his hair
up and designed Los Angeles. A flotsam of movements, emotions
and myths with a texture as different from Europe's as Kipling's
East is from West. And the Shakers are part of it, a moment in
the perpetual theme of Utopia in a new land, alive as ever still
in the Movement. Speck on a tide of world-building.

A group of French heretics formed in the seventeenth century,
they fled to England and were there caught up in the tide of
evangelistic fervour produced by the poverty of the industrial
revolution. Visions in Manchester, accompanied by shaking
and marching, 'swiftly passing and re-passing one another like
clouds shaken by a mighty wind', as they themselves described
it. One of them, 'Mother' Annie Lee, had worked in the cotton
mills since childhood. Became their leader, was imprisoned and
then, in 1774, she and her followers sailed to a new world and
freedom. Their cut-price boat from Liverpool nearly sank
several times and the Captain threatened to cast them adrift
for blaming his ungodliness. But after three months, they
reached New York; upriver to Albany, where they started
evangelizing, and within fifteen years there were a dozen
Shaker communities scattered throughout New England. Their
philosophy was based on the visions of Mother Anne: sexual
equality, celibacy, joint ownership. They weren't just visionary
ascetics. Pioneer to the core, they also stressed self-sufficiency
and invention, becoming famous for the products that give
them their livelihood, from the first washing machine to herbal
medicines and seed. Their ideal was the whole man, and their
most famous theologian was also a silversmith, botanist and

cabinet maker. And their lives had a light side. Toys, picture-
books and candies featured in their school budgets; plays, pop-
corn parties and sleigh rides. Their broad view of life was a
liberal communism come true. At their peak, their eighteen
communities had some 6,000 members, from Maine to Kentucky
and Ohio. But given their American setting, they embodied the
USA's contradictions. Aspiring to permanence, they were born
in a spirit of restlessness, alive to the call of new myths; essentially creative, they also enforced celibacy. The first blow was
the Civil War, when their pacifism aroused hostility from both
sides. Several communities were destroyed and during the boom
period that followed, with the West and the big cities calling,
the young people drifted away. New England's whole story
writ small, less ruthless and smaller scale than the bigger
USA's, but conceived and destroyed by the same quest. Today
there are two communities left; Shaker Village and Sabbath
Day Lake, up in Maine. Each with a handful of followers, all
over seventy.

Half an hour later, on the dot, the little old lady at work in
the garden beckons us into the Shaker shop. Lavender bags,
greeting cards and pamphlets on Shaker life; they still follow
the principle of self-sufficiency, she explains. She introduces us
to Mr Thompson, their curator and handy-man, lean, bright
eyes and hollow cheeks, must be in his early forties.

He asks our names – his is Bud, he says, as he takes us to the
museum. We're the only visitors, so we have him to ourselves;
friendly and extroverted, he nevertheless gives an impression
of being strangely involved with it all. 'The fields are all Shaker
property. They were pretty prosperous once, I guess their
frugality did that for them. See the barn over there?' Points
to the farmyard at the back. 'They used to keep a prize herd
in there, Guernseys, over a hundred head, and about twenty
yoke of oxen. They still own around nine hundred acres. Must
have been quite a sight when they worked it – they had songs
for each task, planting, scything, and all that. Sang them in
time to their movements. The old ladies still remember them.
That's what brought me here in a way.'

Perhaps he's sensed our curiosity at his obvious warmth for

the place. 'I was working as a folk-singer, tramping around after
local songs. Theirs really interested me. And there was something about this place – so when they told me they needed
someone, I reckoned I'd stay around a while. I've been here
seven, eight years now. This building, it's now the museum, but
it used to be the meeting house where they held their services.'

Inside, he points out a disc in the floor which marks the spot
where they testified and began the shaking and dancing that
was the heart of their way of life. They've since given it up, he
adds, they've all grown too frail for it. We can see two of them
through the window now, in their bonnets and ankle-length
dresses, walking up and down the pathway enjoying the colourful flowerbeds. Hard to imagine them possessed with whatever
visions they were that only this new world allowed them to
enjoy and share in peace; the little round marker stares up in
blank rejection of any attempt to gauge what they really
experienced here.

Bud's voice breaks in. 'These things in here, they made them
themselves and even invented half of them'. Points to a neat
wooden contraption. 'That's the first steam-driven washing
machine, won them a gold medal in the Philadelphia exhibition
in the 1870's. Dried milk, flat brooms, they were the first people
to make them. Not to mention dozens of medicines and their
Shaker furniture. Ironic, though – their inventions were divine
revelations, so they refused to take out patents. Then outsiders
copied them and turned around and served injunctions to stop
the Shakers producing them. Just wasn't their world, I guess.'

Portraits of Shaker elders, benign faces and high collars.
Phials of medicine and old dresses; but unlike the dour black
Amish serge, these are full of faded colours. Bud nods when
we comment on it. 'That's what I like about them – they're
never pious. Even the old ladies here, they still have a big sense
of fun, they all like to enjoy things. They tell you quite frankly,
that's why they're Shakers. And it's why they're against
specializing. They feel people should have a taste of everything
life has to offer. They're not really so other-worldly. See this
paving stone? That's typical – after they'd been here a while
they found that the rain was eroding their gravestones, as they

were made of soapstone. So they just gave them up. They didn't want individual memorials, their real aims were communal and concerned with here and now. So they took up the gravestones and used them for paving. They put up a monument instead with just "The Shakers" written on it.'

Back outside in the sunlight, he points out the three-storey building where they lived together when they numbered several hundred. No servants: the women cooked in turns and worked at looms on the bottom floor while the men were in the fields. It's still used as a dining-place for the half-dozen survivors. It must be strange, living on among these stark reminders of their Utopia's decline; but there's no decay about it, no admission of defeat. All the buildings are well kept up, flowerbeds tended and hedges trimmed.

Bud suggests a cup of coffee. 'There's something at my place might interest you – the drawings they did during their trances.' He ushers us into a small room beside the museum, sparsely furnished with a simple wooden table and high-backed Shaker chairs. Its chaste atmosphere matches its occupant's solitary, ascetic exterior.

He delves in a cupboard. 'Here they are, photocopies. Funny but they're all done by women. The men weren't so prone to trances.'

They're a bit like William Blake illustrations, though more abstruse. Pen and ink drawings full of Rosicrucian-like symbols, some of them identifiable, the Serpent, the Tree of Life, steps, altars, musical instruments, the sun and the moon, geometrical figures, numbers, indecipherable inscriptions. Visionary comments on future life in the USA? They would hardly look out of place in a museum of modern art. But apparently no interpretation was left by the women who drew them.

Bud tells us more about himself and how he came here, confirming the impression that the Shakers aren't so remote from the present. He left school at an early age, though his family weren't badly off; married young and soon divorced. Uncertain of what he wanted, career prospects left him cold. So he took to the road as a folk-singer until several years later he reached Shaker Village. 'I've no idea where I'll go next, though I'll have

38

to be moving soon. Guess I've stayed here out of some feeling that this might have been the life for me. Apart from the celibacy, that is. But now' – he shrugs – 'I've tried to involve people in modern Utopian experiments, but I guess they're just too busy to debate the way they live.'

A bell rings. 'That's their lunchtime. I have to go over and give them a hand.' We exchange addresses. Then he hurries across the road to escort the old lady we talked to last night. We'd thought of asking her more about her long life in the village; but now, in this stillness of dream-like figures moving through the bright sunlight towards the large community building, the idea seems intrusive.

Five miles away, Route 95, Massachussetts Turnpike to Boston: wheels flay the burning asphalt, seventy, eighty, eighty-five, Pontiac, Chevrolet, passing and re-passing at ninety. This year's model makes the pace.

Oliver Macaulay, 63

MACAULAY, *Oliver, 63 (Oliver Wendell Holmes Macaulay when the occasion calls for it): b. Kentucky, share-cropper's son, now a hilltop farmer ('I gone up in the world'), upstate New York. Generous paunch and belly-laugh, braces patched with bailing twine. Works a hundred wind-smacked acres (sixteen cows, chickens, old tractor), helped by wife Nora and son Dean; other four children have left the land.*

Good set of farms up here once, she was quite a neighbourhood – all gone – couldn't keep up with the costs – down in the valley she's good bottom land, some's got a thousand acres. Up here aint noth'n but rocks – folks reckon we're stubborn staying – fact is we can't afford noth'n else – only thing is to leave the land like the rest of em – I won't do it – bailiff's gotta come for us first.

(*A stock joke down in the valley and the prosperous market town to which their neighbours have retired, they're referred to as 'Ma and Pa Kettle' and legendary for their improvidence. But maybe there's some envy in this of their lone tenacity. They have their own way of seeing things.*) In Kentucky it was corn and cotton mostly, little patch down in a holler – six boys and two girls – got along all right. Till the Depression – cotton price fell, hot summers too – remember Nora, 1930? Corn was drying on the stalk and rats was lying down dead in the porch. And dead still. Just crickets buzzin. And seed-pods poppin – too many of us – couldn't make it no more – our first little boy was born. So we quit – folks was headin out West, but that was a pretty good ways for us, all we had was twenty dollars – friend of ours was coming up here – just had to go where the ride was going, right up here in the back of his pick-up – wasn't much better – folks on the streets, no work – no place to go – hungry – baby too, Nora's milk dried right up on her, wasn't getting enough to eat – met this lady, Mrs Rogers – big old house down in the valley – seen us standing in the street and took me on as hired man, only twenty dollars a week but that was pretty good right then – kept us from starvin.

(*After three years with Mrs Rogers, they managed to strike out on their own, with the down payment on their farm with its sixty or seventy acres of pasture. Good days, especially with the New Deal: paid off the farm and bought another fifty acres. A family concern: milking their twenty odd cows before school and taking their eggs and vegetables and home-baked bread to the local market. Tractor, pick-up, milking equipment. His spare Kentucky figure vanished, Oliver Macaulay admits, though Mrs Macaulay has kept hers, pale and narrow; Dean's like his father, thick-set and ruddy-faced.*)

Them days, see, the living was good – pretty nice off a hundred acres – farm food's the best you can get, you wouldn't get no better food in that White House – still up and down, mind, winter months we'd sometimes be wonderin where the next few dollars was coming from – downtown they'd understand, we were all good friends, pay when you can – up here folks was the same way – six or eight farms right along this track, and we were all pretty good friends. Grange, the farmers' association, we'd be down there every week, talks, fancy dinners, hardly missed a meeting in years. Same thing around harvest time. Folks'd all work together and the ladies'd cook the dinners – Nora's cooking was the best on the hill. Filled me out, see, I was a skinny young feller once but a farm life fills you out. Like Dean there. Other kids is the same, all got a pretty good figure on em. And there was plenty of neighbourin, even winters – wind gets her teeth in the hills, but we'd still have pretty good neighbourin – git out together and shift that snow – and tobogganin – boys'd go rippin down that hill and end up pretty near in town. Good set of kids – folks could raise a big family, see, raisin up here was pretty easy.

(*For a while. Then things tightened up again, an ironic backlash*

from the Midwest's overproduction – slashed profit margins,
allotment laws, wheat on only a tenth of your land. The big farmer
could take it all, but the small man was out of the race.)

Take production credit – supposed to help the farmer, but the
little guy can't get her – only the big guy wins, see, the feller
who can keep on growing – prices don't change, expenses go up
repaired the tractor – six dollars an hour – feller that does it
only gets two, it's the boss that gets it, all them fellers does is
rob. They don't want to fix her, see, reckon on makin you trade
her in – veterinary service, she's the same – old vet, Doc Brown,
he'd really look after you – small guy or big guy, he'd come
running just the same – died – last month we needed a vet –
sent a young feller – wouldn't even get down to look at the cow,
he was afraid he'd dirty his knees – bill for fifteen dollars –
wasn't here for half an hour – folks aint the same – all they
wants is to get – don't want to know you.

(*This new USA screened the death that the smaller one was*
dying behind it. At the new canning factory in town, farmers'
children could double the earnings offered by a family farm. Their
other two sons went there to work; one went on to the city, the other
out West. Both girls are married, one still in town, the other in
Ohio. Only Dean remained. The same with all their neighbours;
the debts, the part-time factory work and then another silent farm.
Only the Macaulays hung on. And certainly the others, with their
modest suburban homes, look better off for leaving the land.)

Aint the same, though, that's the truth. Aint no more
neighbourin now – meet a feller in the street, could be you'd
know him pretty well, and he'll just say how d'you do and keep
right on walkin by – boss is waitin for em, see – some of em's
janitors down at the college, younger fellers is at the factory.
Dean, he's working days there now – couldn't pay them bills –
makes her pretty hard – out all hours and we don't take
Sundays off no more – they think we're crazy stayin up here –
most of em's got like city folks – think they're smart. Tell you
somethin – what's so smart about city folks? Them folks is
runnin round so fast they don't even know their tit from their
tail – aint no life – workin for another feller – think they're
smart, see, with them colour televisions. But I bet they aint

got time to watch them. They're too busy thinkin of how to pay her off, wonderin where to git the money so's they can buy a better one. Call that smart?

Sure, I guess it's lonely up here compared to what it used to be – don't get folks passin by now, we hear more planes than automobiles. But it don't bother us too much – day I set my feet on this farm I said Nora, we're stoppin right here – only them bailiffs'll git us out – it don't trouble us. Just winter times – snow blows up – can't shift her alone – and sometimes, yep, she's quiet up here. Summer nights, workin late, we can hear them big new milk trucks roarin down that thruway there. Bringing the milk clear from Wisconsin, from the big concerns out there, rightaways down to New York City. Hear em in my sleep sometimes. But even them big trucks won't move us, not if they come right in at that door. Long as Dean's earning cash, long as I can keep on workin.

Know what they call us? Ma and Pa Kettle. Well, that's a name – and them folks aint got no names no more, you wouldn't know em one from another. Say what they like, we're stoppin here. Right, Nora?

CHAPTER 3

ARRIVALS:
Boston

Dusk comes slowly to Brookline Hill as we sit with Saul and Judy in the porch of her parents' home, Saul describing his Boston boyhood. Already in the little we've seen here the difference from New York is immediate. There's none of that intensity, with its harshness and perpetual motion. Boston's pace is more discreet. Real estate values haven't yet wholly standardized the city's skyline and old countries and ancestries are very much in evidence. Accents, conversations and styles all suggest that no one here is more than half American, from the founding Anglo-Brahmins whose names still swamp the social columns to the Irish whose tone of voice dominates city politics. (Billboard in an Irish-led suburb in the Harvard area allegedly condemned in the interests of university expansion: TO HELL WITH URBAN RENEWAL – WE SHALL DEFEND OUR HOMES WITH OUR LIVES.) Meanwhile the Italians who followed in their migrant footsteps occupy the old part of the city, once a new world Dublin; and the Jewish community remains equally close-knit, despite the gradual drift to suburbia and the patterns of middle-class living.

Nor is it just outward, this maintenance of traditional groupings. Saul: 'It's still your world as a kid, or was fifteen years ago. Not just a matter of Yiddish at home, or knowing you're different from other kids. Sure there was anti-semitism, but that's just the tone of the city – when the Jews aren't on the receiving end, it's the blacks or Irish or Italians. It was more than that, more positive. Families still think ethnically and growing up in a Jewish one you were in it from the start – you know, groomed for something. I guess I was five or six the first time my old man took me down to the diner where he and his buddies all had breakfast – five or six days a week and every guy had his seat at the counter, week after week and year after year, Yiddish only. Jewish-owned diner, of course. Hombergs, black coats and fur collars, up on the bar-stools like crows on a fence, putting down the day's business with their morning bagels and coffee. It was meant to impress me, I could tell – kind of a message that when I was ready there'd be a seat waiting for me. And though I fought it later on, they're great guys, especially the older ones. That's just the Jewish side of it, but most of Boston's still like that, a jigsaw of separate worlds, all going their different ways and pretty much ignoring each other.'

There's a fair slice of it all in this leafy corner of Brookline Hill, which might be taken at first glance for a uniform section of suburbia. Saul and Judy outline it to us. Next door is an Anglo-Brahmin family, sheltered by a high stone wall; silent house, silent garden, lavender and rambler roses with a few neo-classical statues, Venus in a cockleshell and naked Hermes on the wing, casting back a wistful eye at more aristocratic days. The neighbours on the other side belong to the opposite end of the spectrum, a new Jewish family just moved in with a flurry of activity – a new swimming pool in the garden, then an outdoor bar in the garage and when Honey came home from Vassar in her scarlet Thunderbird there was audible family dissension because with swimming pool and bar, Dad's Pontiac and Mom's Corvair, parking space was getting short. With only a fence to contain it all (high stone walls come much later), their neighbours watch and listen wryly to the traumas of transition to the world of Brookline Hill. A third house, ghostly now, falls between the other two; it's not quite Brahmin class, but robber baron rhetorical, a Gothic monument complete with the towers and castellations with which the nineteenth century rich swaggered away from the Federal style of their European-minded predecessors. Originally built out West by a family of Boston frontier traders, it was dismantled stone by stone and rebuilt on Brookline Hill as a condition of the sale of their land to the Northern Pacific Railroad. The owner was a Christian Scientist, who wanted to spend his last days gazing over Boston again. At his death, he left it to his church. Now its only occupants are a few old Christian Scientists living on a single floor.

Judy knows how to get into the grounds – she used to play there as a kid, though slightly afraid of the ghostly figures who sometimes swept across the forecourt in long, Edwardian-style dresses. Wrought-iron gates creak behind us; box hedges trimmed into birds and baubles are gradually losing their outline. Azaleas bloom on the velvet dusk; an elm reaches out over a long, sloping lawn ragged with advancing weeds. Grass and a few hollyhocks push up between the paving stones. Three storeys of high Gothic windows with curtains drawn coldly across them are topped by marble cornices and intricate, low relief chimney stacks, the work of Italian immigrants and common now in Boston's scrap yards as the nineteenth century houses succumb to redevelopment.

Suddenly, could be a trick of the light, a face at one of the top windows, pulling the curtain aside slightly. Old Boston, a brief glance. Gone before we can make it out.

The next day Saul offers another taste of ethnic Boston. Two of his friends have got engaged and there's a party to celebrate. 'Watch out you're not sacrificed, though, you'll be the only Gentiles there. And let's go late, it can be stifling, the love and identity. And the food – like they say, food is love and there sure is a lot of it.'

Cakes and cream, fruit salad, candy, cookies, Scotch on the rocks, Cuba libre, Martinis and all in superabundance, though the party's been on for hours. Bold-featured women bolstered up in gold lamé and black silk and kisses all round for Saul and Judy – there's no one they don't know there, although as it happens they've no relatives among them. Just as everyone knows every story told, its characters and the particular moments which warrant an affectionate laughter, often at the teller's expense or that of Jewry in general. The older men sit tightly together in the corner, a cloud of cigar smoke over their heads like a symbolic chapter heading. They're nearly all first generation and still have strong Yiddish accents and looks

46

which suggest that relaxation is rare except on occasions like this; their laughter, like the lines in their faces, is one that seems to weave them together. As does their way of discussing the young people, watching them as if they're shared.

Saul was right – we're the only Gentiles, though many of his own age group aren't practising Jews any longer, except to preserve the family peace. There's nothing exclusive about the response to us, big-hearted and hospitable; but no great curiosity either, at least among the older people. It's slightly as if our presence is taken as a foible of Saul and Judy's, a part of the young-will-be-young. When one conversation touches on Yiddish literature, they seem surprised that we're interested. But this isn't true of our own age group; they want to know where we're from, what we're up to in the States and what do we think of it, this wider world with which their parents suggest such limited and private connections. Their eagerness has none of that ethnic wariness; though alert in a possibly Jewish way, its concerns are just young American, their range and uncertainty the opposite of the immediate, definable ends which have linked the older people. Saul for a college career, but disillusioned with much of it, anxious to travel and see more of the world, not just the USA; his brother, who's thinking of leaving Boston to set up business in California; Arthur, the fiancé, an air force pilot, twenty-six and commands a jet. (Saul: 'He says it scares the pants off him, can't make out why he's up there.' And later we hear that just after his marriage he's drafted for Vietnam, then under therapy for a nervous breakdown during training.)

Afterwards, Saul's still discussing it all. 'It's not us any more, but it's hard to break with. You know something? In the old country, the Ukraine, before my grandparents came over, the Jewish community was so tight that if you married outside the faith, that was the end of you. Literally – they'd make a coffin and bury it and for them you were inside it, finished. It's still a bit like that and you're involved before you can choose. For me it wasn't just incidents like going down to that Jewish diner. It was pretty much our whole life when we lived up in Chelsea – that's the old tenement district over the other side of town. I spent most of the time with my grandmother, she had this shop right on the sidewalk with everything on display outside, nuts, fruits and pickles in barrels. And she never talked English to me, always Yiddish, Yiddish stories, and I used to help her behind the counter. The school was right across the road, red brick and a strip of asphalt. It was a regular UN, Poles, Jews, Blacks, Germans, Irish, Italians, we had it all. We fought just like the UN, too. I sat next to Waldo the gipsy boy, he never did learn to write. We all lived in the same tenements, washing lines and busted plumbing, but that didn't matter, we all had our labels. And I was a Jewish boy, I stuck by the other Jewish boys and expected the same of them. By the time they slum-cleared us that had really shaped my outlook.' (We go by there a day or two later, now a six-lane overpass, only the shell of the red brick school and one row of tenements left: with all-black faces. As if they were the latest immigrants.)

'So it's a shock to learn that your Jewishness isn't an anchor any more. It's tough for them, too, when they've worked for you, to find you're made in a different mould. But it's true, and we know their side of it. Take my father – most of his uncles and aunts were killed in the pogroms in Russia and he was only thirteen when his parents died here in Boston during the 'flu epidemic – 1918, I think it was. So he left school and pushed a hand-truck. But he ended up with his own business, a small one, but he got through. It must be hard when you've been through that to see your Jewishness receding from the kids you did it for. But that's just it – their Jewishness was very much a way of survival. Just because they did make it, our problems are different, we don't need to think as a closed group. We can't. If you do stay within it now, you're smothered, a kind of love victim. You know the bit about the proverbial Jewish momma – and it's true, like a lot of Jewish jokes about Jews. And when you're married both your mommas fight to be baby-sitters and pass it on to their grandchildren. No kidding.

'But we can't live like that, you have to break away at some point. That's just what the old people did, but it's hard for them to see it that way. Vietnam, civil rights, the content of

what college teaches you as opposed to the label you get from
it – our problems are different. I guess they seem fancy to them
when their big problem was just to survive. Though it is the
same thing, in a sense – we have to define ourselves, like they
did. But nothing stays still here. The definition has to be
different.'

Boston's clattering streetcars have a slightly Parisian flavour
and the passengers at the casual stops an unusually individual
air. Or perhaps it's just the newness of summer, girls cheery and
old men dozing and others loosening their business collars, that
makes it seem un-American. These and the driver's nonchalance,
tic-tac of the change machine, a feeling of space, few billboards
and big magnolia blooms brushing the windows. (Judy: 'When
I was a kid, the streetcar had this line on the doorway – if
your head came below it, you rode half price. My brother took
me with him to get baseball tickets one day and he made me
bend my knees, just in case. But he didn't say why and he
never told me to unbend them. I spent I don't know how many
years riding streetcars with knees bent, I figured you had to. I
kind of associate it with Boston.')
    It's this faint eccentricity which really characterizes the city,
a taste for variety in people and things, perhaps because it is a
place where neither are quite Americanized. Boston Common's
casual green fits easily into its surroundings, doesn't surprise
you like Central Park, crouched among the skyscrapers. Elms
and maples spread their shadows over the gaggles of schoolchildren, flirting students and snoozing hobos, who all look less
hunted than in New York. Nuns stroll through the chequered
sunlight, the founding fathers' bronze heads seem unpreten-
tiously endowed with many a summer's pigeon droppings,
balloon and ice-cream men abound. A lightness and a tran-
quility, carelessly sophisticated: a Catholic restraint on Protes-
tant Mammon by the Irish and the Italians, perhaps; and New
England's pre-industrial touch, filtering in from old village
suburbs like Charlestown and Dorchester. But above all the
city reflects the presence of those Anglo-Brahmins, whose
wealth and conceits are old enough to have built Georgian

houses and remained part European, largely ignoring the new USA and looking down, as Europe had, on the USA's new arrivals, Irish, Jewish and Italian; so that they too remained Europeans, of a different social order. On Beacon Hill their stately mansions still crown the city; well trimmed trees and cobbled alleys, commemorative plaques in the doorways and old ladies walking their dogs out and chatting to them, English style, with parasols, Edwardian brooches and a fading air of command.

Saul maps it out to us from on top of a downtown office block with the city spreadeagled below, long grey promontories and thruways with Cambridge and Harvard just visible beyond them, dabs of green and church spires. In the other direction, Boston dockside; wooden fingers of the wharves touch the grey Atlantic from warehouses and winding streets. Saul: 'The docks down there, the North End – that's the oldest part of the city. Used to be pretty fashionable until the Irish moved in, then it turned into tenement land, an immigrant bottleneck and the poorest part of Boston. That's how it's been ever since – the latest lot of immigrants takes over the North End because accommodation's cheap, a few of them make it into the suburbs, and finally a real few into the old high-class spots like Beacon Street and Beacon Hill. Meantime new immigrants move into the gaps they've left and often as not they're slum-rented by people who've just escaped it themselves. Mainly Italians living there now, there's plenty of them still arriving. Down there, above the Common, that's the mainly black sector. Boston tries to convince itself that it's different in that respect, but there's no mistaking it.' He's right – four-storey tenements, red brick gone grime black, rickety pattern of fire-escapes, rooftop jungle of washing lines, trash cans and lounging figures with that underemployed look that's always doubly conspicuous in the bustling USA.

It's only the Irish who've challenged the heights between Yankee and immigrant Boston. That emerald streak pervades the streets even more forcefully than in New York. A group of dockers with lusty placards arguing a pay claim demand to be photographed in distinct brogue, with Dubliners' poses and comments to match. Every news-stand has a sprinkling of fairly salty magazines underneath its Catholic journals. Donkey jackets and shoulder bags, and the bars are ribald honest; no restraint on midday laughter, drinkers sit around in groups instead of solemn business pairs and the smell of draught beer is stronger than any air-conditioning. It's as if they've made it their city in answer to the way they arrived, not as hopefuls headed west but as America's poorest immigrants running from famine and eviction with little conception of what lay ahead and few means of fighting for it. Only to be faced in Boston with new Anglo bastions ('Only Protestants need apply') as embittering as Ulster's: bastions which stood until James Michael Curley, darlin boy, toppled the Yankee Republicans to become the city's mayor. Changing days for the sons of Ireland under his roisterous momentum, even when it came to them from inside a federal gaol: from the North End's tenements and cellars where they'd hungered for a generation into the suburbs and beyond until in 1946, when Curley retired from his seat in Congress, John F. Kennedy took it over. But the struggle had been fought in Bostonian terms: the Irish carved their own niche in the structure, rather than destroying it. City politics remained machine-based and Blacks and Italians inherited the tenements and lower rungs of Boston's ethnic separatism.

In the decrepit North End, the struggle's still in evidence. Just the edge of it at first in the weekday empty market, trucks backed up to warehouses in a riot of fruit crates, melon peel, old newspapers. Men loading them swear and joke: sweat-gleaming ebony face over a bright yellow jacket; doll-high, swarthy Italian, bull chest and gesticulations; Irish brow with a cap pushed back over a rough head of curls. Quit their heaving when we pass and straighten up to yodel at us, 'Eccolo', 'How bout that,' 'Top o the morning to you ladies'. Echoes of their knightly greetings follow us round the empty stalls past the smell of salted herrings, round the corner and suddenly: Salem Street, little Italy. Four-foot-six wisp of Naples shrouded in her widow's black stares in surprise at our intrusion – fifty yards away was Boston; now we're foreigners, all of us. Fruit vendor on the corner chats with the broad-beamed restaurant owner surveying the world from his doorway, '*E poi e venute la polizia e hanno detto attenzione, no fate piu rumore* . . .', shops with their goods spilling onto sidewalks, barrelled olives purple and green, salt tang of anchovies, pastrami, pasta in bowls, dried figs strung from the ceiling, secondhand clothes, square-cut suits and winklepicker Italian shoes, Jo Tecci's, Ristorante di Napoli and Pollini's Grocery, dried fish and cheap Chianti. Old man asleep in a doorway, cap pulled down over his eyes, conversations outscreaming each other, corner to corner, sidewalk to window, doorway to doorway, across the street, '*Mama mia*' and she spreads her arms, crucified black serge on sunlight, all two hundred pounds of her embracing the world in her exclamation. Peasant figures that might have set out yesterday from Italian villages in their heavy woollen shirts and work trousers with ramshackle braces; women wrapped deep in black against the lost Italian sunlight. Blare of a horn hits the walls as two dark teenagers cruise by in an open Chevrolet, bare chests and hunting eyes, slow enough to be admired, racing the engine and dwarfing the shops with their prize from another USA. Girl in a dress-shop doorway lets her eyes get held for a moment; mother sees, she drops them and turns away again hurriedly, caught between her two worlds.

Nearby in Paul Revere Square, time has dealt a well-earned blow to older Boston's claims to fame. Beneath its Brahmin centrepiece, a rhetorical statue of Paul Revere riding off to Concord with news of the British Redcoats' landing, a riot of Italian babies are taking their first oblivious steps. Little boys splash in the fountain with a healthy disregard for the horrid patriotic couplets behind them. The women seated in the shade are raven-haired, hard-smoking Sabines, chatting and keeping an eye on their men, clustered at the far end, where the eldest doze quietly, each with a piece of cardboard placed meticulously beneath him to preserve the seat of his trousers. The smack of cards drifts through the sunlight; a few players in pairs, with the benches as tables, but the big game is in the corner, under the shadow of the wall. Heads bowed in concentration, mobile of figures round them watching every turn of the cards, greeting each one with a babble of comments, debate, advice; not a word of English. Suddenly the chatter mounts to a shout, players jump up, arms wave, spectators take sides, heads turn, the old men nod quizzically, boys stream across the cobbles, windows fly open overhead and cowled madonnas scream down at the seething little square – 'Che coso c'e adeso?' 'Luigi facendo rumore', 'Al diavolo con gli uomini' – goading the two contenders on, until they finally march off, each with a band of supporters, pursued by taunts from the little boys in the safety of the fountain. Two minutes later they reappear with the policeman from round the corner. He arbitrates quietly, then jumps on the bench and harangues them all in Italian. After which he loosens his tie, takes off his cap and joins the spectators. Peace slides back. Old men nod, little boys shout, heads move in a studied circle, women chat overhead, leaning out from window to window between the everywhere washing lines.

As Saul and I wander round, a man makes room for us on the bench when we ask him about the card game. An Italian form of poker, he explains. Mid-forties, watchful, sculpted face. Then it's his turn for questions. Where are we from? He perks up at the mention of England. 'I was working there, in Bedford, London Brick Company. In England is okay. Money no good, but they treat you like a man, give you a job, say: "Look, you do it," and you get down, you do it. But here – good money, but is rough. Push, push, every guy pushing. You start at the bottom, is rough, understand? Every guy push you. No freedom, the boss always there, tell you "Do this, do that." And when they done with you, you through. Give you check, tell you get out, work finish, same day. Is rough.' Pauses. 'You know what – bosses is Jewish, that's the trouble.'

Saul grins but checks himself and the man doesn't notice and carries on. 'But in England, they get stupid. Fifty-seven, fifty-eight, let all goddam niggers come, the Jamaicans come in, mess up the place. Bad people. That's why I leave. Same here, too many niggers. Just give trouble, they don't work. And this Irish, drinking, fighting.' Looks round at the crowded square. 'Here is all right. Plenty Italians. But you know, is hard for

Italians. People don't like us, call us wop, people here is prejudiced. Irish people, they don't like us – that's why I leave
England, too many goddam Irish, *Mama mia*, always fighting,
want woman, money. Six years I come now. I become American.' Drops his voice in confidence. 'You see, I born in Napoli.
You been to Italy? Napoli? Is my happy city, I born there.
But Napoli done, finish for me' – and he puts it out of his life
with a movement of his hand. 'No work, is too hard over there.
That's why I come to America. I got papers, American citizen,
citizen of the United States.' Looks at Saul. 'You American,
no?' Saul nods. He pats Saul's shoulder almost sycophantically
– and suddenly it looks as if he's asking for approval, as if it's
all been a desperate attempt to prove his new Americanism.
As his own experience, presumably, has taught him to prove
it; a hint of the strains that must still weigh on the early years
of poor immigration.

Saul asks him his voting preferences and the answer comes
back emphatically. 'I vote a Republican. Republican – Com-
munists finish.' Smacks his fist into his palm.

Saul: 'Are you happy here – glad you left Naples?'

He shrugs, less decisive now his opening performance is over –
perhaps he was trying to convince himself, not just us. 'Happy?
I don't choose. I just go where God send me.'

Saul: 'What about your kids, though? You planning on
sending them to college?'

Tilts his head. 'Maybe. I hope. In Italy I think so. American
boys go to college. But now – is hard. We need the money,
fifteen, sixteen, they working. And my big boy, nineteen, is
different. He gone away – but no college. Gone to Vietnam.'
Lips pursed. Hand moves thoughtfully over his strong, unshaven chin. The conversation seems to be over.

Below the square narrow streets slope down to the waterfront, twisted and cramped and overbuilt from the days when
the Irish arrived to settle on every vacant spot and make a
home in every room. Ellis Island imagery. Fire-escapes chase
each other in zig-zags up soot-black walls; from them you
could almost hold hands across the littered crack of the street.
Paper trash, sunning babies, cats slyly on fishbone corners,

two little boys in a doorway engrossed in making a fishing line, ball game in a dusty schoolyard ringed by collapsing wire netting, two men hoisting a chair on a patched-up piece of rope from street level to third floor, and always the women's faces, watching from the sidelines, arms thick with overwork, framed in strings and tufts of washing. One leans out and bawls down at the schoolyard. *'Guido, hai comprato il pane?'* Answer flies up in English, a curse. Scream back, window slams. The North End's summer scent, rotten fruit and bad sanitation, stirs and settles back like sludge.

Afternoon silence on the wharves by the line of old sea-captains' houses, built in imposing grey stone with the embossed wooden doors that once guarded supplies and cargoes. Shades of Boston's founding fortunes – textiles, boots and salted fish for the Caribbean plantations; the China trade, tea and spices from Canton's river markets, tall masts of Massachusetts outstripping the Bristol and Liverpool merchants to build up the Brahmins' wealth, discreetly invested, often elsewhere, after the heyday was over, so that Boston settled back as the USA's first dowager city. On the far side, above the harbour, the after-Brahmin imagery of the city's return to life with labour for her industries. Old immigrant shanty houses, their first and harsher USA. Driftwood, corrugated iron, rag curtains, cardboard patches, tar paper, holes for windows. Fenced off now, condemned. Gulls are the only movement. The tide sucks at slime green piles. Flies tussle with the silence.

In the cobbled streets behind the wharves, coffee smell and fish stench make a giddy combination, buoyed up on the lazy heat. Snatches of tipsy laughter from the long, low corner bars, ships in bottles on the walls. Fish sheds. The flash of packing, slither of fish guts men in aprons slashing gutting turning round without checking a single movement, cod, sole slap sprawling herring pitchforking packing salting; barrels and crates are heaved and scraped across the sidewalk into the trucks. Foreman shouts instructions with a distinctly Italian accent. An old black man, his stick-like body the barest statement of existence, spits, strains at the next barrel,

GOIFFRE'S FISH-MARKET
CLAMS   LOBSTERS
BOSTON MACKEREL
COD STEAKS

skin wracked on thin limbs, heaves, checks, barrel poised like a
continent on his back.

Olga Green, 57

GREEN, *Olga, 57, grandmother and part-time hairdresser, poised and always well turned out, lives in upstate New York in a small town black ghetto. Often mentions her family history: maternal grandfather escaped north from slavery via the underground railway and settled as a farmer in upstate New York, where he reared seventeen children: their faded pictures in a family album, stern black Victorians looking the camera straight in the eye, high collars and ankle length skirts. Her father was also a farmer and worked part time for neighbours, as he hadn't much land of his own.*

He'd had to leave school early, so there wasn't much opportunity for him – best he could hope for as a Negro was to be a waiter in a hotel, head waiter was considered the highest type of job at the time – mother reached 8th grade – pretty good for a girl in those days, but all she could get was domestic work. (*Childhood on the family farm she describes as threadbare but contented; partly because so isolated, little to compare it with*) – a shock to me when I first went to school and learnt what it meant to be a Negro – learnt to live with it and fight it. Literally. Every time we came home from school we had a fist fight with the other kids – taught that we were inferior and abused us – all through your life, so you taught your children to fight the same way – not much to fight for except for your pride, of course – weren't encouraged – assumed as a Negro you'd grow up and continue much as your parents – in school they told us to take domestic science and manual arts and to forget the sciences that might have led to the professions – 'no jobs in such fields open to your people'. That's how they put it – hard –

you were in an American school which taught that everything was possible, it was only up to you, but suddenly it didn't apply to us – you'd start to think: maybe there is something wrong with me, maybe I am different – high school – wasn't segregated – would have been better if it was – taught you to think of yourself as inferior – distinctions and prizes depended on belonging to clubs from which Negroes were excluded – right up to my children's time – some relationships with white people, but they were very limited – one white friend, a girl, who was always urging me to become a personal maid – insensitive of her, but it was kind of realistic – the only field open.

I did pretty well in school, guess I could have gone on to college – but friends of mine who had been to college couldn't get jobs – wasn't any opening for the Negro professional in those days, certainly not for a Negro woman. They'd end up teaching in Southern schools or even go back to domestic work. With college degrees. I decided to get married and put everything into my children – changing so slowly – seemed the best thing.

(*Married as soon as she left school; she and her husband moved into town, where he worked as a janitor and set up their present home, clapboard modest, close and warm, relatives around the corner. On thirty-five dollars a week they were comfortably off in ghetto terms, own house, modest furniture, new clothes. Then the Depression: his salary was halved. With less to lose, many blacks weren't as hard hit as whites; but those who did have decent jobs were almost always first fired, and this meant relatives to support. But like others they lived through it to see opportunities expand very slightly: 1940, for instance, the local police force offered posts specifically for Negroes. Her husband applied, but his age and lack of qualifications ruled him out.*)

I guess we realized then how we'd missed out on the way things were changing. It came too late for us. Anyways, we had the children, two boys and a girl, it was going to be different for them – boys did well at high school, then they went on to college and my daughter went to Rochester, to the Business Institute – why I sent the boys to college in the South, to segregated schools – the race question was something they'd have to face, they should know how to deal with it, and they wouldn't learn that up here where people pretend it doesn't exist – of course they had difficulties – most times they came out on top – did accomplish a lot – even made white friends – met Negro leaders and were inspired by them – learnt far more than they would have if they'd stayed at home, where things were easier.

(*One's now a psychiatrist doing case work in the air force, other works in Chicago in the social services. Daughter had a harder time finding something that matched her training, but finally made out quite well with a worthwhile secretarial job.*)

Things are so different now, prospects really seem good for their children, that kind of makes up for our experience. When the first opportunities came it was hard to have faith in them – all we need now is to convince the young people to go right ahead and take them – not over yet of course, but it's changing. People's view of themselves has changed – going to meet problems, but they don't reckon on losing – see themselves differently – a new pride – until quite recently there was always that impulse to try and escape from your Negro background by marrying lighter than yourself, it was a man's badge of honour – now Negroes are finding their own beauty – girls whose hair I do, like the boys, they think of beauty as including their own –

a relief to know that your grandchildren won't ever have to think of themselves as inferior because of their colour – may have to fight, but they won't have any doubts – in the old days people only escaped, they disassociated themselves from their race, from their own parents and family sometimes, that was the kind of dilemma they faced. But now it's on a community basis – one gets up he has to look back and pull everyone up with him. Else he has to stay down.

You know something? In personal ways I believe we're becoming less close, less intimate – having to fight for things gave us a lot we might not have had – that will go – we'll lose contact with our music, our poetry, our comedy, the things that pointed up our indignities, we're already losing all this, except on television – no longer be a community. I think

Negroes will lose that sense of depending on each other when we're truly integrated – our sympathy, the tenderness we always had – had it because we needed it, with the way things were for us. But it'll go, like everything else.

Funny – in my own family – my grandchildren don't recognize, they no longer know Negro music because they go to a mainly white church and of course the Church has always been the musical background for Negroes. Already when they hear a Negro service on the radio or television, they say: listen, that's the way the people sing in Granma's church.

CHAPTER 4

SOLO:
Maine

Saul and Judy decide to join us for a few days in Maine. Beyond the gabled Massachusetts harbour towns, Salem, Marblehead and Gloucester (gables long out-numbered now by the luxury weekend homes and all-WASP country clubs), motels and billboards fade away. Settlements become sparse and threadbare, fishing boats, bedraggled farms and an occasional timber truck conveying the tenor of their lives. Despairing 'For Sale' notices spell out a ceaseless epitaph for a world of small-scale industrial skills, shipbuilding and woodcrafts, outmoded by a bigger one. Slowly the map of Maine comes alive as the jagged coastline stabs at the sea, rocks topped by lone pines that trail the Atlantic mist.

Bar Harbour is deserted, only the Nova Scotia ferry riding at anchor in the bay. White sea-light and a single street, rain-washed and almost empty: a waiting-for-Godot quality, as if it depends for its very existence, now that the fishing trade has died, on holiday-makers yet to arrive.

Round the corner at McKinley, a small wharf is advertised as the ferry junction for the islands opposite. The ferry, 'The William Silsby, capacity nine vehicles', is waiting there, suggestively empty. Next trip is in half an hour, the woman in the ticket office tells us, and it's the last one today. Destination, Swan's Island. Not much guidance from the map; a few square miles with a single road connecting its two settlements of Atlantic and Minturn. Saul and Judy have never heard of it. Nor does the woman in the ticket office have much to add. 'Well, I don't know what to say, never even been there myself. Not many people there. They're nice, all right, but you know' – she hesitates – 'islanders, kind of old-fashioned. No real stores there. Better buy some food if you're going.'

We do so and minutes later the harbour's slipping away behind us. We're the only passengers. The three crew-men lean on the side, chatting in heavy, clipped accents. One of them looks at us and grins. 'Visiting the island, are you? Staying at one of our new motels?' We tell him we're camping and he laughs, open-faced. 'Lucky for you – only place to sleep there is in what you bring with you. There's a fine little camping spot up at Charles Tawney's place, right by the sea there.' The island's in sight, a streak in the mist, wooded to the water's edge. 'See that hill in the middle there? Right there, you can't miss it. Follow me in my Studebaker soon as we get off the boat – I'll get you into Atlantic and she's straight on from there. Look.' And he points to a movement ahead; a dolphin rolling lazily through the sun-bright bowl of the sea.

'What do people here do for a living?'

'It's a problem. All lobster fishing. The old stone quarry, she closed down. Now the whole island's tied up inside of a lobster-pot, winter and summer, the same thing. Did it myself. Looks easy, but come winter, it's tough on you. Nine or ten hours on a freezing sea, and now the lobsters are getting scarce. Last winter we were frozen up, cut the island right off, we couldn't get the ferry out. That's why the young folks stay away, too rough for them. Go to school on the mainland and then we don't see em again. Used to be a grand place, over a thousand people here and plenty of life. Now there's only three or four hundred, scarcely any young folks left.'

The island draws closer, its lonely coast varied only by spruce and firs. A single wharf comes into view and two minutes later we're following the ferry-man down the rough, dusty road. A few isolated houses, most of them run down and unpainted, wooden shacks with shingle roofs. Small jetties stand on ramshackle legs, heaped with slatted lobster traps. Signpost at the T-junction: 'Atlantic' one way, 'Minturn' the other. The ferry-man's no mean expert at the narrow, pot-holed road; his old Studebaker has vanished, leaving only a cloud of dust to show that he's turned towards Atlantic. It's round the corner, where he's waiting for us: a few houses, one store and a large wooden school. Roadside figures watch discreetly. A self-appointed diplomat, the ferry-man seems to be introducing us to this private, miniature world. Enquiring faces glance at him, then at us before they wave. He points ahead. 'Straight on till you come to Charles Tawney's – come by if you need anything, that's my house, right there,' and he points it out, small and green-roofed, overlooking the harbour.

Further along the rutted road, which dwindles to little more than a track, there's a single house, very distinct with its fresh paint and prosperous air. The teenage girl on the doorstep has a bored, vacant look, almost the first young person we've seen, apart from a few schoolchildren. We stop to ask her the way to the camp ground. Her trimness seems at odds with the island. 'The camp ground? It's round the corner. Go down to the farm there, across the field and it's right by the shore. You'll meet my great-uncle Charlie – you mustn't mind him, he's kind of funny, but he'll look after you okay.'

The little that's left of the bumpy track passes an up-slanting bluff, crows hopping in the heather and gulls gliding down the wind. Below it a wooden farmhouse stands like some forgotten toy on the sea-front slope, warped by the gale that flays the few small patches where the soil has been turned. An old wagon with worn shafts: the remains of a battered Buick; then a shed with windows askew, a rusty harrow choking its doorway and horseshoes nailed up outside, and a weathered barn, keeling over and propped up by lengths of driftwood. Two gnarled apple trees startle the eye with their white blossom. Beneath them a sprite-like old man is fastening a halter onto a workhorse.

He looks round at us beady-eyed, cherrywood pipe jutting out of his mouth. Sunken and stubbled face with the soil engrained in its creases, craggy jaw and a felt hat, green-brown, shapeless with age. Pushes it back from his forehead and peers down at our licence-plate. 'Foreigners, eh,' and he gives a cackle, snatched by the wind. His jaw jumps out. 'Ain't about the water, is it?'

'No, we've come to the camp site.'

'Eh, that camp site, yes sir.' He removes his pipe from thin, cracked lips with blackened teeth roots behind them and points to the pines down by the shore. 'She's there, see. Plenty of firewood, first ones y'are this year. Well, they come and they go, come and they go,' and he waves an emaciated arm, with another nervous, high-pitched cackle. 'You go right ahead, folks, and if there's anythin you're needin, you come and ask Cap'n Charles Tawney. You'll be needin water, see. Use that well there, I won't be looking. You ain't suppose to use it, see, on account of the feller from the state has been here and he says it's dirty, but that's a goddam stinkin lie, you go right ahead and use it. I been sick all day, see, so I'm gettin my goddam taters planted, I'll be seein you folks later.' He checks the halter and turns the workhorse. 'Whoa, Prince, goddam ya,' and away he goes, as if the horse is pulling him down the stony field that slopes right to the water's edge, eroding into a sudden drop.

When I go back up for water, he's hopping along behind a crude plough, slicing a fresh strip in the slope. He sees me coming and shouts at the horse, 'Whoa, Prince, whoa, goddam ya,' and horse and plough lurch to a halt. 'Goin for that water, are ya? I'm goin to help you some, she's kinda tricky with foreigners.' He steps up towards the farmhouse, the breeze flattening his overalls against his frail, fleshless figure. 'I been sick all day, see – in a manner of speakin. Had a ball game on the radio, but I didn't like to say. Don't want you foreigners getting the wrong picture, see, we're hard-workin folks here. Anyways, I got goddam ulcers, and that's God's truth. Now, let's see.'

He lifts up the rough wooden lid that keeps the world out of his well and lets down an ancient bucket fastened on to a long pole. A distant smack as it hits the water. He hauls it up doggedly, peering down at he passes the pole over his shoulder. Water's spurting in all directions as the bucket emerges. 'Gotta catch it quick, see, I'm goin to get you folks a dipper.' Runs spider-like into the house, cracked door flapping behind him, and reappears with a bent can. 'There y'are, hold on to that,' and he spoons what's left of the water into our thoughtlessly new container and lowers the bucket again. 'I'm not seein ya, mind you.' He tries to wink but just clenches his face so that little beads of sweat sink slowly into his stubble. 'Goddam state says she's impure, but she's the finest goddam water in this goddam state of Maine. Cap'n Charles Tawney's been drinkin her all his drinkin life, see, and that's a goddam stinkin lie them foreigners come and tell me, comin up here with their "impure water". Bah. That's what I tell the Bangor-feller, I tell im straight, see, if you don't like our water here in this beautiful Swan's Island, you can git right back to Bangor and start drinkin that Bangor-water that's floralised, piped and air-seditioned, God knows what they do with their water before they start drinkin her down, but that's what I tell the Bangor-feller. I don't go mindin his business, see, I don't have nothin to say 'bout what them Bangor-fellers drinks. Bah.' Juts his jaw forward and pushes his hat back again from a brow that's pale above sun-and-soil brown. 'Tell the truth, I never did fancy them Bangor-fellers. Ain't been there for, let me see, comin on thirty years now, but I never did fancy em. Well, he's gone and he won't be back – Cap'n Charles Tawney knows em all, they come and they go, come and they go.'

He looks up suddenly, hawk-eyed. 'You ain't from Bangor-Maine by any kinda chance, are you?'

'No, I'm from England.'

'From England?' He hesitates. 'You mean you're from London-England? Well, now, ain't that somethin,' and he pauses, still taking it in, perhaps a little disbelieving. 'Well, I never did meet a feller come right from London-England before. We've had a couple of foreigners here, New York, Boston, Bangor-Maine, but they never did come from London-England. Mind you, I know about it some, got it in my schoolin, see, didn't have much schoolin on account of I was sick, but they did tell us about it, about all them kings and queens and other things you got in your country.' Kicks the lid back on the well and suddenly changes the subject, as if he's still a bit taken aback and needs more time to consider it. 'Yes, sir, that's the finest water in Maine and don't you be afraid of it.' Pulls his hat forward decisively and replaces his empty pipe in his mouth. 'Come on, I'll show you somethin, I gotta git them taters planted, account of I didn't work today. Tell you what – we'll take the Buick across to that tater patch of mine, I use her to bring the horse in, see.'

He jumps into the old Buick, which I originally took for scrap. No windows or seat in the back, just a pile of cardboard boxes and one of the broken window-frames. No key. He turns the ignition with his thumb and it rumbles miraculously into life. 'I'm goin to show you that tater patch see, show you how we seed em here.' Drives the fifty bouncing yards down the slope, revving fiercely. 'Gotta keep her goin good, else she quits on me, see,' and to prove the point he takes off his foot and the engine dies obediently, right by the potato patch.

Clambers out and pokes at the soil. Picks up a handful, dry and thin, and runs it through his fingers. 'Goddam powder, see, just powder, that's what I live off all my years, land's runnin out on me, see, and them goddam crows, bah,' and he throws the soil defiantly at a black shadow overhead. 'Few weeks back I planted my green peas, see, and they come up mighty fine, but them goddam crows had every one of em.' Goes across to the horse and hitches up the plough again, gives it a rough shake and a shout and horse, man and plough trundle forward, turning the dry, stony soil, the three of them like a single object linked together by a struggle for which they've all grown too old. Forward, turns and back again, felt hat and cherry-wood pipe against the flat line of the sea, with the satin-breasted swallows twittering round him as dusk slips down. 'Whoa, Prince, confound ya,' and the old horse turns to stone. He picks up a bucket of seed potatoes and throws one across to me; it's sliced in half, with two fresh shoots. 'That's how we do em in these parts, cut em and leave the two eyes, see.' Drops them one by one in the furrows, muttering all the time as he does so, something about the crows, and kicking the soil over them with a fiendish look on his face, half savage, half glee. His expression is often like this, I can't tell if it's pain or laughter. Stands back when the patch is finished and looks at it, a slash of soil pathetically shrunken by the dusk. 'It's powder, see, goddam powder,' and he spits in contempt.

Soft slap of the sea on the rocks only twenty or thirty yards

3

away. He unhitches the plough and kicks it aside, then solemnly
ties the workhorse to the fender of the Buick. 'Go ahead with
that water now, that's the finest water in Maine. And if you
folks is needin somethin, just come knockin at Cap'n Charles
Tawney, he's goin to fix you up, see,' and he waves goodnight
as he sits in the car, pitching his afterthoughts into the dusk.
'She ain't noth'n but goddam powder, that's the trouble with
her, see,' and he gives his thin, dry cackle again as he sets off
up the slope with the horse in tow.

Sparks from our fire drift down at the sea. Dew falls enquiringly. Glow-worms tilt at the grey moonlight. A foghorn carries.
A single light in the farmhouse and the ceaseless roll of the sea
beneath a deepening scarf of mist, spilling and dying, spilling
and dying.

The morning stillness is ripped apart by the growl of a bulldozer
digging a pit at the top of the slope. In its intervals of silence
engines chug on the pearl-soft sea, dropping and picking up
again as the lobster men go their rounds. Saul returns with
water and a branch of apple blossom. 'Greetings from the old
man – I caught the workhorse for him. He reckoned it was
bleak down here, maybe the ladies needed some flowers. Said it
was a good while before the apples came along and anyway the
crows would have them.'

The lifting sun burns into white, contorting the seaweed.
Shadows of the pine trees shrivel. Suddenly there's an outlandish
cry, 'Ho there,' and the old man appears, grinning at us awk-
wardly, as if he's so unaccustomed to it that it hurts his taut lips.
'Thought I'd just come down and tell ya, road at the top's open
again. They've finished with that bulldozer, see, drive right up
there if you want to. That's my nephew's work, see, buildin a
fish pond, he is, says he's goin to make some money. Kind of
a fine scheme, aint it? My nephew, he's doin all right, that's his
house down the road, little ways down from here, see.' Jerks
his head with determination. 'Them folks is all right, see, they
look after me some.'

It must be the house we passed yesterday, where the girl told
us the way. 'Great-uncle Charlie' – it all fits in, except for the

uncanny remoteness of the old man's hermitage from the world two generations and a few hundred yards away. He reaches inside his overall with a look of mischievous glee and brings out a tiny black kitten. His face creases up, a delighted sparkle in the sunken coals of his eyes, 'Chee, chee chee,' and he sets it down, his knotted hands moving as gently as if he were holding rice-paper. 'First time I bring im out, see, so we're going to see how he likes it. Got four more little uns back there, this one's the biggest. He, he, there he goes,' and he watches anxiously as the tiny black object stumbles forward. 'Must be about a hundred of em I've reared up there in my time, see, keep me company, they do, and besides the rats don't like em. A feller needs some company, see, come on then, kittycat.' He bends down and picks it up, tucks it back in his overalls and wanders off again abruptly, trailing his fragmentary comments behind him, 'Yes, sir, a fine feller, a fine little kittycat,' half to us, half to himself, as if he's aware that soon we'll be gone and the sea his only audience again.

We decide on a trip round the island. Traffic regulations don't carry much weight: drivers just use the middle of the road and swing across at the last moment, waving cheerily. It feels as if our identity has already been circulated. In the Atlantic General Store, one room with wooden shelves, a woman is selling home-baked bread to the girl behind the counter. A barefoot boy in an oversized cap buys a quarter's worth of fish hooks and glances at us curiously as he slips out of the door: face is sharp and sun-brown, older-looking than his slight body. Canned goods piled on the shelves, hurricane lamps, rubber boots, hooks, axes and candles, twenty-five-cent cherrywood pipes, the same kind as Cap'n Charles's, yesterday's *Bangor News* on the counter and secondhand clothes in the window. The girl's a bit apologetic, as if she's afraid we'll judge her by her primitive surroundings. She suddenly ignores the woman with the bread, standing quietly beside us. 'I'm not too sure of all the prices, I've been away for a long time. I don't live here now, you see – Portland, that's where I really live.'

Hardly a patch of cultivation in the scrubby, sea-whipped landscape as the road swings round the island. It's more

68

derelict away from Atlantic: deserted houses, weathered and cracked, boarded up windows with broken frames and 'For Sale' notices so old that they're almost bleached away. Abandoned boats warp in the sun, colours fading to brine-grey. Old jetties tilt in the mud, shredded platforms and broken legs, Only the gulls seem alive, along with the bobbing bright lobster-pot markers.

A few miles later Minturn appears, a handful of houses and one-man jetties straggling round a wide bay. A lone fisherman sits painting his lobster pots. His hands keep weaving as he talks to us in a heavy, guttural accent. Born in Sweden, he tells us, and came here as a stone-cutter when they were still working the quarry, which then employed two or three hundred men. When it closed, he turned to lobsters.

Saul: 'But you think they'll last? I've heard that down in Massachusetts the lobster beds are cleaned right out and people can't make a living any more.'

He nods, reaching for another trap. 'Ve can't tell. This lobster's a funny feller. The government tries to control him, they vas seeding the lobster beds here. But ve tell them it von't work. Ve know this lobster, you got to let nature have her vay. And you got to know vhere he goes, vhat the old devil is thinking. You see, about now he's close in, hungry. He just cast off his old shell and he hasn't eaten for a vhile, so he's coming close in, you don't have to look far. You see, you got to know him. Patience. That's vhy the young folks don't like it.' Shakes his head. 'But is true now, I vouldn't advise them to take up this lobster vork. Prices is high, because ve feeding rich people, New York and California. But this lobster is all ve got now. Is a big vorry. Prices go up, but the catch going down, every year is going down. That's vhy folks is leaving the island. But ve old people can't leave. Vhere vould I go – back to Sveden?' He laughs, not sadly. 'Young people, they get a new life, but our life is right here. So ve just got to vait and see.'

Further on the road grows dustier and comes to an end below the quarry by a big, deserted wharf for shipping the stone out to the mainland. Most of the jetties here are abandoned, slowly subsiding stilt houses covered with old ropes and traps, an oar, a corroded anchor, as if their owners were unwilling to admit defeat by removing their trimmings. The chug of a lobster boat underlines the strangely exaggerated stillness. The quarry is like an amphitheatre, empty except for the cry of a bird and the crystal rainwater holding its reflection up to the unlikely summer brightness in which only the past is alive and the whole more like a recollection than a concrete experience.

The road turns inland, but it's almost impassable now. Deserted houses watch over it. Purple lilac blooms push at the windows. Inside one, sunlight streams through a gap in the roof and picks out an old envelope: the postmark's just legible, Bangor 1956. And further on it's much the same. The newly painted sea-front homes belong to people still young enough to operate a lobster boat; here it's often hard to tell if they're inhabited now. The fruit trees are in timid bloom, but the wild grass has almost choked them and wiped out the garden paths. Once a face appears at a window, a woman with lank hair pushing back a makeshift curtain to peer out at the sound of a car. And a little way on an old man stands up from his wood-chopping and raises an enquiring hand.

Back in Atlantic the day's almost done. There's only one man by the harbour, working on his boat engine. He chats with us briefly, seems a bit dour, but maybe it's just shyness.

'Ever been out on a lobster boat?'

'No, but we wouldn't mind trying.'

Glances at us sceptically, the professional at the dilettantes. 'What time do you folks wake up?'

'When we have to.'

He can't help smiling slightly as he delivers his punch line. 'Five-thirty okay?'

'Okay.'

He looks disbelieving. 'See you here if you want a ride, then, five-thirty tomorrow morning. You're not the first has said they'll come. Always glad of company. Never had it yet, though.' And he laughs his islander's challenge.

Sunrise begins as a streak of orange firing the low smudge of the mainland and touching every object, rock, pool and filigree pine branch, with an identity of its own. Five o'clock. Just as we're leaving, the sun's disc tops the skyline, bathing Cap'n Charles's farmhouse, still shut as tight as a clam against the quick chill of dawn.

Atlantic is up and about already, the one time of day when its figures move briskly. Their greetings suggest an intimacy about sharing the early morning. The silver-black sea is polished calm, a low tide exposing the jetties so that they look more than ever like details of a Disneyland Venice. Our sparring partner of yesterday evening tries to conceal his surprise at seeing us, then grins in spite of himself and gives us a hand onto his boat. Big and reddish sea-soft hands, plain face, younger than most here, can't be more than his early forties, heavy-boned and awkward looking; but this first impression fades as he unties the mooring line, packs it deftly into the corner and flicks the engine into gear. Jetties and box-like houses dwindle as we head for the point and out along the rocky shoreline. The white boat is neat as a dime, a pulley on one side of the wheel for hauling up the lobster traps and on the other a large tray of bait. His broad back confronts us silently as we skirt the empty shore, broken by the occasional cottage with its rowing boat moored in front.

He slows after a few minutes and rocks to a halt by a rust-red marker. Hooks it up with a long pole and slips the rope over the pulley. Switches the winch into action, rope tautens, then a splash as the trap comes up. Scrabble of panic-stricken claws as he throws the seaweed aside, flicks the trap open and reaches inside: a baby one, throws it back, then another, measures it, jams its claw with a wooden peg and drops it into the empty bin, pulls out the bait bag, empties it overboard, cloud of gulls scream down, refills it fastens it back and pitches the trap in again. The marker bobs and settles above it. It's all over in less than a minute, his artist's hands never faltering in their un-hurried, intricate rhythm. He chugs on to the next red marker, gulls bickering in our wake and wheeling up and away and then back as another lobster pot appears.

Once another boat passes and the occupant waves. Lone cormorants skim across our wake and occasionally a seal bobs up and watches us inquisitively. The boat engine chugs and lulls, as the hands weave through their formula; hook, winch, trap up, crabs fly measure drop in the bin bait gullscream bait back splash, gulls sheer away again. The lobster man is still terse and businesslike, no time for conversation, as the mauve and orange lobsters rise towards the top of the bin. Stench of the bait mounts slowly into the sea-blinding heat.

He stops in the shadow of a craggy point within sight of Cap'n Charles Tawney's farm. We can see the old horse grazing, the tilted barn and a puff of smoke from the rickety farmhouse chimney. The lobster man's withdrawn as ever as he eats his sandwiches, scanning the sea. His reserve precludes the exchange of names, as if he accepts us only as spectators. Just dourness, this silence, or is it a response to the fact that his way of life seems so threatened?

Saul asks him about the lobsters, how the change of seasons affects them. 'Right now they're just coming out, so they're still small,' he explains. 'By September they'll be a pretty good size, those little fellers I'm throwing back. That's the best season, September, two or three hundred pounds every day. There's some that's caught five hundred pounds at the top of the season. But after that you've got winter in front of you. Can't go out half the time and you get back nearly empty sometimes.'

Saul: 'Do your kids come out with you?'

He shakes his head. 'No, they don't like it. Anyways, they're not here any more. Gone to high school on the mainland. Eldest boy's due for college this year. Going to be a doctor, he says – University of Maine.'

He cranks the engine again abruptly, as if he's given too much away; we edge on along the coast, back into the broken rhythm that lasts the whole way round the island until Atlantic reappears. He sets the wheel towards the harbour and begins cleaning the boat. We try to help and he looks appreciative, but goes over it himself, until we're almost afraid to move, for fear of leaving a mark somewhere. He ties up and unloads his lobsters with the man at the lobster cooperative who weighs them. Just over a hundred pounds; but he doesn't show any

reaction. Grins in his remote way, unable to resist a parting
shot, as we thank him and leave. 'Going back for a nap? Oh,
them crabs – I was keeping em for you.' He hands us the
crateful. 'Cook em in salt water, mind, they don't taste the same
without.' Nods again, as if he's shy even of his own generosity.
'Okay, enjoyed having you.'

Atlantic and the coast road are dozing in the afternoon heat.
Then suddenly a siren wails and a red truck pelts by with three
or four men clinging onto the back and a ladder, hose and
buckets on board, tearing up a cloud of dust. We step up in
pursuit, like the others: a pick-up coming the other way spins
round almost without slowing, old Fords and Studebakers pop
up from jetties and side roads, horns blare lights flash and
bystanders shout for a ride, all like some demolition derby.
Then it suddenly occurs to us; we're headed straight for the
camp ground, there's only two more farms before it and
precious little to burn beyond. None of us can remember if we
put out the fire this morning – pictures of the old man dancing
round with cries of rage; without an intersection ahead there's
no way to avoid the issue. Perhaps it's the sense of the foreign
menace and even some ritual provision for it that have aroused
such enthusiasm. The farms flash by and there's no slowing
down; then mercifully the siren dies as the fire truck bounces off
the road by Cap'n Charles's nephew's home. It slows up by
the edge of a wood, as if they're content to take things easy
and even let the fire build up, now that the actual chase is over.
The others aren't to be outdone. The flock of old cars follows
and apparently no one objects to their driving across the field
and the odd patch of cultivation. The crowd builds up, all pointing accusingly at a column of smoke between the trees. Men
and boys unravel the hose, while the firemen advance, until
they discover an old car chassis, smouldering placidly. The water
gushes out, gulps and expires. Someone suggests a bucket
chain, but the fire's virtually over, so they kick it aside instead
and stamp it out triumphantly.

The older men lead an informal enquiry full of elaborate
recollections of other Swan's Island fires. It's the first time
we've seen so many of the islanders together. Ruddy and

open-faced, with broad hands and loose-hanging arms, each of them has a greeting for us as they turn and see us watching. As before, they give the impression of having already heard of our presence. Eventually the crowd thins out; shades of an earlier USA where firemen were always volunteers, on the principle that cooperation was essential to survival.

One of the women comes up to us. 'Aren't you the folks from the camp site? I'm Cap'n Charles Tawney's niece, I hope the old man's looking after you. He's – well, he's kind of old-fashioned, but he's not a bad old fellow.'

He's sitting on his doorstep when we get back, playing with the kitten again. Jumps up when he sees us, as if we've reminded him of something. 'Hear them folks had a fire down there. Just goin down meself to see if I can help em some. Didn't get much done today, I been mighty sick again, and that ball game, pretty good ball game. Couldn't get me battery workin, radio's a good age, mind ya, must be thirty years now, but she's still goin all right. Only the battery that's giving trouble, so I fixed her up to the car, see.' Points to a wild tangle of wires leading from the Buick engine in at the farmhouse window. He begins unhitching them. 'Goin down to my friend's place to get that battery charged right now. Hear you been lobster fishin.'

It's pleasant, as if he's half accepted us as a regular part of his landscape, describing his own day to us and already knowing of ours. 'Would've taken you out meself if I was a bit younger, see. I heard all about it, see, I was watchin out for you, seen you in the bay there, must've been ten o'clock this morning. I was a lobster man meself, you can't tell Cap'n Charles Tawney nothin about lobster fishin off this beautiful Swan's Island. Weren't so fancy in them days, mind ya, hand winch and a little dory, I had to swim for it once or twice, don't mind tellin ya. Clams and lobsters, plenty of em. Aint so many now, they say. Come and they go, come and they go,' and he closes his eyes and tilts his head back, laughing his high, cracked laughter. Deposits the kitten and jumps in the Buick. 'Well, I'm going down to check on that fire and get me battery fixed, see, bye-bye kittycat,' and the Buick bounces out, misses the apple tree by a hair's breadth, turns erratically onto the road and rumbles off in a cloud of dust, Cap'n Charles's face just showing above the bottom of the window.

He's back on the doorstep the next day. Seems to be waiting for one of us and gets up to lend a hand with the idiosyncracies of the well. Reaches inside his shirt pocket when the operation's over. 'Somethin I hunted down for you. Up there in the attic, it was, aint seen it meself in a while, can't keep track of nothin no more.' He passes me a battered photo. 'That's the old wagon, see, last time I use her for travellin, that was when the new ferry come and they was dedicatin it, kind of big occasion it was, must have been, let me see' – his tired eyes close with effort, as if he's lost all sense of time – 'must have been ten, twenty years ago.' Jabs at the picture. 'That old ox there he's been buried a few years, see, must have been a good while back.' Sure enough, the wagon's drawn by the motley combination of Prince, the workhorse, and an old ox, with Cap'n Charles seated on top, pleased as Punch, clean-shaven, jacket and shirt buttoned right up and a new hat perched on his head. It's startling to see a younger version of his face.

A car buzzes by on the road and he waves a derogatory hand. 'There they go, there they go, always up to somethin. That's folks nowadays, always goin here and there, no time for another feller,' and he spits decisively and sits down on the step again. 'That's it, see, m'dear, no time for another feller, that's the young folks these days. Matters the like of this old house, they aint got no interest in em, but there's history there, see. Hundred years old, she is. And the old shed over there, that's where my father worked as a blacksmith and his father and grandfather before him. They was wealthy folks then, used to own half of Atlantic. Shoein all the horses and fixin them old fowlin pieces. Had a mill here, too, used to grind corn for the whole island. Yes, m'dear, it's a fine spot, to my mind the most beautiful spot in this whole USA, accordin to what I know of it. Aint nothin to be ashamed of, aint no prettier spot to speak of on this whole coast of Maine. Them young folks is always tellin me get the place cleaned up, get electricity an that. But I tell em I was born here, lived here all me life, see, apart from a few little

journeyings, workin on this and that, aint nothin to be ashamed
of and I'm goin to keep her that way. Born right here and I'm
goin to die here. This house, she's on her last lap now. I'm just
hopin she'll keep up till the time I'm dead and gone. Folks tell
me I oughta leave, but I aint leavin her, if she falls down on me,
why, I'll just build me a little cabin right over the road there.'
Pauses. 'I got them kittycats, see, them's pretty good company.'

'Did you keep up with the blacksmith's work?'

'No, m'dear, I never did. Time my father died, see, there
weren't much callin for that any more. His main line of work was
fowlin pieces. When I was a boy, see, we was on our own here,
couldn't get much meat from the mainland, it was potaters
all the year round with a complement of fish taken at certain
times of the year and sometimes a little salt pork, that was all
our staple, see. Only real meat you could get was a few wild
birds, ducks an doves, so most of them folks had a fowling piece.
Had a real run on em durin that Civil War, see, my grandfather
had to fix em all up when the folks round here was enlistin.
Tell you what – I still got one if you want a look at her. The old
man made her himself, see. About three and a quarter foot long
she is, drilled her right out himself, she was like a real cannon.
Held over a pound of shot and they used her down in the Civil
War, in the war they had there.'

Pushes the battered door open, hesitates, then beckons me in.
A smell of cats and kerosene fills the dusty, narrow hallway,
light showing through chinks in the wall. 'That's the kitchen in
there, see, do meself a bit of cookin, taters mostly, crush em up
soft, got trouble with me teeth, see, can't eat much more these
days. And the fowls, they give me a few eggs.'

The ceiling's pitch black with soot and the floor scattered with
candle grease. In the kitchen, an iron boiler. A kerosene stove,
small and encrusted. A hand lamp on the window-sill, its glass
chimney cracked and blackened. A dusty calendar hangs on the
wall, old-style Hollywood pin-up cover. Date 1949. Below it
a single wooden shelf: a few dented pots and pans and a tin
with some oats in it. Wooden table and two chairs, one with
a hole in the seat. One egg, a few potatoes and packet of Jello
on the table. The broken windows are patched with cardboard.

Through the few remaining panes the apple blossom can just be seen. 'Them young folks is always tellin me get that electricity, see, but I don't hold with it meself, on account of the fire hazard.' Speaks hurriedly now, as if my presence has suddenly made him aware of the silence. 'Them's as bad as that Bangor-feller, they won't drink that water neither, say I oughta get taps an all. I tell em what's the use of taps when you got the finest water in Maine right in that well, that's what I tell em.' He still seems a bit surprised at himself for having brought me into the house; old turtle with a guest in his shell. 'That gun, she's in the front there.'

Back to the room facing the road. Curtains made from flour sacks hang beside the dusty windows, but obviously they're no longer used, cobwebbed into permanent folds, as if the house itself is so dark that there's little point in excluding the night and no intimacies to hide. A broken couch with threadbare blankets and springs spewing out beneath it, occupied by the querulous kittens. A few colourless strips of carpet, another table, a splintered chair and a pair of ancient radios, reception panels yellow with age. Another old boiler, the flue's fallen off, disconnecting it from the chimney, though it must have had its day, as the ceiling's soot black again. Candles stuck on the mantelpiece; candle ends on the floor. Another lamp. Cardboard boxes, crammed with yellowed newspapers, the odd book and faded clothes. A colour photograph on the wall is the only new item – his great-niece and a young man, her brother, the old man explains. Both of them are smartly dressed, hair brushed, young and fresh, smiling photogenically. Two blue-grey shafts of sunlight push past the curtains and pinpoint the drifting dust.

He rummages in a corner and pulls out the rusty gun, its stock chipped and polished with age. 'Yes, sir, my grandfather made her, old-fashion muzzle-loader, made her right here in the forge. Last time my father used her, I was just a young feller, that was when we had them ducks. They was comin in every night by the brook there, where we got that new fish pond. This old gun my father had, it was famous in these parts, so he planned to see how many he'd get. I helped him build the duck blind, see, and when them ducks come in, he loosed right off at em, he-he, thirteen he had, I believe that must be some kinda record for this whole United States. Yes, m'dear, we had some times. Tell the truth, that brook there, she used to be a nice little spot. I weren't too happy when they started that goddam bulldozin. Mind you, that's progress, aint it. Long as they don't progress me. Now, about them ball games, there's one in Boston, one in Chicago, I been down to my friend's place, see, and got that battery charged again.' He turns both radios on and fiddles with the reception until the commentaries crackle through, one from Boston, one from Chicago. Then he sits down with a vague expression, gazing out of the window.

Bunched up on the battered chair with one ear cocked towards each radio, running crab-like from one to the other whenever the excitement mounts either in Boston or Chicago. Picks up one of the kittens and plays with it every now and then, bare-gummed grin and his face alight round the thin, crusted lips. The house is like a fortress; apart from the sound of the ball games there's only the mewing of the cats, their plumping down from the sofa and soft-footed slinking through the shadows, to vary the contrast of its silence with the birdsong outside. Sometimes he doesn't seem to be hearing the strident radio commentary, but then he suddenly comes to life and hops from one side to the other, passing a few muttered comments. Finally, after an hour or so, he snaps both radios off and stomps into the kitchen. Comes back a few minutes later with two mugs of coffee and a bowl of mash, a boiled egg with oats: eats a few spoonfuls himself, then feeds the rest to the cats. 'Boston, that's a fine place. I was workin there one time, must be, let me see, 1927 it was. Used to get around some, see, a year here, a year there, catch as catch can, that's me. But tell the truth there aint no place like this piece of Swan's Island. Most of my life was raised here, see. Never did go to school proper on account of I was sick, always kept me runnin for cover. That's why I'm on me own, see, never did get me a wife.'

'What did you do before you went travelling?'

'Well, I growed up on the farm, worked here with my father,

but I always wanted to go to sea – too much salt water in my forebears to let me stay ashore, see. They was old quarter-deck men underneath the square-rigged sail so I couldn't keep away, m'dear, I was up for the merchant marine, but I couldn't manage that on account of the health problem. So I told meself I'll get me own boat, just a little dory, see, and go in for the fishin line – come on kitty. So I started saving a few dollars and after three or four years I was able to buy me a dory and start some fishin, right around here. Used to work on her summers and that time it was hard work, didn't have no ice-packin, you had to sell em the same day. Up at dawn and out on the sea and you got through your fishin quick, cause about noon the afternoon breeze gets mean around this coast of Maine and you got to get back in cover, just with manpower, see. Couple a times I was nearly caught, fightin that old bitch out there. This elbow, she's still a little soft from pullin that nine foot oar, feel her.' He thrusts it out, fleshless brown over thin bones. 'That's from pullin that oar, see – plenty of good friends a mine got drowned off a Swan's Island. And when you got back, you weren't finished yet. Haul up the dory, clean the fish, and still seven miles to the nearest market, your fish didn't keep in them days. So I had to load that wagon there and drive her right across the island at a good smart clip. Hard days they was, lobsters and scallops, mackerel and a few herring. Sometimes you was pretty lucky to get them fish there in time, some days I didn't get back here till after the shades a darkness was fallin, and them was long summer days. Kept on till I was fifty-two, fifty-three or thereabouts. I come back on the soil then, must be thirty years or more I was on that sea, goddam er. Just with my own little boat, see, that's the way it's always been.'

Peers out as another car goes by. 'There they go, there they go. Old days if you sat on the step, you'd see ten, twelve people pass inside of half an hour. And they didn't go runnin by like today, used to stop and talk in them days. You mightn't credit it now, see, but this was quite a flourishing island and the city of Atlantic, she was quite a city then. Fishing was good and the stone quarry, see, it was full work every day, people had their roots here. There was plenty of young people, three or four schools when I was a boy. But the young folks now, they don't want to stay. Don't blame em, mind you, it just aint there any more, m'dear. Aint a thing that I did forty or fifty year ago that could still be did today. Nothing, see, aint a thing.'

He pushes his hat back and stands up. 'Matter of fact I've got an old picture took when I weren't long out of school. See if I can hunt her down.' He rummages among the cartons, yellowed letters and accounts, until he finds it. Blows the dust off. It's just recognizable, a spindly, rather pale young man, perhaps in his early twenties, awkward in a double-breasted suit, looking straight at the camera. 'Aint brought her out in years, nobody to look at her, see. Yes, m'dear, we had some times. There was young folks growing up all over this Swan's Island then. We had three dance halls runnin and a few nice little dances, Saturday night was one, see, Wednesday night we had another, catch as catch can right through the week. We'd take that old wagon along, fill her up to overflowin, there was always so many of us half of em couldn't have got inside. Had our own little band see, I was quite a dancing man meself, but they never did let me dance, always wanted me playin, see. Matter of fact that accordion come in handy afterwards when I was over in Portland, Maine, that was in the Depression, see, I was drivin a coal truck. When the work dried up, me and my friends went around singing the hillbilly beat for our supper.' Takes his hat off and wipes the bald crown of his head. 'Matter of fact, I still got her, that old accordion a mine. Like to take a look at her? She's upstairs. Come on, m'dear.'

He leads the way up the dry-rotten stairs into a little bedroom. 'My mother's room in here, see, that's her wheel over there.' Delicate, cobwebbed spinning wheel, a chair and a bed with a lace cover. They look as if they've never been moved, though the room seems cared for. He pulls the accordion out from a corner. Its bellows are frayed and some stops are missing, but he squeezes it gently and sure enough a note emerges. Runs over a simple scale, foot tapping, a note or two blurred, but the hillbilly jingle is there. 'Square dances we used to have. I used to play for em, the Plain Quadrille, the Marching Circle. Waltzes too, the old people, they always did like a good waltz, I was one for the bright ones too, River Shannon and all them numbers. Always liked to see someone doing a good job with a waltz. My Wild Irish Rose was the favourite, he-he,' and his face lights up at some undisclosed memory. 'But I always liked the square dance best – let me see.' Plays a few notes. 'Golden Slippers, that's the one,' and suddenly he swings into it, tensed as he reaches back for the tune, notes slipping, tries a few words, but he's forgotten most of them and the tune gets ahead of him. Frowns, eyes closed, then his face relaxes, lit up by the half sunlight, as he catches a couple of lines and swings away triumphantly, feet tapping, voice cracked,

> *O, them golden slippers,*
> *O, them golden slippers,*
> *Made to walk the golden streets with me, me, me –*

rhythm stronger, voice rising, away now except for the odd missed note; then suddenly his voice rings out, throaty but startlingly firm: 'First four right and left, ready, change and the same again,' echoing down the empty stairs. The cats look up at him in surprise, but his eyes are still closed as his voice remounts. 'Swing your partners and PROMENADE' – misses a note, then another, and collapses to a halt. Opens his eyes. He seems almost shocked. Mutters something indistinct and puts the accordion down. Then he gathers himself, face reset, and rubs his lips. Puts the accordion back in the corner.

There's one more room across the way. He pushes the door open. 'My nephew was staying here, see, my great-nephew, that is, he's a good boy, likes it here. He's been goin to high school, see, he graduated yesterday. Asked me to come, but I wouldn't go, the others went, but I stay right here.' The room has a lived-in air: the windows are cleaner than the others and the sun picks out the grain of the floor. The wall is covered in magazine cuttings: pop stars, the Boston Redsox and Jane Fonda in Western gear, all hip and thigh, pouting lips and skin-tight jeans. He looks at them expressionless and closes the door again quietly. 'Well, I gotta get back to work, gotta plant my green peas again on account of them goddam crows.'

Back outside birdsong and sunlight. The apple branches lift very faintly but otherwise there's hardly a movement. We have to go into Atlantic to check the time of tomorrow's ferry.

He's waiting for us when we get back. He's parked the old Buick down by the camp site and sits sideways on the seat, gazing out at a sullen sea. Sniffs the air as he sees us. 'Storm's comin,' he announces. 'Goin to be a real northeaster, like the one drowned my grandfather. Tell by the wind, see, smell her comin.'

Sure enough, an hour or so later an irritated little squall whips up the water's edge and turns to a gale, gathering the swell and running in at double pace. Pines turn their backs in flight. Gulls hang suspended, outscreaming the sea. The waves darken to midnight blue and finally to mud colour, rocks just spumes of breakwater white. The tent starts flapping wildly as darkness closes like a fist, clenching out the bluff and the farmhouse.

Suddenly a wild silhouette appears under the dancing pine trees, arms flying, clutching his hat, fighting his dogged way towards us, a sprite caught in the eye of the storm. He has a rope over his shoulder, frayed and joined in several places. 'Thought you might be needin her to batten them hatches down, m'dears, she'll keep you fast, see,' and his cracked voice drowns in the wind as he turns full face to the sea and waves a skinny fist at it. 'Old bitch, see how she is, I've known her for seventy year and she's always beating a feller, beatin his door, beatin his dory. I been here all my life, I knows the stinkin ways of her. You'd best batten down, see, I got me radio fixed now and they say she's goin to be a bad one, I'm goin to mind them kittycats,' and he stumbles away, arms flapping, words spinning away on the gale that whips his thin, scarecrow outline, tearing at his overalls.

Then gradually its fury dies – we must have had just the tail end of it. Half light shifts back again, quailing over a penitent sea, and the mainland reappears. The old workhorse is up on the slope, browsing as if nothing has happened. A last glint of sunlight touches the shore.

The driftwood in the fire that night burns with a trickle of violet flame. An old square timber, sea-worn, with a rusty bolt through it. Makes us wonder where it's travelled. Its ashes blow back at the sea. Seems irreverent, burning it.

A full moon lifts through the pines. Tomorrow night we'll be in Quebec and Saul and Judy back in Boston. The sea's roll and sigh are hushed. We can see the old man's house above us, a black spot at the top of the slope. It looks more pixie-like than ever in the starless, moon-washed night. Nine o'clock. No light. He must be asleep. We forgot to tell him we're leaving at dawn.

Louis Forbes, 38

FORBES, *Louis, 38, ex-fighter, hobo, hustler, cleaner in his hard times (at the end of his disability cheque) of cars, dishes, restaurant floors, sleeps in a children's playgound in Chicago's North Side with the elevated railway rattling by above his head.*

North Side, she's mellow, man – hippies here has plenty of bread, stake you a smoke or a bite to eat – and tourists – give you a quarter, they're so scared they can't say no. See them out-of-state licence plates and you git right after em. New Yorkers, they're mellow, pay you quick – not like Chicago guys – stop in the middle of the street and bawl you right out if you ask – and there's fancy restaurants – always get work if you want her, nigger work, washin, scrubbin.

(Lean, wiry and quick-walking, glides along despite a limp, as if he's really going somewhere. Carries his things in an army satchel, an old jersey for chilly nights, a folder with two colour pictures, bread and a bottle of cheap wine, the sickly-sweet type, around fifty cents in the cut-price liquor stores. Porkpie hat and a trim moustache. Left eyebrow badly scarred, jerks occasionally as he talks; cheeks slightly ashen and sunk. He's black. Looks older than his age.)

Growed up in the state of Missoura, near a city by the name of Cape Girardeau – old man was a tenant farmer – livin was pretty sweet down there – sun'd be shinin most days – didn't eat meat too often, little pork and maybe a chicken, but the livin was pretty easy. Melons – me and my big brother and sister, we'd pick one pretty near every day – long as we could pay the rent – till the old man died – I was ten – two years schoolin, I was pretty near writin my name – quit school – help my big brother on the farm.

(*Soon afterward they got notice to quit – landlord had sold the property for building, black tenant farmers didn't argue. Moved to Cape Girardeau, right beside the Mississippi, three teenagers and their mother, one room, one bed and no electricity; rent was only ten a month, rats kept the value down. Louis held odd jobs for a while, warehouse work, sweeping, cleaning, but they never lasted, the pay was low and with two years schooling his prospects were nil. When their mother died the children split up. Louis's sister lived in as a maid; his elder brother headed north for Chicago. Louis reckons he died, as they never heard from him again. He stayed on in Cape Girardeau, selling mainly stolen hub-caps till caught on the job one night. Police beat him badly, had him jailed for a year, then ordered him out of town. He made for St Louis, on advice from a penitentiary friend.*)*

He'd bin in the fight game in St Louis – fixed me up with a pretty nice job working for his manager, cleaner in the gymnasium – one of the fighters treated me mean, a white guy, I never knew why – nigger boy – one day I blow it – bang, laid that bastard right on the floor – manager walks in – stands there and watches – other feller comes back at me – bang, I lay him flat again – manager pays him off and tells him git the hell outa there – three weeks later I got my first fight – won four in four weeks – grew my moustache, figured I'd look like Clark Gable – fans got to know me real good – turned pro – I fought in every city – Chicago Stadium, New Orleans, Minneapolis-St Paul, Kansas City – won around three out every four – one fight I made two grand – never seen money like that before – I could be the golden boy, maybe I'd end up champ, make myself a hundred grand – spent her, man, I spent like crazy – met with Lulu – real fine wedding right there in St Louis – got her picture right here and the little boy too (*the ones in his satchel, overcoloured photographs of a young, attractive woman and a proudly dressed little boy*) – twenty-two then – spent like crazy – got real psychic, my psychic was automobiles – won a big fight in Buffalo one time, walked right out of the ring there and

bought me a new convertible, white convertible, Pontiac – drove
her right on back to St Louis.

(*Until a bad car smash broke his leg and injured his back. Four
months in hospital and another three out of the ring. Even then he
wasn't ready to fight, but by now he owed his manager well over a
thousand dollars.*) Wasn't right – friends ask me: Louis, man,
where's that punch? Couldn't raise her – no footwork either –
lost three or four fights – couldn't quit – weren't a cotton-pickin
thing I could do outside the fight game – Lulu kept on scratchin
at me cause we'd lost the big money – kept on fighting – won
a couple – losing most of em – guys was telling me I should start
fixing fights – but I never did lay down – no more automobile
– no house, way we'd spent the big money – rent was gettin
hard to find – one day I get back home and the apartment's
clean empty – walked right out and left me, taken our little
feller with her – figured if I could make a comeback I could get
her back again – big fights, two, three fights a month – didn't
know where I was – wouldn't remember what round it was – lost
six fights in a row – in Milwaukee, against a big Swede, a wildcat,
I'll keep my cool – he starts clinchin real close – says stand up
you nigger bitch – come on you nigger bitch – got mad, I went
right at him – too quick for me – mean, kept me going – I was
cut right to ribbons – couldn't go back – manager dropped me
– still owed him a few bucks, so he gives me a job cleaning –
one day when I come in late, guess he was just waiting for it,
he bawls me out, gives me twenty-five bucks and tells me don't
come back again.

(*Applied for a job as a trainer, but his fight record was against
him. Then returned to his manager and begged to be taken back as
a cleaner; manager had him thrown on the street. Decided to try
and find his brother – maybe he'd lend him money to get Lulu
back again, though he didn't know where she was. Came up to
Chicago to look for his brother but never had any news of him.
And Chicago was a tough spot to be down and out and black.*)
I figured she was pretty nice in the North, seemed like a black
man could go where he likes – but it ain't so different – all a
black man can git is nigger work, stockyards, sweeping, less
you're one of them college niggers – had luck, I got work drivin

a cab – bread was good – then I mussed her right up – drivin this lady, a rich old lady – starts callin me boy – 'you nigra drivers is all the same' – drive her slower – I stop the cab – 'lady, if you don't like nigger drivin you'd better git on out and walk' – she telephones the boss – 'sorry man, she knows the mayor' – weren't nothin more he could do – my back was gettin worse – had to git on welfare – ain't much, but she keeps me going.

After that I kept real low – figured it was twice I got mad, with that big Swede and that mean ole lady, and all I ever got was trouble – I'd just keep my head down – folks aint give me nothin and I ain't givin nothin back – times I used to git pretty mad thinkin about that mean ole lady – knowin a black man can't get nowhere – used to go on the freedom marches, civil rights, I was there – but nothin aint come of it, once I got beaten real bad, that don't get you no place – get that disability cheque and live real easy – sure man, I'd like my freedom, walk around the Loop nights, visit all them fancy places – can't go down there, not if you're a one dollar nigger, you gotta be twenty dollar style, carry all twenty dollar bills if you wanta git your freedom – no address, they'll put somethin on you, beat you real bad – don't do no protestin no more. And I tell you somethin, I wouldn't want to live like whitie – ain't got no joy, man, only bread – ain't got no livin up there. Mornings I can sit right here and watch em driving down from Lake Shore into them little offices, see the same faces every day. Never do see em smiling –

keep real cool – pretty nice, the North Side – sleepin here two summers now – got to like this little park. Only winters she's pretty cold, I move down back of the Loop, sleep on them old packing cases back of the big stores there – cops git mean, I move down to the South Side, aint safe for a black man up here, not when there's riots comin – feel like I'm gettin too old for Chicago, I feel pretty lonesome – aint made it, you're through – a mean city – you could be layin down and dyin and all folks'd say to you is git the hell outa my way – if the cops don't get you, the gangs will. I seen too many alley fights, I don't go in them pool halls no more. Too many draw-knives and them cops beatin black men to death. See you're a nigger and bang, they git you. Only thing ever brought me here was chasin up that little broad, I loved that broad.

Figure I'll git back to Cape Girardeau, see that old Mississippi again – aint rich, but the livin's cheap down there – aint just a white man's city, a black man can live all right down there. Maybe next month, month after, I'll git back to Cape Girardeau where the livin's easier.

CHAPTER 5

MANSCAPE ONE:
New York – Illinois

After French Canada's depth of rambling fields and ancient barns, there's an added irony in seeing upstate New York again; a younger manscape already spent in the empty holiday towns alongside Lake Ontario and big dilapidated Oswego, still bravely proclaiming itself THE PORT OF UPSTATE NEW YORK. Its architecture's a lucky dip of French Renaissance and Arabesque, Victorian and neo-Tudor. Their centrepiece, the Erie Canal, cuts a haunted way between them, roisterous westward highway of the nineteenth century boom which made New York the Empire State, with its millionaires and political bosses and the big industrial towns, Buffalo and Rochester, that sprang up overnight in its wake: opened in 1825 'to create a new era in history, to erect a work more stupendous, more significant and more beneficial than has hitherto been achieved by the human race', as its founder Governor Clinton would have it; twice enlarged in less than a century, first 'Clinton's Ditch', then the Middle Canal, and finally the Barge Canal; only to be relegated as the West it had helped to create outgrew the Empire State and found new routes and transport east. It divides the city, as empty as the lake horizon. Below the abandoned warehouses two or three fishermen cast their lines at the still, grey water. A few figures talk in huddles in the dank canal-side bars. In one of them a solitary Indian downs his shots in complete silence, waiting impassively for the barman to fill his glass, then throwing it back automatically. He never looks round. It's the same in the stores and on the sidewalks, an un-American desultoriness; no present without a future.

Wherever the canal passes it's like this. At Montezuma a proud notice announces that the town once flourished thanks to the local passenger boat that plied the first of the three canals; but drivers whip by on the thruway without so much as glancing at it. All that's left of 'Clinton's Ditch', highway to a new USA, is a sunken little hollow overgrown with reeds and shrub, straggling through the sleepy town and vanishing in the empty landscape. In nearby Clyde, on the Barge Canal, a former junction for the barges carrying flour from the Rochester mills, weeds push up through the sidewalks and old couples line the benches; Italian faces, many of them, descendants of railroad labourers brought three generations ago from immigrant Boston and New York City to make the robber barons' fortunes. Centrepiece of the village green is their tribute to the USA, a statue of George Washington, with a faded plaque: Erected in 1885 by the Sons of Italy in America, Chapter 947, Clyde, New York. The buildings echo the same spirit of barge tolls reckoned by the thousand: none of New England's clapboard white, but square-faced burghers' Victorian, four storeys, high Gothic windows and rhetorical cornices in Italian Renaissance style.

Round the corner in Canal Street the huge warehouses are boarded up. Their silence dominates the town; New York City's equivalent would be Fifth Avenue abandoned. In Jimmy de Renzo's Half Barrel Bar the man beside us livens up when we ask him about the canal. 'Used to be quite a few folks here had worked on her – aint many now. They hardly use her any more – pleasure boats mostly and just a few barges, maybe ten or a dozen a week. That's why the town's gone downhill, gets smaller and quieter every year. Folks that built her thought the canal would go on forever. But since she pretty near closed, it's been dead.' He turns to the barman. 'Right Jim? Folks here was asking about the canal – I was telling them, doesn't look like Clyde'll make a comeback now.'

Jim concurs. 'No, sir, don't look like it.' He comes to join us, as if reminiscences are all that Clyde now affords. 'From what my old man used to tell me, Canal Street here was really something. Them brick buildings over there, they was beer-halls and boarding-houses for the barge men and passengers, all the way to New York City in top hats and fancy dresses. And girls – there was more girls up here than in New York City. Often

the town'd be so full, folks couldn't find a place to sleep. But
no – aint nothing doing any more. They were hoping she'd
pick up again after they built the Barge Canal, but she never
did, railroads killed her. Only reason folks has stayed is the old
ones don't want to move and the young ones don't know where
to go.' He looks round. 'You interested? Aint many folks are
these days. Follow Route 31 out of town, you'll see some old
stone locks by the highway just a couple of miles out. Ask for
Mrs Beal at the junction with the old road – there's one of
them right aback of her house. Then try Lyons – museum there
has quite a bit about the canal.'

Beyond the town, road and railroad link up and all the history
of New York suddenly runs parallel – the two early canals
reappear in the fields and the bigger Barge Canal reaches unbroken to the horizon, but without a boat in sight; even the
railroad only has an occasional freight car, whilst the once
major Route 31 is a byway now that the New York Thruway
runs a few miles to the south. Suddenly, on the edge of a field
right behind a modest house, there's a glimpse of a huge stone
structure. Sure enough, Mrs Beal ushers us in unsurprised.
'Sure, you take a look at her. Don't you stay out there too long,
them mosquitoes is big as elephants. They ploughed the first
canal under, most of it's in that corn field there and I sure wish
they'd do it with this one, them mosquitoes is getting so bad.
But you go right ahead now.'

Behind the house in the dank shadows huge stone slabs form
a double rampart alongside the second, Middle Canal. It's some
ten or twelve feet high under the heavy vegetation, with hardly a
stone out of place. Where the ramparts end, eighty feet away,
the canal bed vanishes again between the whispering cottonwood trees and into the open cornfields. Apart from the
mosquitoes' hum, there isn't a single nearby sound: just the
accentuated silence of a corner of human history forgotten by
the world it produced.

We follow the old road by the bank until it suddenly peters
out into a cluster of shanty cabins. There's only one person in
sight, a very old, very black man seated surrealistically in a
very ancient chair surrounded by battered furniture and scrap;

chickens scrabble in the dust and a puppy plays on the doorstep beside him. He averts his eyes, then looks after us cautiously. Only the lush line of the trees shows where the canal runs on. Beside it, snatches of cultivation, more crude cabins and a few haggard faces answering our glances suspiciously: it's half unreal, as if they too were left by the boom and haven't seen a stranger since. The canal bed is a fairy-tale avenue canopied by the cottonwood branches and buttressed with bits of a concrete embankment. The towpath is just detectable and beyond it the first, smaller canal shows in patches of fetid green through the deep scrub and brambles. The hoot of a freight train, muffled and gone. Mosquitoes bunch above the puddles and somewhere the cry of a marsh bird drifts theatrically through the trees.

In the modest county museum at Lyons the cheery lady curator tells us to make ourselves at home. Engravings and early photographs echo the Erie's epic history – Governor Clinton's long struggle with New York City's Tammany Hall, whose bosses were afraid to back it; the eight year Odyssey of its construction with immigrant Irish from New York City working in still unsettled country with no roads to bring supplies and often laid low by malaria. Then the triumph of its opening: 'they have built the longest canal in the world in the least time with the least expense and to the greatest public benefit' – displays, pageants, parades and banquets in every new canal town as the Governor's flotilla went from Buffalo to Albany, three hundred and sixty-three miles, with brass bands all the way, and down the Hudson to New York City. Boom time followed – freight costs slashed and quantities spiralling every year, manufactures from the East and new agricultural wealth from the West. Over nineteen thousand boats in its first year alone and forty thousand migrants heading west along its course. Towns mushroomed in their wake: in Rochester, population three hundred when the canal building began, the world's biggest flour mills ten years later; Palmyra, Newark, Clyde and Lyons virtually born overnight: New York City boosted into the world's greatest port. Saloons, brothels and dance-halls at almost every stopping point, earning the Erie its nickname,

'The Great Ditch of Iniquity'. A new land opened to the west. by the early seventies the former migrants' eastbound produce was outstripping the freight from the coast, symbol of the turning balance between the old and new USA. And in this there's the first hint of its supremely American outcome – already the farmlands of eastern New York were finding it hard to keep up with the pace. Finally the canal's success rounded even on itself. Others were built along routes further south and by the 1840s, although the Erie had been enlarged, the railroads were competing with it. By 1900 only one fifth of the West's freight still went by canal. A brief lease of life afterwards when the Barge Canal was built, to fight back at the railroads; but soon it was barely paying its way. It still carries some grain eastwards and fuel barges to the West; but most of the craft on it now are pleasure boats, idle for most of the year.

The museum is full of genteel reminders of the world it left behind. Photos of local worthies being thanked by Eisenhower for their part in Republican campaigns. A little old lady who's brought the museum a hand-made silver locket given her by her grandmother, one of the town's first citizens. And the pictures that the curator shows us: parades through the crowded streets and the canal in full swing, freight piled high on the jetties in front of the big stone warehouses. 'There's not much left of it now,' she explains, 'apart from the Barge Canal, of course. Clinton's Ditch and the Middle Canal, they filled them up long ago, except where they joined the Barge Canal. Not that Lyons changes much – it's still a pretty conservative town with a lot of Yankee blood and even a few Dutch names from over on the Hudson River. Irish too, their ancestors really built the canal. And Italians and Germans, theirs worked on the railroads. You might not believe it, but there's quite a few Lyons folks still look on them as immigrants.' She pauses. 'I tell you what – you should talk to the Misses Wilson, they're sisters, been in Lyons all their lives, I'll telephone to warn them for you. Go right on up along Maple Street to the big house at the end there – the dark one with the wide porch.'

There's no mistaking it, a huge Gothic fantasy amongst the

maples, with high gables, a long veranda and pointed turrets at either end. An old lady is waiting at the door, in a long white shawl. She shakes us fraily by the hand and peers up at us intently. 'So you're from England – now isn't that wonderful.' She looks a bit surprised at June but apparently accepts that time may have varied the British somewhat. Raises her voice. 'Daisie – visitors from England, Daisie. Come on in now.'

Another elderly figure appears and greets us with a mischievous smile. 'This is my sister,' the first one explains – 'you'll have to shout because she doesn't hear too well, she's eighty-seven.' She twinkles. 'I'm only eighty-three.' She bellows at Daisie, who listens through a brass ear trumpet which she keeps attached to her waist. 'These folks come from England, dear, they want to hear all about Lyons and the old Erie Canal.'

They usher us into the hallway, the first one enveloped in her shawl and Daisie with a head of white curls and bangles and beads everywhere. When we're inside, Daisie repeats her sister's performance – takes us over to the window and peers at us flirtatiously. 'Well, now, so you're from England. We used to travel over there, it must be fifty years now since we've been to England. I expect it's changed a bit?'

Her sister chips in. 'Sit down, my dears.' She points to an elegant period sofa, while they sit opposite in high-backed chairs. Daisie offers us cigarettes from a large silver box with a trace of dust. When we accept, they both follow suit, lighting theirs with difficulty and puffing away with mischievous glee. The younger sister points at the sofa. 'Most of our furniture is English – that davenport belonged to the Governor of New York, the one after Governor Clinton – he was a friend of my grandfather.'

Daisie breaks in. 'Great-grandfather, Beth.'

Beth looks piqued. 'Well, our great-grandfather, yes, dear, you must be right – he was from England, near Tintern Abbey, that's near Wales, isn't it? Oh, it's so long since we've been there.' She suddenly leans forward conspiratorially and repeats her earlier advice. 'My sister's very deaf, you know' – and she winks at us wickedly as Daisie's cameo face is turned. It's like this continually, each sister alternately playing us off against the other, unaware that she's doing the same.

Daisie sits up straight-backed, eyes bright under her curls. 'But why do you come to America? There's so many things in your country, we have hardly anything here.' Her face reflects a Brahmin's scorn for the modern USA which made their town a backwater.

Beth taps the cigarette box. 'This came from England – and the Queen Anne table behind you. And this little cup of mine' – she picks it up, hand-beaten silver, mounted on a wooden dragon – 'I got that in Peking, yes, we went to Peking, in the old days, of course. We were always travelling, the trans-Siberian railway, the Pleasure Gardens, the Great Wall. The Chinese warriors had cups like this on their belts when they went into battle – it's in the old Chinese pictures, you know.' Her voice grows firmer. 'The museum wanted to buy it, but I wouldn't let them have it – people these days don't appreciate things.'

Daisie makes her comeback. 'That picture up there' – she points to a portrait of a princely Renaissance couple – 'my grandmother painted that, she copied it from the original, it was in the Uffizi Museum. Of course, it was different in her day, she knew everybody here. We used to know them, but now it's different.'

Beth nods. At least they agree on the limitations of the present. 'People nowadays aren't interested in anyone – no reason why they should worry about the older people, is there?' She looks at us as if willing us to disagree. A car screeches by. She looks annoyed. 'Those machines, the way they drive them. Where do you think they're all going? Everyone's so hurried these days. It wasn't like that when we were girls.'

Daisie lifts her ear trumpet. 'What's that? When we were what?'

'Girls, dear, I was telling them about Lyons when we were girls. This was the last house on the hill and above here was all orchards. The older families lived up here and the others, the canal people, they lived down near Water Street. There were really busy towns all along the canal here. Clyde, Lyons, Newark

– what they used to say was, Newark had the money, Clyde had nothing and Lyons had the aristocracy.' She laughs, pleased with herself. 'It's different now – sometimes we don't even know who's come to live here on the hill. Even the canal people, they live on the hill now, the Irish and Italians, you know.'

Daisie chirps up again. 'You know what we used to do in those days? We used to go sledding down the hill – right down to the bottom there. Winters we were quite cut off, the canal would freeze right over – of course, there was lots of us here, girls and young men, there were lots of us, weren't there, Beth?'

Beth: 'Yes, you're right, dear. And when we went sledding down that hill, we'd end up by the package boat office at the end of the street there. And the men would take us out on the boats right up to the court house out on old Route 31 – then we'd walk back along the canal.'

Daisie: 'Skating and barbecues on the bank. Sometimes the ice would break and we'd all go down together, but we didn't mind a soaking, there was always lots of us.'

Beth: 'You could take the passenger boat all the way down to New York City. And all our things came up by boat, the things we'd ordered from Europe. Now you can't even go by train, they don't have passenger trains any more. They all fly or they go by car. We don't agree with all that flying, we don't go travelling any more. The day they closed that passenger line I knew we were going to stay right here, I knew we'd never leave Lyons again. I was right – we've never left Lyons since then.'

After a glass of dry sherry, they come out to see us off, puppet-like figures waving to us from under the wistaria. Below the hill on Water Street a few figures lounge in the doorways of the grandiose five-storey buildings. The ground floor of one of them has been converted into a garage and another into a bar; but most of them are boarded up. Round the corner, dusk gathers slowly alongside the Barge Canal. A plaque on the wall: Grand Avenue. It must have been where we're standing, a wide stretch of asphalt beside the canal, a parking lot now, until it peters out in the bushes.

As dark falls there's hardly a sound; and in Water Street, as we leave, exactly three lights are on in the fifty or sixty yards of big buildings on either side.

Turning south towards Pennyslvania through New York's last farming valleys, the landscape gradually broadens out in a green foretaste of the Midwest; Palmyra, birthplace of Joseph Smith the first Mormon visionary, echoes another of its founding dreams. A sign describes an old brick store as the spot on which the first Book of Mormon was printed in 1831. Another points up to Cumorah Hill, where Smith, a local farmer's son, is said to have found the golden tablets on which the prophecies were written. A path winds up to a large gilt statue of Moroni, the angel who appeared to him. Given the epic outcome, the Mormons' flight from persecution to build a new world in the Utah desert, Cumorah's smallness and stillness are startling. It can hardly have changed since then. A single farm straggles below us, broken-topped silo and two small barns. Crickets are the only sound and no one in sight apart from the farmer, ploughing a small, sloping field. Only the blue westward haze gives a hint of the land beyond it, its scale and its promises. Moroni's glittering statue is out of keeping with these modest beginnings; Joseph Smith would probably find it more startling than its original.

There's something of the same contrast between the Mormons' past and present in their information centre nearby. Mormon stickers and posters and pamphlets ('With over thirty-five detailed maps and a Rapid Route Section indicating the fastest routes between the main Mormon sites for travellers with limited time'), plus a non-stop publicity film; closing shot is Mom, Dad and kids smiling from brand new convertible with Salt Lake City and Temple in background. It's as if every once-unique vision has ended up with the same choice; either the Shakers' twilight or reduction by the Image Machine to a uniform Madison Avenue jingle. The lady from Utah in charge of the centre makes us think of blueberry pie rather than this year's Chevrolet; but like the glossy pamphlets she's swamped in Mormon sales talk which gives an urge to pinch her to see if she'd react at all.

Down the road at the Joseph Smith farmhouse two oldish couples stand on the porch surveying the quiet countryside. They greet us and introduce themselves: Brother and Sister Day and Brother and Sister Thomson. 'Me an' Sister Thomson, we just got in from Salt Lake City,' Brother Thomson tells us, glowing with a pilgrim's pride. 'First time we ever left Utah together. Brother and Sister Day here, they're looking after Joseph's place.'

'We take it in turns,' Brother Day explains. 'It's one of our duties as Mormons.' He pricks up his ears when he hears we're from England – his son is over there at the moment. 'He's on his mission – the young folks, they all go out on a mission before they settle down and get married. He's in – what's it called, dear, the place where Jethro's on his mission? Kent, that's right. My folks were from England, you know – my grandfather Day was a Methodist minister, then he heard the Mormon message and came right on over here, brought a hundred converts with him. Sailed over to New York City and then they bought their wooden wagons and got themselves right-a-ways over to Utah.'

The way he describes it is so immediate that he might have done it himself. It's much the same when he and his wife take us round the neat old farmhouse. They blossom with pride as they show us the place where Smith carved his name on the door – 'Joseph' they always call him, as if they knew him personally. Meanwhile Brother Day rambles on with his family history. 'My other grandfather, Grandfather Bennet, was blinded in an accident. Gold-mining in California, lost his sight in some explosion. Then he heard the Mormon message and went to visit the apostles in Utah – knelt right down in front of them and they placed their hands on his head and blessed him. Next thing, he opened his eyes and saw them standing in front of him.'

Their convictions seem to bound their world. There's something reassuring about his description of miracles as such matter-of-fact events and the Utopia-centredness which makes Kent so vague and remote, simply part of a pagan beyond. Yet there's also something disturbing in its modern combination with Madison Avenue publicity: as if any creed, however

4

98

eccentric, has access in this age of McLuhan to near-totalitarian methods. It turns their homely, Bohemian conviction into something of a bludgeon, just an offshoot of the American Dream, with its evangelist's view of the world typically sustained by their ignorance of it. It's when the conversation drifts round for some reason to horse-racing that the contrast comes home. Suddenly they're different people, as their voices shrill in condemnation of racing, betting and smoking in turn; to double the effect, both are judged worse in women than in men. It's as if their flight from intolerance has ultimately come full circle to their own indulgence in it; an ironic innuendo of success in the USA.

A few hours later and further south the big Alleghenies ride the horizon, last fold of Appalachia and barrier to the waiting West, farms sprawling at their feet and villages with hardly a sign, no need, no other strangers here, ('You should stop by in the winter,' says the lady in the diner, 'prettiest place in the whole USA with the clouds reflected in the snow and the sun shining down on them hills.') Over the Pennsylvania line New England's modesty is gone: a huge old steel viaduct carries the Erie Railroad west, the successor, itself superseded, to the canal and its passenger boats, with few signs of settlement, stone quarries and massive cuttings and lumber trucks pounding east until outcrops of industrial Pittsburgh loom through the mountain mist, ridges gouged with surface mines and smokestacks puffing at the sky above the Allegheny River, slow-broad green to industrial grey. Butler, a biggish mill town cramped into a cleft in the mountains.

It's more twentieth century than New England's factory towns, but still close enough to the East to share its perpetually shambling look of the industrial revolution. Smoketrails scar the mountain sundown. Six o'clock siren blasts through the valley and soon the sidewalks are jammed as the day shift heads home and the night shift goes to work. Yet there is something strikingly new about it compared to all we've seen so far. Suddenly, undramatically, its images of the end of a day have a self-contained character, the stamp of a total USA after the halfway European flavour of its prelude in the East. The

rival gaggles of high-school kids in bermuda shorts and sneakers
eyeing each other across the street, transistor radios in hand;
the traffic cop whistling and waving and back-chatting the
passers-by; the truck driver who stops at the lights opposite
the Chicken Basket diner, catches the young waitress's eye and
flexes his biceps for a quick laugh before he trundles on again;
the late-shopping housewives, all curlers and kids and overloaded with packages, filing out of the supermarkets; the
teenage mechanic slouched at the wheel of a customer's Cadillac,
coasting it singlehanded cool round the back of the traffic cop
with half a hunting eye on the schoolgirls; the battered rows
of tenement houses scrambling up the pit-scarred slopes and
another bigger and fresher scar smashing the green woods aside
where they're building a new thruway. ('Mind, that aint nothing
new,' the man in Clinton's Bar tells us. 'They're always building
some new road, ever since I can first remember. Least, in the
new bits of town, where the money is. Six-lane highway up there
and down here by the railroad crossing it's still them old cobbles
and holes. You know what they say about it, the country club
set that run this town – us folks down here don't pay no taxes,
so why the hell should they pave the streets?')

It's in the laundromat that we meet him, next to the crumbling Clinton Hotel. He's painting the walls a cheap-looking green
that matches the economy lighting. He glances at us unsolicited,
as if he feels free to talk because we're obviously strangers.
'They're generous bastards,' he observes. 'Told me to get the
cheapest paint and be sure I do it in one coat. That's how they
make their first million, right?' He grins. All he's really achiev-
ing, apart from covering the obscenities, is to heighten its
morgue-like desolation, in keeping with the figures who use
it. They're all silent, apart from himself, a sample from the
USA which can't afford a washing machine. An old lady with
crumpled clothes and mud-coloured sneakers that flop as she
walks; housewives drawn with overwork and a man with the
build of a king trucker folding a pile of freshly washed diapers.
The painter obviously wants to chat, their submissive silence
must get him down. When he asks the inevitable where are you
from, his face lights up at our answer. He was stationed near

Oxford during the war at a US air base, he says, and there he
met the love of his life. 'I sure should have married her – Alice,
her name was. Her dad used to run a little gas station a couple
of miles out of town. Say – I'll be through in half an hour –
how about us having a drink? See you in the Clinton Bar.'

When he joins us there, most of the drinkers are watching the
ball game on television. He glances up at a player's profile
flashed briefly across the screen after one of the home runs, the
crowd still roaring in the background. 'Wanted to be a champ
myself, when I was a kid, that was. My folks was immigrants,
they spoke German, I used to be kind of embarrassed about
them because they hardly spoke any English. Got my sights set
right there on being a real American boy – Big League ball-
player, that's what I reckoned.'

'So what happened?'

He laughs. 'Hell – I was dreaming. Nearest I ever got to it
was collecting players' autographs. Didn't stop me dreaming
though, my old man encouraged me. They had a rough time.
Came over here with the stars in their eyes and spent most of
their life in the mills, Pittsburgh mostly, then up here. Then
the Depression took their savings. So they kind of fixed on me,
reckoned I'd make up for it.' He takes a long drink. 'Dice was
loaded wrong, I guess. I had it all planned out pretty nice – when
I started work the Depression was over, things were picking up
again and I was saving quite a bit. We was planning on building
a drive-in with nice little lights and grass out front – little way
out of town here where you can't smell them goddam mills.'
He shapes it all out with his hands. 'And I'd build a place for
the old folks, little cabin by the side – then I'd plough all the
money back in and turn her into a real motel.' He shrugs. 'Soon
as I'd saved a bit, they grabbed me for the goddam army. Then,
when I came back again I planned on bringing Alice over – didn't
work out that way, that's all. Got married to a local girl and
never did save me another dime. Save' – he laughs at the idea –
'I still work at the mill, see, grinding, filthiest work of all, and
by mid-week the money's gone. That's why I'm doing the
painting there. It's all them payments – they keep getting
bigger. I'd quit the mill tomorrow if there was a chance of

making it – but that's it, not a dime to start with and payments due every goddam week. Anyways I couldn't back out, the job carries a pension, see, and life insurance – quit and you lose em, you have to wait till retiring age.' He pauses. 'Only seventeen years. Granpa's Drive-In I'll call it.'

'How many children have you got?'

'Two – eldest girl of ours, Jenny, she's the prettiest girl in town. Or was – got married a month ago and now she's gone to California, guess we won't see too much of her. Seventeen – kind of young. He's a nice boy all right, but well – she seems just a little girl. That's why it kind of took me short. The way things are around here, you're so goddam wrapped up in working, planning, trying to save then suddenly, wham – the kids have grown up and gone – and you're still planning. Our boy, he's already fifteen, army'll have him pretty soon. Funny thought, him in Vietnam and us still making them goddam payments.'

We watch the ball game for a while and then he gets back to the subject of England. It's the same as with his kids – he seems to expect time to have stood still, thinking of his English girl as being the same as when he knew her, over twenty years ago. He describes how she looks then suddenly asks if we'd look her up for him – apparently it doesn't occur to him she probably moved long ago. He drains his glass. 'I gotta get back. Seven o'clock shift tomorrow morning.'

He shakes hands and disappears down the half-awake, broken street, his figure no longer distinct from the others, a twentieth-century Paul Bunyan cut down to human scale (only his dreams frontier size) by the pallid neon lights

that pulse on and off all night opposite the old hotel, gas station and laundromat, alternating red and green (we realize he never told us his name) HAMBURGER CHICKEN DINNER HAMBURGER CHICKEN DINNER OPEN 24 HOURS HAM-BURGER CHICKEN DINNER HAMBURGER CHICKEN DINNER HAMBURGER CHICKEN DINNER OPEN 24 HOURS HAMBURGER CHICKEN DINNER (only told us his nine-foot dreams, 'I used to go with a blonde over there,' and we wonder if she remembers him and how, her fresh-faced American boy, sagged and dying of monthly payments, of never was a Big

League player nor nice little lights and grass out front and dwarfed by the neon red and green) HAMBURGER CHICKEN DINNER HAMBURGER CHICKEN DINNER.

Beyond Butler's billboard frontier (FIRST JEEP BUILT HERE, a despairing claim to uniqueness) the ragged little industrial towns, Gothic halls and cobbles and cables and derelict mine-shafts in between, vanish with the Alleghenies. As the foothills fall away, suddenly Ohio's there in valleys rolling unbroken green with a first sense of the big land's richness, permanence, after those eastern images of arriving and re-building.

Rough stalls line the road, piled high with farm produce proclaimed by homely, hand-written signs: FRESH EGGS, SWISS CHEESE, HOME MADE BUTTER, UNCLE SAM'S BAVARIAN SAUSAGE. The girls who serve us at one of them, ruddy-faced and country-dressed, giggle helplessly at our accents; they belong to it all completely, as if a peasantry took root once the East was left behind. It's the same with the names, Elm Farm, Greenville and Pleasant Farm; they come from the soil, out of the here-and-nowness of it, as if there's no longer any need to allude to a past or wider world. The side roads are like *Gulliver's Travels*: we're suddenly the only newish car and half the others ambling old pick-ups, any urge for this year's model a remote absurdity. Wild apple trees bear witness to the legend of Johnny Appleseed, who wandered the pioneer Midwest to offer seeds to all he met and perhaps remind later Midwesterners that even their past may have something in common with their hippy children's dreams. The barns have a character of their own, occasional signs of their ancestry in Pennsylvanian stone foundations or big, low Vermont gables, but otherwise no two are the same except as rambling monuments to the contentment of generations which seem to have enlarged them time after time. The farmhouses too: hardly any are new, but they're freshly painted, with names and dates under their eaves, Schweiner 1911, Adams 1898. Pairs of blue Norway spruces stand at every other gate, a nineteenth century settlers' habit. The corn's so thick on either side that it brushes against the roof of the car; the far apart villages are often no more than a dozen houses next to a grain elevator, post office, store, wooden school and plain, squarely built little church gazing out over the fields which begin again without a pause. Children play in the open street and look up in surprise at an unknown car. At one of the railroad intersections, where the usual grain elevator dwarfs every other building in sight, an old man leaning on a fence watches us in anticipation. Suddenly we discover why, as we hit the local pot-hole, almost bouncing off the road. He roars with delight, as if he's been waiting half his life for some unknowing alien. In all this self-sufficiency there's at last the intimation of a USA which hasn't only realized its Utopia, but has never been hustled out of it. It's a remoteness that comes from contentment, not from having been left behind. Figures raise their hands as we pass, kids, farmers on their tractors, old ladies in white bonnets standing proudly by their fruit stalls. As its details coalesce, the names, the farms, the easy pace and all ages working together, the Midwest's isolationism is more understandable.

It's only in the bigger towns that it looks blunter and less deep-rooted. With their banks and stores and cemeteries built in a sobered up baroque, they seem to be searching for an image, some tangible identity which history has withheld from them. Notices echo it with their mixtures of the bland and bizarre: 'UNIONTOWN SESQUENNIAL' and 'CANEFIELD AMERICA'S CLEANEST TOWN', the Kiwanis Club, the Elks, the Greenfeet. Each town duplicates the last with a horizontal precision, golf courses, trees and streets laid out diagrammatically, plain-faced houses and model lawns with new car, trailer and speed-boat parked unfailingly in front as if there's some minimum property law. Without the East's historical details, they still aren't tempered by the West into its personality. Even the local radio programmes have the same limbo flavour, as if nothing's quite identifiable in this void of alienation. What sounds like an outdated pop-song turns out to be a revivalist hymn; what sounds like a hymn is in fact a commercial; ice-cream socials and road deaths are announced with the same meaningless swing.

Yet even these towns had Utopian days if Mansfield, Ohio, is typical. Louis Bromfield, a native son and fashionable writer in the thirties, described how it grew from a settler community into an agriculture centre before becoming an industrial town. Later, believing that this tokened the passing of an ideal USA, he bought up several declining farms in Pleasant Valley, close to Mansfield, and tried to make them viable. His efforts only showed how little the USA's savage momentum allowed for such nostalgia; by the time he died, in the fifties, his farms were bankrupt and only saved by the contributions of friends, who preserved them as a museum and agricultural institute. Visiting it is not unlike our brief experience of the Mormons. From the nearby hilltop, where the museum curator has told us that Louis Bromfield's ashes were scattered, you can sense how it held his imagination. With the afternoon haze over the valley it's a new world paradise. Alfalfa and half-cut hay reach emerald and olive green to the densely wooded horizon. Roofs of the old farmhouses nestle down between the trees. An ancient apple tree nearby has small gnarled fruit, but fresher and sweeter than any supermarket offer. This for Bromfield was the world which gave the USA the chance of being the closest thing possible to a humanitarian society. It seems doubly ironic that after such struggles to achieve it, its lifespan should have been so brief, roughly two or three generations. Yet the portents are everywhere, from the beer-cans littering the hill to the 'For Sale' notices where the land is being sold as lots. And even this record of it all has only survived at a standard price. The samples of Bromfield Foundation news-sheets given us by the curator are mainly conventional red-baiting tracts in Bromfield's liberal, pacifist name, roundly abusing Castro and commending Brazil's rulers for their anti-communist witchhunts. Perhaps if he'd lived to see this happen, Bromfield would have realized that any new Utopia would have to be fought for in the very manscape of tenement skylines and immigrant accents which he deplored.

Westward through Indiana and into the flatlands of Illinois it's finally the country that superseded his ideal, green undulations gone and the first of the checkerboard farm lands, with that big Midwestern sensation of hardly a rise or a turn in the road and seeing the trucks way ahead like insects hovering in the heat, shimmer slam and silence again, only the sun's diamond glint on the next grain elevator rising up like a silver cathedral, gone in a flash of railroad junction, freight cars and a swirl of chaff and the next one glittering pinpoints up still several miles away and always in the same spot because the road hardly turns, dead straight east and west so that you feel the sun swinging round in perfect twenty-four-hour time, first at your back then at your side and finally sinking down like a stone through the big midwestern sky.

until we right angle north for Chicago in the wake of the big trucks crashing down the four-lane highway, six-lane, eight-lane. Stopping at a railroad crossing the sense of green remoteness is over as the freight cars pelt by with their names reminding us that it's the hub of a continent, the Baltimore and Ohio lines, the Santa Fé, the New York Central, Canadian Pacific, Chicago and Illinois; all converging northwards on that smudge with a smell like a monstrous gas leak that reaches us on the lake wind while the city's cranes are still dots in the distance.

CHAPTER 6

CHICAGO CHICAGO:
Chicago

From on top of Chicago's Prudential building, 601 feet high ('Prudential's investment in property within your sight is a billion dollars', with pink granite walls and marble floors, the world's fastest elevator and its highest moving staircase), the city's a concrete anarchy, the most USA view in the whole USA, the reverse of New York's symmetry and through movement: a whirligig city, pulsing round its grimy navel in the 'El', the elevated railway that snakes through the huddled tenements and under the skyscrapers on the Loop, the commercial sector. It gives you the feeling that the total USA of time and space, anguish and empire, has crowded round concertedly and thrown bits of itself in the centre along the tangle of railroads and encircling Chicago River. None of that chaste harmony that Eastern skylines often profess: the city's more like a wild old whore with a century's mementoes from battling robber-baron clients all piled on for a final strip show, tearing one extravagance off (the Morris Hotel, fifty storeys, 'the biggest building in the world ever to be torn down') only to add a gaudier one ('Another Improvement for Chicago – Richard M. Daley, Mayor'). And she's such a success and law to herself, she doesn't need any hollow make-up, those bangles proclaim her the all-time queen, unashamed of the pocks and scars, slaughterhouse stench and tenement veins that tell she's been through it all (through a frontier existence to stockyard fortunes: through the continent's toughest strike-breaking to its biggest private empires), The Gothic skyscrapers' giddy towering over the other USA of back-alleys and washing on roofs make it a huge medieval city dotted with bizarre cathedrals; medieval too in its single-mindedness, every vanished empire-builder raising his own monument to lone-man private enterprise, expressing its every gross caprice in a clash of styles and statistical follies shouted by the city guide. No pretence there, either – it's not the museums or art galleries, but these latter-day temples of mammon that are detailed first and recommended for a visit: the Wrigley Building, all gleaming white tiers as if to suggest its origin ('Floodlit by several of the most powerful batteries of lights in the world'); the North American Building, five hundred feet of Italian baroque with fluted tiers and cupolas, more tiers and a final dome, outdoing Manhattan and Mandalay at a single stroke; skyline drops to tenement grey and then leaps up ecstatically in a huge jade green tower topped with a splash of Byzantine gold, ostrich feather cornices and a pinnacle like a rocket launcher – the Carbon and Carbide Building, none other. Half of them date from the twenties, when Chicago came finally into her own as the junction of the Midwest and court of the kings of Big Money days: the huge, squat Merchandise Mart ('the largest building in the world devoted to one single business') that might have been built by Mussolini, erected in 1928 at a cost of thirty-two million dollars, and later bought by Joseph P. Kennedy; the Conrad Hilton, 1927, ('still the world's largest hotel – so large that if a visitor were to spend one night in each room his stay would last eight years'); the Tribune Tower, another folly, inlaid with 'fragments as well as whole decorative pieces from the world's most famous buildings, including Westminster Abbey, the Vatican and Notre Dame'; 'the world's only skyscraper opera house' in the Klemperer Insurance Building, built like the conning tower of a massive submarine at the cost of twenty million dollars by a businessman fond of light opera. Even the more recent buildings join in the carnival of green and gold glitter and folly and hootenany superlatives, 'the world's largest post office and probably the only one with a major expressway passing through it'; United of America, 'the world's largest marble-faced structure'; the Palmolive Building crowned with 'the famous Palmolive beacon, the most powerful ever, with a two billion candlepower and brighter than the full moon at a distance of thirty miles'.

Finally it's so universal, this clamour of rival ostentation, it even acquires a unity written huge in a single word, CHICAGO CHICAGO on every hoarding, sticker and sign, the whole defying everywhere else just as its parts defy each other, as if they know it's the hub of the world, or not just that but the world itself and so to hell with the rest of it, with its cosmopolitanism and historically ordered styles, its aesthetic harmonies and hypocritical liberalism glossing over all its flaws. To hell with New England's modesty, with the slickness of the East, with the West's fad futurism, it's me, CHICAGO, and I don't give a dime for your judgements. The only unsung superlative is the one that rings it round south and west, beyond the stockyards: the USA's biggest slum, the huddled Polack tenements and broken South Side terraces where you can go for eight or ten miles and hardly see a white face. Even with this there's no attempt to mute the contrast: the same rapturous coverage for the circular Marina Apartment Buildings, standing at the heart of it all like twin high cost fashion models using a background of poverty to accentuate their luxury, 'a symbol of Chicago, with forty floors of parking space and eighty floors of apartments, marinas for the tenants' boats, an ice-skating rink, restaurants, a bowling alley, bank and complete shopping facilities'. No sign of inhibition, either, round the penthouse swimming pool on another apartment building down on Michigan Avenue, where they're holding a cocktail party (see the glitter of jewels and drinks from right up here on the Prudential) against the same derelict backdrop of the South and West Sides. All around it's the same brazen image, me, CHICAGO, take it or leave it, I know what I am and I'm proud of it, the all-time greatest epic of doing and lone-man-made-it city in history.

At street level it's the same concrete chaos with a demoniac coherence; not just the sense of everywhere violence, more complicated, a brutal saga of time translating a Hamlet ideal into a super-Darwinian reality, angel and ape identified. The same jangling sweating fury and hotch-potch of opposites: the gang war slogans on the walls, the monster billboards and non-stop movies in theatres like gilded palaces, the demolition and construction; the buzz of commuter helicopters, the

limping of children with ragged shoes, the loud conversations
in thousands of dollars, the hobos on the Magnificent Mile
begging for a loose quarter or fighting amongst the refuse in the
South Water Street Market over an edible leftover. The traffic
a free for all without signals, just challenges, blaring and losers'
curses. The Loop with its mammoth department stores and
cut-price liquor shops at one end, its glittering face slashed by
alleys overflowing with trash cans and refuse and ringed by the
rattle-black Elevated. The drunks and overdressed Lake Shore
ladies jostling each other on State Street, the Loop's narrow
jugular vein with more neon than sun at noon. The desolation
of broken sidewalks and tenements probing into the heart of
the city, a diamond's throw from the Marina Buildings, nibbling
at Michigan Avenue ('a concentrated area of high-rise apartment
buildings and of private residences as well as exclusive clubs,
hotels, restaurants and cabarets'); the lots between the tenements where the Gold Coast commuters park their Cadillacs,
watched from peeling doorways by the whores and the unemployed. So that its human logic completes the same spiral as
that of the buildings, from Chicago against the world and one
Chicago against another to its final self of man against man.
(Little wonder that Streeter, one of the city's first real estate
kings, declared himself and his Lake Shore property an independent, sovereign state.) Even without this particular style and
its hard, straight-in-the-eyes look from every other Chicagoan,
you'd never once forget where you are, with the same CHICAGO
CHICAGO at every turn, in the press, in every commercial, in the
snatches of conversation and the non-stop news coverage from
a dozen radio channels. It's a city so self-dazzled that the whole
USA's self-concern is a pale shadow beside it; anyway here it's
not self-enquiry but an uninhibited self-proclamation suppressing the very idea of dissent. Even the violence is reported in a
weirdly disc-jockey tone, a non-stop celebration of another
statistical miracle.

Contrary to myth, only the ghettoes provide a peaceful inter-
lude: the parks full of Puerto Ricans buying tamales from men
with push-carts; Little Poland, where Polish granpas line the
benches thick as peas in the narrow triangle between Milwaukee

and Division, while teenage girls walk arm in arm with grand-
mothers whose wrinkled faces are hardly as high as the girl's
shoulders. The cook in the Polish corner café jokes and flirts with
customers and gives his favourites an extra helping; the men
bang their spoons on the tables and sing the old Polish songs.
But its warmth is old and private, it doesn't extend to the
outer present of all-superseding Chicago. There's no laughter or
hello for a non-Polish speaker, even when his face becomes
known. The essence of these havens' warmth is their separate-
ness, back to back, apart from the rival teenage gangs which
threaten each other across the street, often in different languages, while their elders watch resignedly. Every group and
area seems to relate, if at all, in this way: the Gold Coast towering up in a wall of luxury apartments, with the West and South
Sides squatting opposite in angry reply; the Old Town hippies,
Blacks or Chicanos freezing into immobility as a squad car
cruises by, then back to the image of man against man, the
hippies' studied avoidance of names or the fight that paused
beginning again. At times that straight-in-the-eyes challenge
can be a form of openness – like the teenage girl who greets us
on the Lake Shore boat trip with, 'Say, where'd you get that
hair-cut, oh that accent, listen Momma,' and Momma joins in
quite naturally. But essentially it's hostile, a who-the-hell-are-
you aloneness with its corresponding victims. The single figures
on park benches pouring furtive shots of liquor from bottles
hidden in paper bags. The old people in cheap restaurants
eating with desperate concentration as if it's their only joy in the
world and they're terrified someone will snatch it away. The
solitary men in the rooming-house where we're staying on
Division, most of them permanent residents, building private
dream worlds in their airless little rooms. (One has all four tiny
walls covered with huge girlie posters; another builds model
aeroplanes and seems to fly them day and night, hear him
through the thin walls, 'Zooommm', 'brrrr' and sometimes a
crash followed by a delighted cackle.) When they speak – and
it's rarely, though some have been neighbours for several years
– they almost all address each other by room number rather than
name. Once at the drinking tap, as we pass: '127 died last night.'

And they only seem to go out alone, their figures swallowed up in a trice in the city's swirling and screeching through its twenty-four-hour day.

Nine on the Loop . . . and the traffic mounting since dawn is up to a crescendo now, flooding down the Magnificent Mile and spilling over the big bridges, screech at the lights and belt forward, screech and belt, screech and belt like bloodhounds after the cross traffic and when one innocent lags behind as the lights change they surge straight at him. See the blood lust in their eyes. It's a blonde who nails him, stops him howling dead in his tracks push-button rolls her window down sticks her head out and yells at him watch the lights you son of a bitch and she keeps him there, pinned right down, while the traffic wildcats round them until the lights change again and he screeches off to answer her screech and reassert his four-wheeled manhood. She looks relieved, as if she just got her morning's fix. On State Street and Lake Street the executives leap out of their cabs towards their plate-glass palaces, secretaries hot-foot behind them. Outside the National Bank ('building Chicago and the nation since 1863') the guard keeps his hand on his gun, nice and relaxed so we all feel at ease, and looks a dawdling Black over (a non-white face stands out up here, they're mostly down at the cheap south end, the only ones with time to dawdle), chomps a little on his cigar and fingers the nice polished handle then he suddenly flips it out the man jumps the guard grins polishes the polished handle and chomps a little on his cigar. Whirling lights compete with the sun: 9:21 COCA COLA TEMPERATURE 80°. Crowds mill fresh for battle and no one makes way for anyone, least of all the well-dressed women, not summer dresses but jewels and glitter as if they're off to a cocktail party, elbowing each other aside into the big department stores, stuffed leopard $800 and family helicopters on view.

Except down on Van Buren Street, where there's little to hurry for and the only glitter is broken glass and the dimmer strip lights in the cut price liquor stores. . . .

Only mid-morning, but already it's sultry up on Chicago Avenue. The two policemen doing duty at the door of the district court look openly irritated. Their guns jut out from their tilted hips in silhouette against the sunlight and they look people up and down, the audience filing into the courtroom and the others across the street, as if they blame them for their discomfort. But there isn't any response. Everyone enters quietly and the sidewalk figures show little interest, obviously used to the court's proceedings. Presumably they're only there because it's hotter inside the houses and for want of a job to go to. A few chat, but most just lounge or doze in the shrinking slashes of shade. Though closer to the Loop here, it's even more run down than Division, as if the city's poverty belt is flinging itself towards the centre in a welt of defiance. It was wealthy once, as some of the houses have balconies and large, now curtainless windows behind which people are still dressing slowly, too early to have been night-workers and too late to have day-time jobs. Several of the houses have been pulled down; through the ragged gaps the Marina Apartments are only a few blocks away. The sidewalks are lined with glass and filth. The dozing figures fan themselves and swat the flies with newspapers.

Inside the courtroom it's even hotter. The two big fans make no difference as they're both at the magistrate's end. A Stars and Stripes droops in the corner. Beside it is the city motto, '*urbs in hortu*', its irony presumably lost on all present. Every one of the benches is crammed and the crowd overflows into the corridor, maybe a couple of hundred people. A dozen or so are Puerto Rican, three or four white, the rest black. Except the nine men behind the bar who, from magistrate to clerk, are white. It's paternity and maintenance suits and they rattle by monotonously at the rate of one every two or three minutes to a background of low murmurs and scattered comments from the spectators. Drab and low-keyed, it seems more authentic than the legendary Chicago of Al Capone and big-timing. Yet ironically its hopelessness gives the crowd an un-Chicagoan air of sharing something and living together.

The magistrate is a small, round man with his shirt wide open, sweating and commentating garrulously. He does almost all the talking, as if everything's a foregone conclusion, with little point in really pressing either claim or defence. His scoldings are wry and paternal, suggesting that he's not indifferent so much as warped by the story's repetition from case to case and between generations, reducing even the defendants to victims rather than offenders. The couples come up one by one. Most of the men attempt a bravado, but the women can't hide their nervousness. Occasionally they twist their skirts and flex and unflex their hands behind them until a laugh line from the magistrate reminds them that the audience is watching; then they put their hands back in front, holding the wooden bar for support. Sometimes the children are with them, and usually they carry on peeping and playing if there's nothing particularly novel about their mother or both their parents standing with lowered heads beneath a line of white faces.

The sequence doesn't vary much. The magistrate looks down sharply. 'How much support are you paying this lady? Fifty dollars? Cheap at the price, uh.' Laughs from the audience. 'Silence at the back there, silence or I'll clear the court.' (He's always like this, suppressing the laughter he's just provoked, as if it underpins his power or masks his hint of sympathy.) 'And when did he last pay you, ma'am? You got your receipts with you, mister – no?' Many haven't got them at all and in most cases they're incomplete. The magistrate tuts and raises his voice. 'Why don't you people keep your receipts so's you know how much you've paid? And you don't even know how much he's paid, do you ma'am?' (It's always 'ma'am', which sounds supercilious, though this doesn't seem intended.) He raises his small, plump hands. 'You see that? She don't even know.' Another nervous rustle of laughter. 'Silence in here – I wish you people'd make less noise, just like I wish you'd make less babies. You know how much you owe in arrears on this support now, Mr Reed? One thousand and thirty dollars. Has he paid you anything this month? Nothing? You got any money on you now?' Then the tattered notes come out, almost always ones, the odd five. (Once there's a ten and he rises to the occasion. 'A ten dollar bill, ladies and gentlemen, today's big winner. Silence there.') 'Fifteen dollars, uh, Mr Reed. Oh Jeez, look at em – why don't you people wash your bills? Silence there, I said silence. Quit crowding round that door, you're not out on the streets now. Okay, Mr Reed, fifteen dollars. You be sure and pay this month's balance by the month end or we'll issue a warrant. Next.' And the figures file back, most of the men in working clothes and still trying to seem unconcerned, the women looking down at the ground. Sometimes, especially when the magistrate has been cracking his jokes, there's a glitter in the woman's eyes.

The clerk calls the next case hurriedly, as if they may never finish. 'James: Dixon.' These two are older. The man doesn't even attempt the usual show of confidence. The magistrate looks at them. 'Back again? I've forgotten – how many children do you have, ma'am?' Her answer's inaudible even to him. He repeats his question. She mutters something. 'Two children – and what's he paying you – or rather what's he supposed to pay you?' He turns to the clerk, a heavily built, crop-haired young man with a frankly bored expression.

'Fifty-two dollars a month, sir.'

'Fifty-two dollars a month – and when did he last pay you, ma'am?'

Her answer's inaudible again. The magistrate nods at the woman's counsel, who repeats the question with an over-deliberate politeness. 'When was the last time he paid you?' She's biting her lip and doesn't answer. He raises his voice and asks again, slower and harsher this time. 'Ma'am, I'm asking you, when was the last time he paid you? February? Good – February, your honour.'

The magistrate turns to the man. 'So it's six months you haven't paid. How old are you?'

'Sixty-one, sir.'

'You married?'

'Yes, sir.'

'How many children by your wife?'

'Eight, sir.'

'And you're working?'

'No, sir.'

'Why aren't you working?'

'Sick, sir, can't bend down '

'So you're on assistance?'

'Yes, sir.'

The magistrate shakes his head and raises his voice. 'You hear that? He's too sick to work, but he wasn't too sick to have children. Guess you don't have to bend down for that, uh?' The man's so nervous he blurts out, 'No, sir,' then shifts at the audience's laughter. The magistrate goes on compulsively, as if he feels that ridicule may succeed where threats have failed. 'So we have to support you with taxes while you populate the world? Got any money on you now?' The man fishes in his baggy old trousers, drops his cap, picks it up and hands up some notes to the magistrate. He counts them. 'Twenty-four dollars. That all? No more in there, you're sure? How about the other pocket? Okay. Twenty-four dollars it is. Now you get up in full with that payment, cause there won't be a next time. Next time we'll put you in jail.' He mops his brow. 'Next.'

There's sometimes a spark of variety. He adopts a special line for a Mexican whose English is poor. 'You've got five kids by your wife?' He points to the woman and baby beside him. 'And this one is yours too, uh?' The man shrugs. 'So she say.' The magistrate snorts. 'So she say – uno mistako, uh, mister?' The woman's counsel breaks in. 'Are you a citizen of this country?' The man shakes his head: 'No. Mexican citizen.' It seems that the magistrate might not have asked, but nevertheless he takes it up. 'How would it be if we deported you? Like that, wouldn't you? Free babies over here and a free trip back home again. Well, we'll deport you okay if you don't pay your support this month – but we'll throw you in jail first. You won't get any assistance in there and you can't make babies there either.' Laughter. 'Silence. You got that, mister?'

One youngish woman tries to defend the man who's up with her. She says he's paid since she complained, but the magistrate thunders at her. 'Who told him to pay you? Payments are made through this court, you know that – I know damn well he hasn't paid you. Have you?' The man shakes his head. 'But you told her to tell me you had?' He nods.

The woman breaks in. 'But, your honour, we're going to get married.'

The magistrate checks it with the man, who agrees, but he's still not satisfied. 'Okay – you bring me your marriage licence by the fifth of next month. Else we'll put you in jail, mister. And don't try and fool me again, miss. Next.'

Another woman, with two small children and carefully, if cheaply dressed, is more articulate than the rest. She stands up at the bar on her own; the man hasn't answered his summons. The magistrate issues a warrant against him and says there's no more he can do, but suddenly the woman raises her voice, the first time it's happened all morning. 'I gotta get some support, your honour – what chance d'you think these two children have got if I can't bring them up decently, I want to send them to decent schools so's they can get a chance in life. Where d'you think they'll end up if they stay in the ghettoes of Chicago?'

The magistrate checks her. She bites her lip. The recorder looks straight ahead without writing anything down.

Noon on the Loop . . . the pace hasn't changed but nerves seem frayed, smears in the make-up and sweat on the shirts and the traffic's snappy now where before it was gladiatorial. Half the people smoke as they walk. A demure-looking woman kicks out at a man, equally demure-looking, thinking he'd tried to jostle her, but it was only a mistake and he rubs his ankle ruefully, only to be jostled himself. Few people laugh or joke and almost all who do are young, except when a wedding procession goes by, horns blaring and tickertape streaming and faces all black laughing and shouting, but the crowd hasn't time to watch. It's so thick you have to hurry or else get bounced like a shuttlecock. The midday blend of haze, smog and neon makes it all seem underwater, figures drown and lights dilate: 12.26 COCA COLA TEMPERATURE 86° the flickering MAGIKIST PEPSI-COLA news flashes flitting across the sky NEGRO BOY SHOT IN RIOT . . . US PLANES KNOCK OUT VIETCONG FORWARD POSITIONS . . . LABOR LEADERS SAY US MUST FIGHT TO CONTAIN COMMUNISM . . . READ LIFE MAGAZINE . . . READ LIFE. The executives file through the gold-plated doors and potted plants of dining clubs. Secretaries pick at salad lunches and make themselves up dispassionately. Waiters snatch at dollar bills and slap the change on the counter. At the corner a shrivelled man is handing out religious leaflets

ETERNITY
WHERE SHALL I SPEND IT?
WITH WHOM SHALL I DWELL IN IT?

which most people drop without a glance until somebody bangs into him and the slips fly, he grabs but they're gone, trampled under and nobody's noticed. He looks lost. Then he turns away and walks off.

Down towards the south end the buildings drop and soar and drop and down a narrow alleyway a few yards from their rich façade an old man with a wooden trolley ferrets through the trash cans. On Van Buren Street under the El that straddles its length on grimy legs, it's still no more than half light among the flickering liquor prices and flophouses one dollar a night; but it's the only part of the Loop whose figures stand chatting, where there's laughter from the barber's shop and the newsboys whistle up and down. Suddenly a crowd gathers as a Chicano stands in a doorway brandishing a broken bottle and shouting hysterically. They wait for the fun as the sirens howl and the cop car screeches to a halt. But as soon as the guns come out, he drops the bottle and gives himself up. The crowd drifts apart. 2:12 COCA COLA TEMPERATURE 88°.

Washington Park ('Bughouse Square'), set right in the heart of the city, has its grass and maple trees, squirrels and even a few swings, but its eeriness hits you immediately. The way the eyes pick you over without actually looking at you. The curious symmetry of old people on the outside benches, with the middle-aged beyond them and the young bloods in the centre. The fact that almost the only women are two lank sexagenarians walking up and down holding hands, with blue and orange hair washes and wild touches of rouge on their cheeks. The way the figures on the benches hardly ever raise their eyes, for fear of a by-stander's catching their glance to beg for something. It's a play where nothing happens, though everyone has to know what might, without actually watching it.

We seem to upset the balance, apparently by our conventionality as the square's one heterosexual and not too eccentrically dressed couple, which increases the bizarreness, as we're just getting used to stares for the opposite reasons elsewhere. A man saunters by, pauses stage casual and comes back. 'Got a smoke, mister?' He nods in acknowledgement, though perhaps he hoped for a stronger one, and moves on. A younger man sees and shambles inevitably towards us. 'Need a smoke.' His hand trembles and a torn sleeve shows the needle tracks on his arm, some none too clean-looking. His face is unshaven and collapsed, fiftyish at first glance, maybe thirty behind the mask. He seems to want to say something when I light his cigarette, but all he can manage is: 'Shakes, see.' He holds out his flickering hand intently as if he's both fascinated by it and somehow hopeful that we'll stop it. It's curiously pale under the dirt. He wanders off still holding it out and staring at it like something he found.

The old man beside us moves closer, rearranging the paper he's sitting on. Pauses, then looks at us. 'They see you strangers. That's why they coming. You don't live Chicago, uh? You gotta be careful. Is bad city. You don't wanta walk in side street. I don't never walk in side street. People got knife, bottle, they kill you. Don't walk by doorway. Walk around.' He hesitates, as voices are raised. 'Look now, see, they fighting – but don't look close or they come fight you.'

He's right. Two of the figures in the middle are flaying at each other wildly, a Puerto Rican and a white boy. A crowd comes round them, sluggishly, as if they're not quite sure it's worth it. The white boy trips the Puerto Rican, scattering his coat and hat and jumps over a bench and makes off. The Puerto Rican limps after him, stumbling over a sleeping man, who growls and rolls over without waking up. He picks up a bottle. A few figures crouch automatically as he hurls it after his opponent and limps back, cursing violently.

The old man keeps his voice down. 'You see – they crazy. When you go out, you go this side – don't go through middle. They got knife, you stranger, they catch you. That's why I sit outside. See?' He half looks around. 'Old people outside. They get away quick. You don't know Chicago, uh? Where you from? From England? I was in Southampton, from there I come to America.'

'Where are you from originally?'

'Little country – Bulgaria. I come – I don't remember the year, was the year the war begins. My brother was coming after me, but he die in Liverpool. I was twenty-one years then – come in *Mauretania*, old boat. Bulgaria different now – different government.'

'Which part did you live in?'

'Small town, two thousand people. My father was farmer, nice house, farm' – he spreads his hands over the litter around our feet. 'Was in a valley, beautiful valley, many acres. We grow perfumes, Bulgarian roses – foreigners buy them to make perfume.' He smiles very slowly, as if it's the first time in weeks. 'I wake up morning and smell perfume, every morning I smell perfume. And melons. Big sweet melons, they lie on the ground like fat sheep. And pumpakin. You know pumpakin? Smell nice.' He takes off his hat and scratches his close-cropped silver hair. Another scuffle breaks out by the fountain. 'They fight again, see. Over there. Is always the middle. Here is safe.'

This time it's two black men, both too drunk to hurt each other. A white woman stands beside them brandishing a large knitting needle and goading them on impartially. Suddenly a mutter spreads. A squad car on Dearborn. The spectators close ranks, screening the fighters protectively. As soon as it's passed they move back and the fight picks up again. Eventually it peters out and only the young woman is left, still waving her knitting needle like some maniac muse of violence. Nobody takes much notice of her.

The two old harlequin women walk by, holding hands and muttering loudly, though not to each other. Our neighbour watches. 'This old age bad. When you young, you strong, get work. But when you old, you get sick, you got nothing. They got nobody to talk. Chicago nobody like to talk.'

'Don't you have any relatives?'

'No' – he sounds surprised, as if he's lost touch with the idea.

'No relatives. Only my brother, dead. I have one cousin, Bulgarian – but I lose track, he lose track. I don't know if he's living now. Only me. I got one friend, Bulgarian, live in same room house.' He pauses. I ask him his name, but he doesn't answer, as if I should have known better, that it's only anonymity and our not belonging here which makes the conversation safe. I try again.

'How long have you been here?'

'Chicago? Nine year – I go like grasshopper, work here, work there, sell paper, load truck, working in grocery. In Depression I was in West Virginia. Was hard, I lose job, no house, sleep in field. They get demonstration, march, but no good. Women was wearing sacking for skirt, people die. I was all right then, young, but if Depression come again, you old, you frighten, can't do nothing. So I save money. Four thousand dollars, save all the time. Then I get sick, stroke, you know? Spend one year in the hospital, Presbyterian Hospital, and when I finish I got twenty-three dollars – can't work, get hard time, Now I work a little, get social security. Is hard – when you got no money, you finish. You want to go in restaurant, drink coffee, put hand in pocket, nothing. Can't say I pay you tomorrow – tomorrow no good. In America is bad without money, you finish, you got no friend. You see here' – he nods at the figures opposite; a man lying crumpled on the bench; another talking hard to himself, eyes focused on thin air; and a woman in a white feather boa, stroking a brown paper parcel. 'They got no friend, they got nothing.' He looks around. It's getting dark. 'I go now. Night come, is bad. Don't forget, no walk in the middle.'

He settles his hat, smiles briefly and disappears hurriedly down the path. The woman in the feather boa sees him pass and curses quietly. A young man minces by with a white poodle on a red lead. The man who bummed a cigarette, the second one with the torn sleeve, stops another on the path. It's hard to tell if they know each other. He holds out his hand. 'Shakes, see.' The second man pulls it closer as if he's admiring it, making an expert assessment. They both watch it, riveted. Then the second man suddenly cackles and totters away down the path. The first doesn't move, just watches the hand as if it's not his. Then he starts crying quietly. One or two people watch without looking. But nobody speaks. Nobody moves.

A scuffle breaks out by the fountain.

Six on the Loop . . . the last wilting executives hurry out on to State Street to the cocktail bars and cabs. The sunslant blackens one side of the street and sets the other on fire. A lull in the little square with the fountain in front of the showy civic centre. Boy meets girl, fewer suits, and the hobos start to take over, collecting the newspapers carefully for a read and tonight's bedding. Men sweat and strain in the side alleys, shifting huge piles of trash. Inside the La Salle Bank a lone black figure scrubs the floor, a fly trapped in a glass mausoleum. The crowds have thinned. A drab woman stares fixedly at the wedding dresses in Sears Roebuck. An old man watches the chickens roasting in a restaurant window and turns away talking to himself, 'two dollars fifty cents', loud enough to hear his accent; Polish, it sounds, almost as rare as a black face on this plusher section.

Suddenly the movement picks up again. On Clark Street the night shift arrives at the huge construction site of the First National Bank ('The Chicago Chamber of Commerce congratulates the First National Bank on its skill in demolition'). Drills putter and piledrivers pound and the workers spread like ants over its floodlit skeleton. At the south end business revives in the cut-price liquor stores. The El rattles by like a monster night bird trailing a little red tail-light. Underneath it's already dark, though at least down here the stars through the rails aren't drowned by neon and figures relax now that daylight's finally gone, a forum in every other doorway. Banter in the cheap restaurants, where people seem to know each other.

At the other end the traffic mounts with a savage gaiety as the evening crowds pour in for the late night shopping and restaurants and movies. The jungle of lights that has languished by day comes into its own now: 7.56 COCA COLA TEMPERATURE 76°, the sky flashing and popping and whirling with liquor and cosmetic ads. The baronial movie houses swallow the crowds like outsize whales with gold teeth and velvet throats. A part of Randolph's cordoned off and a yellow monster goes to work waving a claw with four-foot nails that rip the asphalt up like paper. Even Chicagoans seem surprised at its appetite; or perhaps they're astonished as us at the sight of real red earth under this world of concrete and marble that seems to have commandeered all existence. You can still hear the sound of it, chomp and tear, in the underground Greyhound station two blocks away where the crowds drift and doze in a waste of Coke and coffee machines, strip lighting and piped music. A soldier in uniform sleeps on a bench, 'I love you' tattoo'd on the back of his hand. A group of college kids lounge on the floor, one strumming a guitar and some singing half-heartedly. An old Amish couple sit side by side, the woman asleep with her bonneted head resting on her husband's shoulder while he stares straight in front of him, heavy beard and broad-brimmed hat and dressed from head to foot in black, untouched by the world around them. Eyes close. The announcer drones. A little boy, trimly dressed like a miniature executive, suddenly pulls at his mother's hand and jumps up and down, excitedly: 'Momma, look, Momma, a hippie, look, Dad, I seen a hippie.' The hippie looks injured.

The door across the corridor in the rooming-house is usually half open, revealing a pair of feet on the bed and a portable television tuned to a high concentration of gunfights. Occasionally it's ousted by taped revivalist style sermons, spiced with live exclamations of 'glawry Lawd' and 'hallelujah'. Then one day he bounces in, slim, dapperly dressed and black, in his mid-twenties, maybe less, with an alligator grin and a way of darting about like a highly strung impresario. Gives us a big 'hi there' spreads himself in the only chair and proceeds to tell us his life story. As he talks on non-stop, with the hallelujahs and glawries so savoured that each syllable takes off on its own, we realize it's his own voice that he listens to on the tapes. He's a travelling preacher in the Pentecostal Church. Twenty-seven, or so he says, born in the East, left school at fourteen and later went to Bible school, since when he's hardly looked back. (Nor been back, he later adds. He doesn't know if his father, a garbage man, is still alive.) He supports himself with donations from his various congregations, all of them exclusively black, almost the only principle of Pentecostal organisation being considerable segregation. This doesn't bother him, he says, in fact he's all in favour of it, people are happier that way. And it hasn't been any problem to him. Very few Pentecostal preachers can live entirely off their takings, at least in black areas, most of them holding a supplementary and often menial secular job. But Brother Eldon's a skilled exception. With a regular circuit between Chicago and St Louis, he's been making it since he began. He tells it all with a huge verve, thin hands weaving the air and a hallelujah in every gap, as if it's a sermon in itself. 'Yes, brother, praise the Lawd, he really loves my ministry, the folks really love my preachin. The preachin and the healin I've done – if you could see the folks I've saved. Hallelujah.' His grin never slackens. 'Brother, I've healed cancers, tumours – folks have real faith in my ministry. Hallelujah. Especially the ladies. Brother, when I get going good I can really roll em around, if I told em to drop down dead, they'd drop right in front of me. Aint that somethin? Hallelujah. I can take em up there, brother, take em right to the gates of heaven and tell old Peter to open up.' He shadow boxes. 'Open up, brother, praise the Lawd, here's brother Eldon swingin em in. Yes, brother, they like my preachin. I can get em real wild or keep em quiet as a little mouse. Hallelujah. Aint that wonderful?'

Once he's got a foothold, he blows in whenever we're there, proclaiming his skills with a fluency that hardly allows us a word edgeways. ('I like talkin to your kinda folks. Church folks can be pretty dumb.') Occasionally it's late at night after he's got back from a service and we're given every detail, including his takings for the day. Usually it's forty to fifty dollars, but one night he bursts in whooping out his hallelujahs like an evangelical cowboy. 'Glawry, folks, I seen the glawry, the Lawd was really there tonight. Brother they love my ministry – guess how much I made tonight, guess how much they gave the Lawd.' He digs into his coat pocket and brings out a fistful of bills. 'Eighty-three dollars, brother, glawry hallelujah. I was really performin tonight, I just had those ladies rollin, weren't nothin they

wouldn't do for the Lawd. Oh glawry, them folks is poor but
God's really movin, brother. Eighty-three dollars. I can make
the last payment on that television there. Praise the Lawd.
Aint he wonderful?'

He's always like this, the same mixture of hallelujah and
cash returns. At least it gives him a bizarre candour. He seems
genuinely proud of whatever pleasure his preaching gives; yet
equally proud of telling us how he's extracted the last five
dollars from one of his regular church ladies who'd saved it for
new shoes for her children. He might be one of his own audience,
so equally dazzled by both his parts that he sees no conflict
between them and assumes the same of us. And he flaunts them
to the full. Tells about the girls he had before he went to Bible
school ('but, brother, I didn't make out with them broads like I
do with the Lawd, hallelujah'); his political sentiments (his
first vote for president went, he says, for Goldwater); the
softening up techniques he uses to elicit contributions; and how
he used to keep two cars, a new one for taking girls out and the
one he's still got, a battered Ford, for visiting the ghettoes.
Despite the clichés, it's hard to tell where the truth ends, and
he certainly seems to believe it all, delivering it with the same
hallelujahs and fixed impresario's grin, as if applause is ringing
in his ears. Perhaps not surprisingly, he doesn't seem to have
friends.

Then one evening he invites me to join him. He's preaching
down on the South Side in one of the little store-front churches
that sprout in every other street in most black ghettoes. It's
Saturday. Dusk by the time we leave in his Ford, which he
drives in true Chicago style, blaring everyone out of his way
and holding forth non-stop with an extra sprinkling of glawries.
He seems to be warming up for his preaching. He feels at home in
Chicago, he says, and we go round the long way, screeching
down the Gold Coast past the luxury apartment buildings where
tuxedoed socialites and their bitter-lemon blondes are piling
into convertibles, like ads for expensive cigarettes. His head
darts to right and left and if anything catches his eye he switches
lanes for a closer look, regardless of the surrounding traffic.
'Brother, it's glawry-land up here, another couple of hundred a

month and I'd be living right here. Praise the Lawd. Hallelujah. Times my ministry's been good I've lived real high. Praise the Lawd.' Blares his horn, leans out and bawls at the neighbouring driver, 'What's the trouble, brother, you stuck?' and screeches round, swinging south and suddenly the skyscrapers and dainty parks and blondes are gone. The big sweeping avenues give way to narrow streets and small shops and battered cars. Everyone seems to be outside (night now but still sullen hot), strolling, murmuring, kids racing, groups on the steps of the little brick houses with broken windows and broken porches. And for mile after mile there isn't a white face to be seen. When the kids notice us, they stop in surprise, though it's nothing more, no comment. But Brother Eldon suddenly seems nervous, crouches lower over the wheel. 'Brother, see how they live down here, oh glawry, aint it somethin? I'm a full-blooded Negro myself, but I really hate how these folks live. Glawry, brother, I wouldn't live here. It's real wild, they'll cut you, rob you, burn your car. I tell you, brother, if we walked down this street together they'd beat us before we got to the corner. I don't agree with no civil rights, these folks has got to blame themselves. Glawry. They're so dirty and wild, they don't know how to care for themselves. See down there' – he points down a side road – 'that's Blackstone Avenue, brother, I wouldn't walk down there if you paid me, not if the Lawd himself was there, that's where the Blackstone Rangers is, teenage hoodlums, they burn the cars, kill each other. Oh brother, these people. Glawry. Maybe the Lawd'll help em, here we go, hallelujah,' and he swings round another corner, scattering a group of kids. 'See those kids, oh brother, aint safe to drive in these streets.'

He draws up by the sidewalk. The street's cramped and dimly lit. Some figures sit murmuring in a porch. A group of teenagers stand on a corner, mock-sparring with each other. Again, not a white face to be seen, sidewalks littered with glass and trash and kids playing in an empty lot. A man staggers up to us and Eldon steps hurriedly aside, but he just mutters and staggers on. It hasn't the smouldering quality of Harlem on a summer night, perhaps because it's less concentrated, beat up little houses instead of Harlem's tenements. There's more of a tattered hopelessness, a despair that seems too deep for aggression, though Brother Eldon clearly thinks differently, glancing hurriedly over his shoulder until we reach the spot where he's preaching.

It's simply a small converted store with the window painted over so that you can't see in from the street and a notice on the door: 'Service tonight 8 o'clock.' We're ushered in and immediately he's the focus of attention. Most of the people there are women and as he introduces me they clasp his hand with a modest murmur. It's as if his presence alone is a cure and more than enough to explain my own: and certainly, with his sharp suit and air of being on top of the world, he stands out even more than me. Apparently the contrast, far from setting him apart, is just what they expect of him, their share in his reversal, outwardly at least, of the system. Most of them wear white dresses and cheap hats, old, but carefully kept. Faces are tired and figures heavy, often too big for the rickety chairs, so that they look like sacks of straw, dumped there involuntarily. Three or four men are sitting together by the wall on the far side, also poorly but cleanly dressed. One is drunk and falls off his chair and eventually they persuade him to leave, but otherwise everyone's rather subdued except for the children sitting up front, the girls the only splash of colour in bows and hats and party dresses. The room is small and already crowded, a dirty beige patched with linoleum over the cracks in the floor and ceiling, which sags. Dimly lit and no ventilation. The heat seems to be crammed in, too much for the room to hold. A few religious prints on the walls, an old piano and some plastic flowers. At the far end there's a rough altar which looks like a couple of packing cases draped with a sheet and a red paper cross. A young man appears from behind it, strongly built, in a white surplice. Brother Eldon introduces us. He's the local deacon, who runs the church. The same subdued handshake and only a murmur of conversation, as if to say it's not words we're here for, it's for the song and salvation, to do what words have failed to do.

A few more figures drift in and shake hands with Brother Eldon. Then he makes his way to the piano and tinkles out a gospel tune. One of the women gets up and starts singing and the others join in, the words indistinct, something like 'I'm coming, Lord', but what matters is the sound, repeating, mounting, eyes closed figures sway, the kids too swaying with song and suddenly the deacon adds a rip-run on an electric guitar. Song after song and as each one ends a different voice deep in the crowd sings out into another and the voices rise again in a blues swell that reaches back with eyes closed to carry them out and way beyond the cramped room, the cheap clothes, the tinny piano. One old woman up at the front has picked up a pair of cymbals and plays them wilder and wilder and the others follow her, hands clap feet stomp and the sound rebounds, mounts and mounts. Brother Eldon's the only one who seems aware of what's going on, turns round to wink at me, rattling away at the piano. Then as the sound ebbs for a moment he gets up and starts to pray, gliding round the space out front, coaxing them on, 'Sweep down oh Lawd, come on Lawd, oh glawry, you're there Lawd, come on down and take these folks, take em on up to the glawry land,' and all the while they're murmuring, 'Thank you Lord', 'Yes Lord', 'Oh my poor soul', 'Yes Lord', eyes still closed, sometimes a shout then back to a moan. Never a break as Brother Eldon retires again and a woman testifies, deep Southern accent and speaks to herself, their shared self, barely audible, 'I'm calling on you, yeah Lawd'; then one of the men gets up and again the voice is broken, all that holds it together is the sound, almost a cry, and the others' murmurs confirming their oneness with him, 'I drive my truck, I drive all day, sometimes I feel like I'm finished, Lawd, feel I'm out on the highway there and I can't git no further, Lawd, feel like I wanna be free, feel too small, can't do nothin, help me Lawd, help me Lawd,' then he bursts into a gospel song, a huge old magnificent voice and the others join in. Wilder now and the woman beside him sways, eyes closed and hands outstretched, bumps into one of the chairs but she obviously doesn't notice and the guitar wilds up goading her on, spinning spinning, then breaks and there's just the clapping, feet stomping and cymbals' throb and the heat banging the ceiling and driving back down on the spinning figure, black face over white dress in a pained sweat of ecstasy, hands outstretched and fluttering like a trapped butterfly's wings then holding her stomach in agony with her head jerking and now another woman joins her, white skirts whirling round and stumbling against the chairs and the others come forward to make a ring and the two of them sway from side to side. The deacon's become a whirling figure up on his own behind the altar, head thrown back and throat straining, huge voice and guitar pounding with no attempt at a tune any more, just the same crashing chord crashing round the little room so that the heat crashes with it his voice just a roar of pain and the old lady goading him on smashing her cymbals closer and closer and one of the women up at the front moves out of the crowd and spins slowly, face frozen. The other tilts forward then falls back on the pulsing circle and they're no longer separate figures just a single swaying mass and one of the men has slipped to his knees, he's smashing his head against the wall, smashing it and crying out and suddenly the spinning woman gives a scream 'I seen him, I seen him' and falls to the ground twisting and moaning and slowly the tempo slips back; cymbals, guitar, handclap and the low swell and roll of the voices gradually regaining their strength. Until another figure comes forward and it all begins again, the whirling and imploring hands the clenched face the guitar's smash ending in another body slumped back on a frail chair, another one and then another. Brother Eldon is the only person who doesn't seem to be carried away, stepping up when the pace lulls to pray and preach and goad them back, waving his hands, and darting about, as the voices come in; 'Help me Lord', 'I wanta be free', 'Ain't got nothin here Lawd', 'Touch me boss, help me Lawd', 'Come on Jesus, I wanta be free'. It's only the sound of him they need, for another song to begin and another figure to twist and fall somewhere in the way beyond where they've all gone together until gradually there's just the guitar and a low clapping and stomping, still throbbing, but the fever's gone and finally sound and voices ebb and a broken peace settles down.

Brother Eldon steps firmly out front. Spreads his hands, natty figure poised in front of the slumped bodies, some still jerking and murmuring as if they're half answering him and half still voicing their own beyond. Speaks soft then raises a shout and then back to a whisper again, emphasising his self-possession. 'Brothers and sisters, the Lawd was here.' ('Yes Jesus', 'Oh Yeah') 'And brothers and sisters I'm gonna tell you, I'm gonna tell you about the Lawd, all about freedom, hallelujah.' ('Hallelujah', 'Yes brother') 'That's right. Remember the Children of Israel? They took em into Egypt, sisters, they took em way down into Egypt and set em building pyramids. And they toiled, sisters, they suffered, like some folks is sufferin today.' ('Yes Jesus, that's right', 'Yeah Lawd, yeah we're sufferin') 'But the Lawd their God did not forsake em, he didn't forget em, no sir, hallelujah, he told em you just gotta love the Lawd, and everything's gonna be all right.'('That's right') 'Praise the Lawd. Aint he wonderful? He told em if you're looking for freedom you gotta raise you voice right up and listen to what my preachers says and they listened, sisters, they raised their voices. They cried hallelujah Lawd.' ('Yes sir,' 'Hallelujah') 'That's right. Praise the Lawd. And the Lawd sent a plague on old Pharoah, everybody got mighty sick, cept them children of Israel and that's cause they loved the Lawd, they praised him, hallelujah.' ('Hallelujah') 'And them children of Israel, sisters, they didn't do no hollerin. They didn't do no drinkin and fightin. They just raised their voice to the Lawd and hallelujah, he gave em their freedom, that's right,' ('Hallelujah', 'Praise the Lawd', 'Yeah brother') 'that's right, he set em free and that's where we're going, brothers and sisters, praise the Lawd we're going there. Ain't no night-sticks up there, aint no linin up for assistance, cause the Lawd's gonna be there. Hallelujah, we gotta keep prayin, we gotta keep on singin out and I'm doin a whole lot of prayin. Sometimes I get tired Lawd, I been down there in St Louis, the brothers and sisters there sure is prayin and one of them sisters down in St Louis, she gave my mission a hundred dollars, praise the Lawd, hallelujah, she seen the glawry, brothers and sisters, and we're gonna git right after her, we gotta get to the glawry land,' ('Yeah brother') 'we gotta raise our voices up and I'm gonna ask you to help our mission. The brother here's gonna come around and I'm gonna start her off, sisters, I'm gonna put ten dollars in there and that's

5

right out of my own pocket.' Takes out a ten dollar bill and drops it conspicuously in the hat that one of the men holds in front of him. The man starts moving down the rows and Brother Eldon keeps on talking. 'I want you to give to the Lawd, sisters, he aint gonna hesitate,' ('That's right') 'not when he leads us out, hallelujah, he's gonna take us right on up there, right on up to the glawry land. He ain't gonna spare nothin, sisters, and he's gonna look for the big givers, like them children of Israel, they gave all they got to the Lawd and what did he do? Hallelujah, he gave it all back to em, brothers and sisters, he took em right up there, hallelujah. Thank you sister, praise the Lawd, thank you brother, thank you sister, the Lawd's watchin you right now, the Lawd's really here tonight, sisters, we're goin on up to the glawry land.'

Notes pile up in the hat. One or two of the women reach down and take their offerings out of their dress fronts. Another takes her shoe off and picks out a five dollar bill. Only one or two hesitate and then, as the hat pauses, they give. Coins from the children. Then the hat's brought up front and its contents tipped on to the altar and counted. Eighty-seven dollars fifteen cents. Brother Eldon announces it as an offering to their pride, then he goes over to the piano and plays another gospel song. They sing in a low, exhausted voice, flowing up again but gently, and one from the back carries over it all, a great swelling above beyond words ceaseless flood of blues voice, not just the voice of one woman with a trailing dress and split sneakers but half the world's, for the whole world to hear, of man tormented by men but outsoaring them, fantasy but a kind of freedom.

Brother Eldon prays. Heads bow. As they continue murmuring, he and the deacon divide the money. The prayer ends. Brother Eldon announces the date when he'll be back. We say goodbye. Nobody talks much. They leave quietly. Brother Eldon seems in a hurry as we head back to the car. 'Praise the Lawd, forty dollars, ain't that somethin, hallelujah. Let's get back quick now, I wanta see the midnight movie. Praise the Lawd, he was moving tonight.'

As we drive back past the store the last figures are still coming out in subdued ones and twos. They don't turn at the sound of the car. Just disappear privately down the sidewalk through the trash and broken glass.

Two on the Loop . . . a ghost ship now, with its neon stilled to release the stars for the first time as the last merrymakers drift home, shouting and laughing and squealing their tyres in the sudden, echoing emptiness. The different sounds have grown distinct, the road gang tearing Randolph apart, the construction site on Clark, a drunk tripping over a bottle, a cab screeching, a Greyhound bus trundling out of the station. A squad car prowls to a halt and picks up a girl who's been stumbling along and finished up with her face to the wall. Men they don't seem to bother about, at least on Van Buren where there's half a dozen or so sprawled on the sidewalk or tottering weakly. In Uncle Sam's all-night diner two men in suits sit silently over strawberry sundaes topped with huge whorls of cream. The only other customer is a little old woman whose tattiness looks out of place in her polished surroundings. She finishes the soup she's been eating fiercely, pays and gets up to leave. But the swing door is too heavy for her and as she struggles to open it she drops one of her crumpled bags. The waiter watches, curious in a detached way, as if it's some sort of experiment. Eventually she makes her escape when somebody opens the door from outside.

The square by the civic centre is hushed. Even the fountain has switched itself off, lending the square a civic smugness at the respectable hours it keeps, as if to rebuke its one occupant, a hobo woken up by the squad car. He walks about stomping his feet and gazing up philosophically at the faintly shining civic centre. Then suddenly figures slip out of the shadows and in two minutes it's in full swing, a booming little hustlers' market with everything from canned food to women's jewelry changing hands. The presiding genius is a large black character with a yellow sweat shirt and a panama hat, respectfully addressed by all as Big Ben, sitting on the central bench with a carton of loose fruit on his knee; he's trying to sell a camera, a pair of shoes and some baby food. The fruit's just a come-on and a means of concealing the camera, which looks fresh from a tourist's back. His main customer is known as Rat, a lean, dart-ing, reddish man with a sniff of what could be an Irish accent and a wristful of watches. He sells two to Big Ben for ten bucks and the pair of shoes. He tries on the shoes and approves. Big Ben throws in a bag of tomatoes. Rat takes a bite at one, mutters, puts it down on the bench and disappears business-like towards the Greyhound station. Two minutes later he's back again equipped with salt and pepper servers. He sits down beside Big Ben, seasons his tomatoes carefully and eats them like caviare. Big Ben watches seriously. 'Tomatoes is pretty nice, Rat. You take some of them fancy diners, you order coffee and a bowl of hot water, throw in a shot of ketchup, salt, pepper and free crackers and off you go, tomato soup. Dime for your coffee. I don't agree with tipping, neither.' Rat concurs. The talk's a hobo news service, sleeping conditions in Minneapolis and casual labour in California with fruit hustling on the side. Big Ben doesn't feel this particular line is quite what it used to be, complains about the insecticide and then expounds on pollution in general. They discuss where they're going for the winter. Chicago gets chilly, Big Ben explains. He's in favour of Texas himself, he knows some Mexican girls down there with hearts as big as the civic centre. Rat sells winter in Nevada like a big-time travel agent. A squad car prowls in the distance and the minor figures flit. Rat looks at his watches and reckons it's time to head down Randolph to take in the all-night movie. Tells us thoughtfully how it's done: just mix with the crowd as they're coming out, then turn around, telling the doorman that you've left your hat inside. 'She's warm in there. And nice seats. I don't go sleeping any old wheres.' Big Ben heads for an alley to get a good piece of cardboard to sleep on before they clear it all away.

Stillness again. 3.46 COCA COLA TEMPERATURE 67°. Just the wind rattling the refuse and the occasional stumbling figure. The hobo sits down by the fountain and dozes off with his head in his hands. The sand-coloured disc of the moon hangs between the gaunt buildings. Squad cars hover. The wind whines. The Loop has paused; muffled shunting of the trains from the junctions a mile or two east.

Then slowly the sounds pick up again, as if they're responding to each other. The fountain comes to life with a plip and the dozing hobo jumps and wakes up. Newspapers thunk on the sidewalks as the delivery vans go round and the vendors haul them into their stalls. Lights come on in the diners as another van delivers bread. The first lonely horn intrudes. The lights change in the parking lots: MORNING SPECIAL $1.25. Buildings start to regain their outline, the sky pales through fire escapes and suddenly through tenement gaps the sun hoists up. The Loop burns, then fades, tenements into their daytime grey and the Loop into its plate glass glitter. More horns. Cabs flip their lights off. The hobo by the fountain pulls out a piece of bread, chews at it hungrily and reads the paper it was wrapped in. Then he gets up and flaps his arms. He seems to be looking for somewhere to go.

Footsteps increase. Their pace has changed, hurried and a little nervous now, the first of the day people glancing round at the last of the night-walkers. Sounds begin to coalesce, the faint roar of the subway, the horns, the footsteps, the first bus grinding. Nightworkers queue at the stops. They've finished repairing Randolph Street, resurfaced as if nothing had happened. A faint trembling underfoot as the first wave of traffic approaches; an advance horn, then another and finally it breaks on the Loop, screech and swerve, horns blare. Bacon smell from the diners. 'Remember that Johnny that used to eat here, little feller with the beard? Died yesterday.' 'Is that right? I won't miss him. He used to smell awful bad, ever notice?'

6.32 COCA COLA TEMPERATURE 72°. Down on Van Buren Street the El screeches by overhead. The lights come on in the liquor stores.

CHAPTER 7

MANSCAPE TWO:
Illinois – Missouri

'Swiss Villages' marked on the map a hundred miles west of Chicago suggest a different set of contrasts, and after our slow-crawling flight from the city the greenrolling and skyblue sky and farms with their silver beacon silos make us want to get out and wave and gulp the big midwestern air, mistfresh and dairy-sweet. Cowbells dong in the long green valleys. Fruit and vegetable stalls again with their mellow custodians and crazy misspellings. Pick-ups trundle. Otherwise stillness; only the tall corn, very softly, platter platter in the breeze.

It's no place though, wide and open under the big midwestern sky, for Swiss canton secrecy. Long before we see the names of New Glarus and Monticello, advancing billboards sound a warning:

SWISS CHEESE CHEAPEST HERE

SWISS LANE   WILHELM TELL

BOWLING ALLEY   RESTAURANT

SWISS MAID DRIVE IN
SWISS CHEESE THE CHEAPEST HERE

In reality New Glarus is just a little midwestern town whose image is like false eyelashes on a corn-fresh country girl. True, there's an old-worldly note in the checker-bright flower gardens, in the chatter of German in the smaller bars, a carved donkey cart at a corner and old men with pocket-watches and princely handlebar moustaches, sipping their beer in a wooden balcony overlooking the main street. But otherwise the Swiss ballyhoo just stifles its small-town easiness, lending its usual grid-pattern centre a slicked-up, artificial air and investing restaurants and stores with the fixed smile and brusqueness that go with selling any image, Injun, Mormon, Manhattan or Swiss, complete with imported cuckoo-clocks, chintzy aprons and overpriced bratwurst. The chalet roof on the Alpine Café sums up the little town: Swiss until you look from an angle, when it becomes an exotic version of a Western false front concealing a building as flat as the rest. Even the 'Swiss' waitresses are German imports, an old man tells us: and the pioneer settlers' carved gravestones (fruit and animals in low relief and the finger pointing up to heaven) were moved from the old churchyard to beside the newly built 'pioneer village' – it's more convenient for the tourists.

This commercial schizophrenia, as Swiss as a ready-mix cranberry sauce, doesn't rub off on the younger people; they're just genuine farm and high-school kids, cheery and curious, hanging on the back of pick-ups and heading home with their baseball gear. But the old men are sore at it, as it's only with them that the claim to uniqueness has any validity. We end up drinking draught Pabst with a couple of them that evening outside the New Glarus Hotel, before we're all driven off by the 'Swiss Band' in the bar. With beetling eyebrows and Alpine hats, they still speak German to each other and a fairly guttural English, although they're second and third generation. But they don't hold with their Swiss image. It's only a few years old, they say, and from pioneer until tourist days there was hardly a piece of Swiss architecture in the whole community: just an old church, which was pulled down to make way for a bigger one. The Chamber of Commerce's Swiss Renaissance has distorted and suppressed whatever used to be genuinely unique. In a way it couldn't be helped, they add. Ten years ago the town was dying as farms got bigger and people left: tourism has kept it alive. But only in a mythical form which has nothing to do with the real past. Most of the local craftsmen have been driven out of business – tourism made it cheaper and smarter to import things from Switzerland: and no one can sell home-made traditional food now, as local factories mass-produce it. From outside, it's the lie that's depressing: the manipulation of the past to distort the mellowness which should have replaced it and allowed them to enjoy their Pabst and unviolated selves in the midwestern peace they created.

It's the food that really upsets the old men. A few years ago a good Swiss meal cost under a dollar, one explains. Now it's twice the price and he can't afford it. Swiss cheese went the same way. Every farm had its copper cauldron and wooden press for making it. Now the local factory has undercut them out of existence. 'And it don't come out good. They take out the cream from the milk. Swiss cheese should make with plenty cream, she shouldn't make just any way. I can't eat this cheese they make. I got a friend, she makes home cheese, real cheese.' He winks. 'Old girl friend.'

The band's begun playing and it's hard to talk. He says good night. 'Tomorrow early morning I leave Swiss cheese for you in the bar. Real cheese. From my girl friend.' And he chuckles and disappears. Sure enough, the next day it's there, as cream-rich and wax-edged as any cheese from an old man's dream. When we collect it, the youngish barman looks at us curiously, as if to ask what lies behind this unconventional transaction.

Swinging down through Illinois the land's flatness unfurls again into the green alienation of agribusiness meeting the sky in a monotone broken only by grain-elevators and lone-buzzing planes. Pioneer Grain Lot 3841, Pioneer Grain Lot 4210, side roads always at right angles, County Road H, County Road J, and sober billboard homilies in the intersection towns:

PILO LUTHERAN CHURCH
WELCOME
WILD OATS NEVER MATURE INTO GOOD GRAIN

NEPONSET POP 500
HOME OF INDUSTRY FARMING AND FAMILY LIVING

Our one brief encounter with it matches its air of disconnection from all but a bare Puritan ethic. The car suddenly dies to a halt on top of a lonely hill: no gas. A passerby picks us up, a farmer in his new Chevrolet, and certainly he's as friendly as anyone is likely to be to an unforeseen couple from another planet. Shakes his head at our reply to the usual enquiry of where we're from: 'Gee, that's a long ways from home.' So long in fact that it silences him and when we ask about Hannibal, our next stop, a hundred miles away, it's, 'No, I never did git down there. Don't git much occasion to travel, only into town and back.' He drops us off at a Sinclair station where we buy some gas in a can and get a ride back from a college kid. Even with him it's much the same, friendly but blank – 'a long ways from home' – but nothing further, not about the Beatles even.

We can't get the gas in without a funnel and as we're sitting there, still stranded, a state patrolman draws up and offers to tow us. But instead of going to the Sinclair Station, which would involve crossing the traffic, he stops at the Mobil one opposite, where we duly fill her up. When we cross over to the other to return the can to the attendant, he looks at us blackly, tight-faced. Although we've paid for the gas in the can, we've obviously made a major blunder. 'Why'd that son-of-a-bitch cop take you to the Mobil station?' We explain about crossing the traffic in tow, but he isn't satisfied. Our New York licence-plate seems to provoke him. 'You gotta give me two bucks for that ride – I gotta pay the kid that took you.' We know he's lying – the ride was offered, he was going that way in any case and it wasn't more than half a mile. We say so and his face hardens. 'Well why the hell didn't you come back here? You jest gimme them two bucks or I'll make trouble for you, mister.' We suggest he calls the cop to settle it and he suddenly loses control, dancing up and down in rage and screaming at us, 'You sons-of-bitches, get the shit out of here, you son-of-a-bitch right out of town'; and he stands there screaming as we pull out, waving his fists right to the last, a little figure lost in the vacuum of bare sky, bare fields and flat treeless little towns.

Until slowly the Western flavour grows stronger, squares with wooden false front buildings and walks dwindling to half pace. Old cars groan in the heat and bat off in a cloud of dust; the cry of a train hangs on the emptiness, a hundred freight cars rattling by and dwarfing the town, whose biggest billboard advertises a hog festival. In the café it's the same, the first of that big open friendliness, regardless of our being strangers and unplaceable ones at that – we get the same 'hi' as everyone else from the bartender in T-shirt and levis. No charge for a refill, even if

you're just having coffee, and when we ask directions they don't
reply with 'right' and 'left' always east or west or south. Everybody drinks from the bottle, hooped over the counter, murmuring; the notices on the rest-room doors aren't 'men' and
'women', but 'boys' and 'girls'.

No sensation of road movement, just that floating, floating
feeling, bends several miles apart and signposted like some
event, only the sun's slow veering round and heat shimmer and
truck blast until gradually further south the big green undulates
again but with a new atmosphere; still and uneasy suddenly,
the wild grass high in the fences, tangled trees and vegetation
lush and loud with insects, the farms older and tottering – first
suggestions of the South. A pair of crippled tarpaper shacks with
two black figures sitting outside: they watch us pass, expressionless. Then suddenly the Mississippi is there, glitter-brown and
belly-sensual, less like a river than a lake between its dark,
sultry banks. In the dank little river towns the houses already
reflect its presence. Big Southern balconies gaze out aloof from
the higher ground; tattered little black sectors limp down to
the water's edge. The river swings and falls away, butts against
its blank walls, breaks up around huge dark islands and swings
again fat and sluggish, with whole trees floating down it and
drowning in its mudflats, scum-edged in emerald green and
water lilies in white bloom; a stogged barge, a tilting jetty, the
filigree of fishing nets, a lone rowboat way out suspended
between water and sky. Otherwise empty,

a sullen expanse between the cottonwood branches and down
the narrow side streets of the damp, ghosted towns, until it
vanishes again. But you can always tell it's there from the way
the horizon meets the sky and the secret inlets where willows
trail in the chocolate brown, from names like Carthage and La
Harpe; and always tell it's turning south, from the tall white
columns and porches shaded by acacia trees, the growing stillness of the heat and finally the poplars pointing over the low
green valley towards the silver span of a bridge across to the
old river-port, pink and peeling by riverbrown: Hannibal, home
of Mark Twain.

*

A long, crumbling main street runs parallel to the Mississippi, dotted with old hotels and raucous little one-eyed bars – there must be at least twenty within some three or four hundred yards. The crusty, capped river faces in the doorway of Dot and Dave's Café are grouped around improbable stories audible right across the street. (One says he was a border sheriff in Texas half a century ago, watching for wetbacks and opium-runners – claims his horse was shot from beneath him by none other than Pancho Villar.) Railroad tracks, abandoned jetties and riverside shacks are overlooked by a wild green hill with right on its crest an ancient house keeping watch through the rich vegetation. Occasionally a barge goes by, its movement hardly perceptible in so much space, water and sky. Without any effort it's all that New Glarus tried to be.

The contrast suggests how unlikely it was that an old world, Swiss or any, would survive rebirth in this man-forging land, at least beyond the Eastern ghettoes and the confines of New England. It's like the names as you travel west. In New England imports fit, Canterbury, Andover and Plymouth; but beyond the Ohio only new ones ring true, those that echo the trek and the soil, Sweetwater, Fortune and Pleasant Valley, rather than nostalgia or delusions of alien grandeur like Venice or Rome. So too with Hannibal after New Glarus – there's no need to protest its past, because it's all there with the river that made it, from broken cobbles to cragged faces: and with those faces it's hard to imagine it yielding to commercialization. ('No sir', says one of the men in Dot and Dave's, 'she don't change much and that's because the river don't change – floods up every couple of years and still brings a few barges by. Town's the same way – up a little, down a little, stays around the same size. Don't reckon she'll ever change much, no more'n that river out there.')

There are motels on the outskirts, but they're out of sight and mind, an adjunct of the through traffic rather than of Hannibal. The old hotels only just survive, now that the river trade's declined, but they haven't turned to the tourist circuit: they're still shabby and comfortable, a modest three or four dollars a night. It's the same with the people. Maybe the old men's stories grow with newcomers to the audience, but they were telling them anyway, tales of northwest lumbering in the robber baron twenties when men died like flies in the camps; of three and four decker paddle-boats docking daily at Hannibal and legends about the Ozark people, as today is market day and some of them have come into town, old pick-ups piled high with eggs and vegetables for sale. Old-fashioned greetings follow us round, even from the younger people and a frail, silver-haired old lady who looks as Southern as they come, but apparently sees us through friendly eyes. No one pushes Mark Twain very much; there's just a museum in his former home, a modest statue of Tom and Huck at the end of the main street and discreet plaques on the old buildings which played a part in the Twain saga – Slim's General Store and Grant's Dry Goods opposite. Neither looks much out of place in contemporary Hannibal. An old paddle-steamer runs regular outings, paddle churning and horn echoing over the river's emptiness; but it's just jaunty, nothing flamboyant, a trip with an old river captain who gathers the kids around him and slows down as he points out beavers and blue herons and the sites of Huck's and Tom Sawyer's adventures.

The museum is equally vivid. Manuscripts and portraits of Twain, with the archetypal look of local doctor and journalist in the Jeffersonian days when this was to be American, rather than provincial. A little boy of ten or eleven who's escaped his parents joins us at the album of photos from the movies of Twain novels. Looks up. 'Hey, you talk funny.' His embarrassed mother calls him, but he won't be got away. He asks if we've been to Africa and wants to be an astronaut. Has he read Mark Twain? Just Huck Finn, at school, but he's seen nearly all the movies and since, as foreigners, we clearly need guidance, he explains the pictures. 'Hey would you like to live here?' he adds. 'I wouldn't mind living here, we live in Kansas City. Hey, you know that bit on the raft when they all get lost in the dark, Huck and Tom and Nigger Jim' – a flicker of maternal nervousness as she hears him saying 'nigger', forgetting perhaps that it's on good authority – 'yeah, that's the best part. Hey, you been on the river boat? You know if there's alligators – okay, okay,

I'm comin. So long.' And he's gone, his excitement reflecting both Twain's and Hannibal's continuity.

The woman in the little store where they sell Southern style rugs tells us the old house on the hill belonged to a Mrs Holliday – Twain's 'Widow Douglas', who lit the beacons to guide the riverboats round the point. Wide stone steps lead up to it and its view over the river. South and east the sad green delta reaches out at a low skyline: westward it rises into the wooded mountains. Way below the river laps at the stone bulwarks of broken quays; the steamer's platter and chug of a barge, while boys whistle down on the mudflats, and fish and boat like Tom or Huck, right down to their ragged shorts and straw hats. Their parents, sitting in the porches of their riverside shingle shacks have a Southern folksiness, black and sunbrown white alike, as if they identify more with the river than with other human beings: they watch us carefully but blankly. They too look unchanged in generations, in keeping with their persistent setting which still conditions everything, the rusty railroad, peeling town, iron barges stuck in the mud, old rowboats with splitting ribs and even widow Douglas's house. It has no plaque and apparently no one's trying to preserve it as it's already overwhelmed by the creepers pushing in at the windows. A columned doorway and a wrought-iron balcony are both collapsing. Inside, weeds are pushing up through the floor-boards.

That night, with the market over and Ozark farmers still in town, Hannibal comes to life with a bang. Literally. Two family pick-ups meet head on at a modest pace right in the middle of the street. As the drivers are equally tipsy, they apparently call it even and retreat to the nearest bar to confirm it, kids settling back to sleep amongst the sacks and vegetable crates. It's at the far end of town, where the railroad tracks converge and every other doorway's a bar, that the action's on: the hullaballoo of a country dance in the Driftwood, a huge old cavern with antique fans whirring ineffectively, strips of ceiling hanging down and two flickering Pabst signs providing almost the only light. A wild little country band, shirts knotted at sweaty waists, with two guitars, banjo and piano going rinky-tink-tink and bang and everyone's dancing, yodelling and clapping; an old farmer, seventy at least, peaked cap firmly set and trousers halfway up his back, stomps and whirls with the flouncy barmaid and several girls are dancing in pairs, hatchet-sharp Ozark faces, young and old whooping it up together, rare sight in the USA. A young man at a crowded table invites us to join them, making room. Introductions all round: his name is Earl, garage hand in Hannibal, early twenties, short and pudgy but with the same Ozark sharpness in his mouth and especially his eyes. He used to live in the Ozarks, he tells us and knows most of the people here. Left in his teens, when his parents died, and he's never been back since. He's making a line at a dark-haired girl with those same bright, gritty-grey eyes, but after every dance with him she goes demurely back to her table, where a stick-like old man keeps unflinching watch. Her granpa, Earl explains – family honour still carries a premium in the Ozarks, where feuding isn't over yet.

After a while he gets restless: says he's fed up with hillbilly music and why don't we cross the river with him to a swinging modern bar only a couple of miles away. He's hard to refuse, so we go with him in his rattletrap old Chevy. He does sixty one moment, twenty the next, sitting up solemn straight like a judge, rarely altering his expression and talking almost non-stop. His father was a hill farmer who could hardly sign his name: his mother also an Ozark girl, from the proverbial next door shack. They never could make a livelihood from the stony Ozark soil and were always planning to move, but never saved the means to do so. He was fourteen when the old man died from the moonshine and worse that he brewed in his still – the doctor had told him to quit, but he wouldn't. His mother went the same way the next year. 'Teacher told us, me an my sister, there aint nothin for you here – you better quit now. My sister had a steady date, she stayed there and married, four kids in five years, looks like forty, like my mother. But I quit, came down here and got my training as a mechanic. I couldn't get work for a good time because of coming from the sticks, my accent was funny, my schoolin was poor. Folks can be mean with Ozark people – they reckon we're kinda crazy and backward. Know what they done to my granpa? Had a cabin a little ways from ours and they came to bulldoze it down – lumber company had the land rights. Granpa sat in the door with his shotgun and threatened to blow em out of the seat. Would have too. Know what they did? Gave his buddy a quart of whiskey to get the old man real slugged. When he woke up, his cabin was flat, couldn't see where it had been. They took out his things and left them there – except his shotgun. Never did see that again.'

The bar's all neon, potted plants and suburban-looking clients as if, in spite of all he's said, Earl's dissociating himself from the scene at the Driftwood. They won't let us in though – it's some special dance evening and they're demanding jacket and tie and dresses for the ladies, for which none of us qualify. Earl's mad, convinced he saw people there in shirt-sleeves and denouncing it as prejudice against either him or us, or both.

We persuade him not to press the point and he drives back erratically, encouraged by the second six-pack that we've drunk since Hannibal. He hurls the empties out of the window, concluding every observation with 'What the hell, I don't give a damn,' and we suddenly find ourselves in a farmyard. But Earl doesn't flinch, just keeps on going, scattering chickens, dogs and pigs and straight out of the opposite gate and down another dusty road, talking very dead-pan about hillbillies and the Cadillac set. Then he announces a short cut and whoops right off the narrow track and straight into a cornfield with half the stalks still standing and a few dry cobs on them, smatterbang on the roof like an air raid but Earl ploughs on still talking non-stop as if he's driving right down Main Street. He halts deliberately in the middle as if he's come to a parking lot that coincides with an idea. 'Hey, did I tell you I was married? Yes sir, little Ozark girl, we got two kids. Goin fishin tomorrow, you comin with us?'

We make it a date. But needless to say our last sight of him is his old corn-spattered Chevy weaving unsteadily down the street back to the wild sound of the Driftwood.

North-westwards next morning into the Ozarks, little farms crouch in the hollows, secret and dilapidated below the narrow, switching road. Fair-haired kids are barefoot and lean; cattle browse in twos and threes; old couples sit side by side, thin and beady in plain porches. Overgrown and densely wooded, it has a magical quality in the lingering morning mist and few signs of activity, as if they're forever concealing something; just the patchy hill farms and occasional lumberyard or quarry, always small and often abandoned, like the modest factories in the brick-faced towns with their cracked streets and air of desertion and unemployment, young people lounging, everywhere threadbare.

Except at Hickings, where pick-ups line the road on each side. Cattle and hogs complain in the back. An auction's going on in a barn, overalls and straw hats and an air of liquor flowing: the auctioneer gabbles non-stop in a prodigious hillbilly twang, ringed round by unflickering eyes. Until they begin to notice us. As more and more faces turn our way the auctioneer gradually realizes that there's something more controversial in the air than even a hog; he slows down, almost stops, as he too takes us in. He picks up again but the glances and whispers go on and they're strangely unsmiling. It feels as if they're telling us to leave. Our next stop, for a Coke at a rough little store – June still inside the car, drawn up in the heavy shadow – seems to match the incident. It's just a shack with a yapping dog and crude shelves piled with shotguns, liquor and biscuits; the keeper, a heavy, swart character, resting a large paunch on the counter, has a curt, suspicious manner. An older man sits drinking in a corner. He asks where I'm from as the keeper opens the Cokes. Then the keeper joins in. 'Like it here?'

'Pretty country.'

'That's right. And she'd be prettier even, cept for all them goddam niggers. You got any niggers over there? Cause we got too goddam many here. Not right here in this little county, we put em out a long whiles back and they aint comin back again, no sir' – he nods at the shot guns – 'they aint so stupid they'd come troublin decent folks. It's up North they're doing that cause folks up there's too goddam stupid to keep a goddam nigger down. I heard one of em on the radio sayin how they're gonna take over, drive us white folks right out and take every white woman, yes sir, that's what they're aimin at. That's all

them son-of-a-bitches want, robbin, rapin, plunderin – right
Jeff?'

Jeff nods non-committally, but there's more support from a
younger, pinched man who's come in from the back. He adds
his piece – it all has a ritual quality, like some formal reception
for strangers. 'Tell the truth Uncle Dean, I wouldn't mind if
they did come back here. Have us a little nigger-huntin – fill
em with lead and send em back North where they like the sons-
of-bitches.'

We can't help wondering afterwards exactly why they raised
the subject – they couldn't have seen June. Hardly guilt – a
dislike of strangers no doubt, and a touch of paranoia; perhaps they took me for an interloper, journalist or Civil Rights
worker. But most of all it seemed like an effort to convince
themselves as much as me of some heroic dimension to the aim-
less little store with its mean, yapping dog and otherwise
silence. What would have happened if we'd gone in together?
They talked so big it's hard to believe that they'd have been
anything more than surly. But it lends a second meaning to the
pinched farms and valleys and wooded stillness; as they recede
the thruway's anonymity and then the low skyline of Kansas
City come as an unexpected relief.

CHAPTER 8

VISIONS:
Kansas and Missouri

It's not just escape from the secretive country people that makes
Kansas City relaxing. It's the city itself, casual and open.
Buildings sprawl, rather than soar, bastions of solid stone pastel
pink and beige in the sundown with the effect of a desert city
floating up at the end of the thruway. And an oasis. It's deep in
trees: on the wide suburban avenues you're hardly ever out of
range of the crickets' sleepy comments. There's a western sensation of space reaching right into the city and somehow fashion-
ing everything, not just buildings but people and styles. Little
bustle or jostling: and people answer enquiries with anything
from a nod and a smile to several minutes' conversation, instead
of the nervously flung reply or indifferent shrug that we've
grown used to. The West seems to soften social boundaries.
Black and white are often together and though the city has its
ghettoes, like the cramped homes on a green hill on the west side
of town, they look less harshly outlined than the East's. No one
hurries you: raised voices are rare and the traffic drifts along.
People even make way for us when we find ourselves in the
wrong lane. True, there's a matter-of-factness in the squat skyline and plain language (ad in the bus: BRONSKI SELLS
FENCE), a taste of what many Easterners see as the sum of the
Midwest. But there's also a sophistication, a cool that tells both
East and far West, with their fads and self-consciousness, to go
hang; as in Chicago, but differently textured – after Chicago's
lonely delirium, the quality of a placid dream.

The only address we have is Kelly's, a bar on the old Missouri
side, ex-haunt of a Kansas friend who found his home city too
remote and left to look for life in Europe. Kelly is his opposite –
a cheery Irishman who's spent half his life on the move in search

of peace and found it here. 'First day I was in New York, two or three dollars in my pocket and wondering where the hell to go, I seen a fire in a tenement. Oh Jesus – people came out like ants. They got more people underground there than we got above it in Kansas City. So I headed for California. But that's the same, so I've come back here. She's a darlin city. Nothin like her. Right Joe?'

This last to an oldish man who's refilling a cigarette machine. A curt reply. 'Used to be. Used to be, before your day, when we had a few things going, Tom Prendergast's time.'

Kelly explains. One of the last of the big city bosses, Prendergast controlled local government for nearly a generation during prohibition days. At the price of democracy, his backroom genius made Kansas a Mecca of pool-halls and speakeasies, this empire being based on the contracts provided for his cement company by the men he'd put in power, often for bizarre projects such as the paving, six feet deep, of a creek which runs right through the city. Finally, with history turning against him, he was ousted by reform groups which passed the mantle of Kansas City on to the sadder modern joylands of Las Vegas and Reno.

After filling the cigarette machines, Joe joins us for a drink, clearly hot for an audience open to talk of better days. 'People does a whole lot of preachin, but say what you like, Kansas City aint nothin to what she used to be. Them days she was wide open – when Boss Prendergast was runnin things. And there was mighty good government – no son-of-a-bitch politicians, just Tom and that was it. You couldn't do nothin less you asked him – but after that you could do anythin.'

The man next to him joins in, must be in his late fifties too, a plumber, Kelly tells us later. 'That's right Joe – why in them days you could shoot a man right on Main Street and that was your business, nobody troubled you. Specially if Tom Prendergast knew you – less he knew the other guy better. Then you'd be in real trouble. But a smart guy took more care than that.'

Joe looks wistful. 'You betcha – Pat, you check me – them days you didn't work for your money. You stood on the corner and she'd fall in your lap. Pool-halls and dance-halls in every doorway. We used to sit on the sidewalk and shoot crap right on

12th Street. And cat-houses – finest girls in the States and every one of them a lady, Tom wouldn't have allowed nothin else. Hell – this city was so crowded you could hardly pitch your dice, that was the only problem then. She was better than any of em, New York, Chicago, San Francisco – folks coming in from everywhere, cattlemen, poolmen, convention men. It was Tom Prendergast fixed all that. Nobody starved when he was boss – never did think I'd see the day when I'd be checkin these goddam machines.'

Kelly leans forward into the forum which half a dozen men have joined now, centred round Pat and Joe. 'What did you do in those days, Joe?'

'Me? I worked for Tom Prendergast, Midwest Asphalt Company. I don't care what they say, the reform groups, the churches and those, Boss Prendergast was a saint.' Murmurs of assent all round, glasses rise and 'God bless him'. 'I'd go down to the asphalt company once a week, Tuesday morning, collect my check and that was the job – except election times of course, he'd expect you to help him out and a few folks might get hurt, but it was in a good cause – keep the city where she was, right in the centre of the map.'

A white-haired man joins in. 'Say, Joe, you remember that joint, the one on 12th Street, right on the corner, with that orange-haired girl from Nevada' – Joe breaks in. 'Hell every place was a joint then – there was one on the State line with pool tables made like trollies so's when the Kansas cops came they'd push em across the room to Missoura. And when the Missoura cops came, they'd push em right back again. And they never did come the same time, that couldn't happen in Kansas City.' Sips his beer reflectively. 'Well, them reform fellers had their way – guess they must feel righteous, but there never will be another city like Kansas City, not any more.'

'Why did it change, though?'

His answer comes back snappily. 'The reform fellers – the Churches and the politicians. No-good do-gooders. You know somethin? Christmas time in Kansas City Tom'd go round personally with baskets of food for the poor folks – used to take em round himself. But then the Church started hollerin, using fancy words like vice and corruption – hell, we didn't need churches here. If a man wants to pray, he prays, you could walk right in a saloon and pray – ain't that right?' And they chortle. 'That's what finished Kansas City – politicians, see, they got in power, Tom was the one put em there, but they turned right around on him. They got no shame. Reform groups.' And he spits on Kelly's floor.

Kelly keeps introducing us to just about everyone who arrives, mainly newsmen from the *Star*, now the city's most powerful institution, and friends of theirs, mostly our age. We end up with a trio who share an apartment: Lem, a reporter from the *Star*, Nick, lean and sharp, and Brent, a burly character whose German-Irish parentage shows in his big laughing face. Both these last two are cab-drivers, though their conversation includes novels, Vietnam and the follies of Kansas City suburbia – so that it's hardly surprising to learn that they're both Chicago graduates. It's very different from the hippiedom and intellectualism of the East, Greenwich Village, say, with its faint snideness and air of superiority: easy and friendly, like the bar. Rambling and big, with an unselfconsciously mixed clientele, age, colour and classwise, it would long since have been prettied up anywhere more fashionable: but here it remains just a red-brown cavern covered with Irish posters and news clippings of local hold-ups. It was a slave market, Kelly explains and subsequently a staging post for the Santa Fé Trail. It seems quite natural when Brent and the others suggest our staying at their apartment.

When we get there someone produces grass and the talk drifts gently on. Nick and Brent describe to us how they came to be driving cabs, for a local company which virtually lets them choose their hours. Brent is relatively easy-going and Nick more intellectual about it, yet they've had much the same experience. At Chicago, working for his Ph.D., Brent was spending most of his time doing the old crossword puzzles from microfilms of the *New York Times* – his grease-pencil answers on the glass made him unwelcome and so he left, sick of the grades and competition and authoritarianism. He's been thinking of opening a book store but doubts if the kind he wants would succeed here.

Nick on the other hand spent time in Germany doing research on Wittgenstein, only to return and find himself just as alienated as Brent; he talks of existentialism and anti-hero novelists. 'I depend on them for reassurance that I'm not just a nut in a private daze. They show others feeling the same way about the crazy demands we face. We're a schizoid society, no time for a self, only actions and self-projection, else you don't make it. It was blowing my mind. And it's not just drop-outs like us who feel it. Even up on Mission Hill, that's the local elegant suburb, the people we chauffeur half the time – they've got everything, so they reckon, but it happens to them. Nicely set up, good-looking wife, right income, kids – but suddenly they pop out of their minds. Divorces, breakdowns, suicides – they suddenly don't know where they are. That's why they're often so aggressive, for fear of that.'

Brent breaks in. 'You see a lot of it even as a cabby. They like to get you sized up to fit into the world as they understand it. And if they can't, they can get pretty mean. You don't look like their typical cabby, so they have to check you out, make sure you're just doing it for kicks – you could be one of their kids, I guess, so if you are at it full time they feel you're rejecting them. That's where the trouble begins. You're threatening that whole façade between themselves and uncertainty. It always starts the same way. "Where are you going to school now?" You're just on vacation, see, it's all for kicks or an old-fashioned dad who thinks you should raise maybe half the down payment on your Corvair. That's all they want to know. But tell them the truth, that you quit school to drive a cab, and they get real sore at you. I had one sit up and tell me straight, "Crap, don't you give me that crap." A real little social column lady, born and bred on Mission Hill. When I told her yes, I chose it, no hard luck story, I've been a cabby two years and no, I don't have other plans, she got mad at me. Started yelling her head off – made me stop and put her down and said she'd report me to the company. Never said what for exactly and never did make the report, that I know of. Others get sullen, they close up, then they don't tip you. But you know what they're thinking – "What's this kid got against me?"''

Nick: 'That story's nothing unusual. I really think they're afraid of people, of seeing in them the selves they've lost touch with, and if you trigger off that fear – by the way you look or what you're doing – then they want you to cease to exist. It scares me too, this harsh choice of opposites and the stupid hostility. If you hesitate, you're out of the race, so what do you do? Quit for good or sell out and do like the system tells you? To me that explains the hate, the way they can hate you for something real trivial like a beard. It suggests you've chosen the other way – that's how rigid it is – and reminds them of their emptiness, so in self-defence they call you a freak. And they're right in a way, because it's their society and they're not going to make room for you. A cab's not paradise.'

Pot calm. Then as the first slip of light appears through the balcony at the back, where the chipmunks are awake and playing tag around the chairs, Brent suddenly comes to life and offers to take us to the stockyards. He knew them pretty well once, as his father had a ranch and used to sell his cattle there, but he hasn't been back in years.

Outside it's Kansas quiet. Though it's just a modest suburb, there are trees everywhere, lifting enquiringly in the cool; a few cars brush the silence. Floating down long, deserted avenues, Brent tells us more about the city, his home since they left the ranch, apart from his few years in Chicago. When we mention the homage to Prendergast, he laughs and takes us past Brush Creek, the furthest-fetched of Prendergast's schemes – and sure enough, there it is, solemnly cemented all the way, fifteen miles from end to end and little concrete bridges over it. Even the city's traffic lights are set in solid concrete columns, another of Prendergast's contracts. Brent chuckles. 'That's one thing I like about it compared to New York or LA – the way it looks so straightforward, a bureaucrat's dream, when in fact it was made by a crazy mixture of despotism, benevolence and violence. The municipal hall, the city hall, the courthouse – he built everything. I guess he screwed a lot of guys, but ever since then, city government's hardly been liberal and it's still full of rackets. Least he had style.'

He points out more Prendergast monuments, like the city

152

hall, thirty concrete storeys, baroque and beige in the paling
light, and setting the tone of downtown, placid and solemn,
almost witty in its disguise of the wild days behind it – the
crap-shooting on 9th and 12th Streets and Henderson's where
you could get even breakfast served by a waitress in nothing
but shoes. It conveys a background that's even more USA than
Curley and the Boston Irish, no longer immigrant-based but
expressing the vagaries and contradictions of the reforging
phase that followed: cruel and humorous, heroic and crude, the
anarchy of unfettered man behind the orderly façade he presents
as the image of himself, its relics doubly humorous now in the
peace that's settled down on the city.

Down in the stockyards there's that same wide open sensation
of the full West having begun in the sea of cattle pens and red-
cobbled alleys deep in straw with the wooden ramps and chutes
overhead stretching to the packing houses and Western figures
in levis and Stetsons who'd look like nature out of art, an import from Hollywood, but for the big-hearted friendliness, the
'Howdy folks' and 'Hi, how're you doing this morning'; and if
you say 'Fine' they don't leave it at that but add 'Sure am glad
to hear it' and stop and talk to us boyish curious when they
gauge that we're inclined. 'Should be around eight thousand head
coming through today, I guess,' says the broad-backed character
who's paused by us, leaning on the fence. 'But that's just a quiet
day around here. Where you from? England? Say – sure am
glad to meet you. Taking a beer? Bring some cold beers Pete.'
And Pete's walk's the same as his, hip roll and arms hanging
loose and a cattleswitch in one hand and he talks to the cattle
as they go by, 'Hey, hey, c'mon there, hey,' quietly. Brent
knows each kind, the sad-faced Guernseys, suspicious Black
Angus and stocky curly-browed Herefords and all round as the
slow-waking sun lights cobbles and old grey wood and Stetsoned
figures hooped over fences (one's the spitting image of Truman,
leathered face watching the cattle, and murmuring to them as if
that's life), all round the sad slow cowsong mounts into the
gentle morning, a single seabreak of sound varied by the city's
waking – the last big trucks cattlecrammed clumbering up the
wooden ramps, muffled shunt and cry of the trains, cars

whooshing over the cobbles, hoofs clatter and herds jostle and the cowhands' whoop and whistling.

Brent with the big blue laughing eyes and stubbled and grinning waves his arms ('I'd forgotten what it was like – that's where my old man's pen was before the floods washed it away'); as we leave the bargaining's begun, the buyers from the packing houses – 'Hear you got some steers for me, buddy' . . . 'You want heifers, twenty-six fifty' – and cattlemen leaning on pen corners keeping their cool, watching prices. Cattlesong drops behind as we float up to Quality Hill, highest point in the city, to watch it wake, the first chimney puffs touching the sky the green traffic copter buzzing by and Braniff Boeings zoop zoop over the trees like a carnival taxi service, sun up now over the freightyards and white ranks of the grain elevators the barges nosing up the Missouri the Prendergast skyscrapers towering benignly over the commuter traffic, briefcases and white shirts. Seen through Brent's and the others' good sharing of the gentle grass-given vision, it's a kaleidoscope of living, with the green sweep of the trees, wide curve of the brown Missouri and blue bowl of the farmland beyond cradling it all like a country town.

Brent: 'May be just a sleepy breadbowl like all those Eastern wiseguys say, full of hicks, maybe she is – but she's great, she's my city.' Stoops as something catches his eye. He beckons us over. Under a crumbling stone wall, relic of the vanished mansions that gave Quality Hill its name, there's a straggle of blue flowers in the grass. 'Morning glories. Isn't that something? Why should I leave Kansas City?'

This lulling quality persists, centred for us on their apartment, where there's always someone to talk to, day or night, but no obligations: books, posters on the wall, with anarchic home-made collages and portraits of Thurber, Malcolm X and Andy Warhol; Nick bent over a chess game all night playing himself Buddha-silent under the bronze chandelier that one of them brought back from Egypt; Lem's brother Jack, seventeen, who drops in from Boston on his way to see a girl in Denver, spending fifteen dollars on grass then short of the cash for a hot dog, like a Western Harpo Marx with hair in all directions and skid row boots going flippety-flop; Brent coming in at four or five after a whole night's cab-driving with half his takings already spent on hamburgers-with-everything, Cokes and ice-cream for whoever's there and then he sits talking the dawn away ('I had a crazy dream, I dreamed this guy got into my cab and said "I'll give you ten bucks for each line of poetry you can recite" but all I could think of was Ginsberg's *Howl* and he said "Call that a poem?" and vanished'). The intervals of Kelly's too, where on our morning after the stockyards the Prendergast men are still reliving the glory days of their gangster saint. The city's apparent tolerance, with virtually a whole block given over to homosexuals where slim-hipped boys line the bars, all in drag and bouffant hair-dos. The atmosphere at the Kansas City *Star* where Lem takes us a couple of times, the whole concern employee-owned and democracy ruling so strong (yet a conservative pressure group) that there's not an enclosed office, all together on one open floor, from president to messenger boys. The modest effectiveness of the local anti-poverty programme, which we also visit with Lem and talk to some of their trainees, mostly young black mothers who'd left school without a chance but are now as striking head-high poised and unpatronised as anyone. And the string of bars as easy as Kelly's where ex-jazz-men from St Louis and other one-time river shrines play out their threadbare days, eyes closed and splits in their shoes with the once cream-coloured uppers, earning a couple of bucks and a meal on pianos with half the keys gone, but still conjuring out a magic to hush even a teenage crowd. (One of them takes us back with him to his unlit apartment – no money for bulbs – and his buddy, another old jazzman, who can't be more than five feet high, asks first if we've brought food, then sticks out his hand and says: 'Jimmy Dowley, trumpet.')

Yet despite this nirvana there's a vicariousness in the air. It's exemplified in the Plaza, a much vaunted shopping centre, built a generation ago and a model in its way but so bizarrely eclectic that it seems to be saying: we haven't anything of our own, so instead we'll just assemble everything we can lay our minds on – Spanish roofs and long colonnades, mosaics of Italian and Mexican scenes, Florentine statues in the fountains and crazy Corinthian-style columns supported by goofy British lions clasping globe to imperial bosom, a Neptune here and a satyr there; without even the hotch-potch uniqueness of the far West's Las Vegas baroque, it always conveys the question of where's the self in all of this? It's the same at the art gallery where everything is gathered together from priceless Ming to Impressionists, but there's nothing that's sprung from local soil since the Ashcan social realists who painted their populist murals, derelicts and barside figures like today's old jazzmen, back in the thirties. All the moderns are from the East or West coast, their ephemeral quality underlined yet unchallenged by this midwestern setting.

Karen, a friend of Brent's who works at the gallery, says as much. She loves the independence of Kansas, but at the same time it's so placid that little's discovered or even expressed, there just isn't the forum for it; now she's thinking of going back to face the harshness of the East or the brittleness of California. ('Us dozen or so who see each other, we're getting more and more introverted because of our isolation.') Her alienation is shared. Sometimes there's almost a sense of doom at the fact of people like Nick and Brent chauffering executives' wives. And each of them seems uncertain behind the spontaneity; it's not just Nick's brooding or the improbability of Brent's bookshop, but the others' wildness too. Ann, a painter, twenty-one, twice divorced pixie blonde scrambling barefoot back into childhood by climbing trees down in the park or jumping into the plaza fountains with garlands for the Florentine bronzes (though at least no one in Kansas City seems particularly to mind such gestures); Rhonda, twenty-three, also divorced and outwardly exuberant with a non-stop spiel of zany tastes, one being the myth of Las Vegas like something seen on a moontrip ('Vegas' she calls it, 'the Las is silent'): 'I wanna go back to LA and Vegas and drive down the freeway at one oh five, I hate the grunt and I really love it and I wanna go back to it, to triple cream-topped milk shakes and six-foot-wide motel beds with a magifinger machine to back-massage me while I'm asleep in a neon palace all pink and green, it gives me a sense of security.' So much so that one wild evening we're all of us set to go there, only we've hardly the money between us to get out of Kansas City, so instead we go to the supermarket to buy Scotch and hamburgers and Rhonda sits bang in the trolley demanding a ride like the other kids. She's usually like this. Yet just sometimes when the others are talking she's suddenly quiet, her face a mask, until she quickly catches herself ('They got passion fruit shakes in Vegas this year').

Together or alone, they all have this fugitive note. (Karen: 'Jack has it over us, everything's so fresh to him and he bounces up and experiences, climbing mountains in New Hampshire and having visions over in Denver.') She's right; his madcap seventeen-year-old doings burst like a whirlwind into the stillness that closes around again when he's left. Often they're way back in the past with talk, say, of the Movement's beginnings in the City Lights bookshop in San Francisco or remembering the day when Ginsberg blew in hymning the big Midwest and reviled by the local citizenry, leaving them still savouring *Howl* years later in his stormy wake; as if even where imagination runs deep, revolution is so in-built for the USA of their generation that to be on the sideline is exile. Even in Kansas City, it seems, and for such free hearts as we chanced to meet and share their bright vision of the world, calm must verge on fantasy . . .

It's real, though, if less searching, on the nearby State campus at Lawrence. We've a date there with friends of a friend, Ralph and Kate, Ralph being an anthropologist who's worked on the neighbouring reservation of the Potowotami Indians. Although we've never met before, they throw the house open to us as naturally as Brent and his friends. Perhaps it looks conventional, house with all conveniences in a flat, spacious suburb and most of their friends campus colleagues, yet it isn't. Nor is the campus, contrary to what the East and Cornell's competitive disdain have always led us to expect. It has that slightly functional air of most State campuses, but none of the power-drunk self-importance which made Cornell seem so naïve. And Ralph's colleagues aren't inhibited by any sense of competition about where they're working or what they're doing.

If they talk about it at all, their interest seems far more spontaneous than their Eastern counterparts'; ironic, if unsurprising, to find a new sensibility beginning where status ends.

Life at home with Ralph and Kate is equally urbane and relaxed. Half the day chatting, the kids barefoot and all easy come and go, so much so with Kate and Ralph that we see almost more of the children, both button-bright but without that hardness that sometimes creeps into New York kids at six or seven. Janie (nine and impressed with my act of scribbling for half the day): 'What are you writing?' 'My diary.' 'What's in it?' 'Lots of people.' 'What kinda people?' 'Funny ones, nice ones.' 'Like us?' 'Right.' At which she starts to imitate me, writing in an exercise book, brow furrowed, though we can't see it, only when it's finished, she says, though she hints darkly 'You're in it' (so that this is returning the compliment). And they make an equal fairyland of the neighbouring fields with a rough little stream whose secrets they confide to us and the nearby supermart with its Christmas stocking atmosphere of ice-cream in twenty-nine flavours, where they chat as quick as teenagers with girls behind the counter. (Strange, such brief world-sharings, ending in 'See you some time.')

Ralph also takes us to the Potowotami reservation, as they're holding the drum ceremony, lasting a sacred four days, whose rituals are a symbolic renewal of the tribe's battered identity. It's a strange sensation, after the Indians' Hollywood image, to turn straight off Interstate 70, maximum 80, minimum 40, and find ourselves on the reservation. Yet its closeness to standard USA – its overlap, even, in that the first figures we see are white farmers ploughing land leased from the Potowotami – only sharpens the everywhere sense of the distance between the two. And it's not just the ethnic quality of the drum ceremony: the gulf's apparent even on the thruway, where crammed cars belonging to Indians hug the shoulders at thirty or forty, the driver never looking up as the newer cars whip by. Then on the reservation itself: derelict and overgrown, except where the whites are farming, with a stillness and sunblown remoteness deeper than anywhere we've been, even the flatlands of Illinois, where at least there's the buzz of a plane or a pick-up. But here nothing: most of the Indians walk. Bowed at the side of the dusty track without turning to see who's coming, philosophical intent on their own, but gazing after us a little against the harsh glint of the sun. Or sitting in the porches of threadbare, pioneer-style homes with a few fruit trees and chickens outside, watching the everlasting flatness in their silent isolation from everything but themselves and their past. (One, George, whom we get to know, later invites us to visit him in the derelict schoolhouse where he lives with his crippled mother and chirpy son, all dependent on welfare since George lost both wife and job in the nearby town of Topeka shortly after arriving there. Heavy hawk-faced and strikingly dark, he's the incarnation of the nineteenth-century portraits of big, solemn Plains chiefs. Sits with his eyes searing the flatscape as if he's watching for buffalo, though as we know he can hardly see without his glasses; another reason why he's not working, as he's not had them for weeks now. Ralph: 'He lost them in Topeka, had them stolen with his other things. They were welfare glasses, so he went to the County for another pair and they told him to go to the State office. He went to the State – and they sent him to the Federal. And they told him to go back to the County – but by then he'd had enough.')

The tribe's history, which Ralph outlines to us, is a fairly typical one. Originally living by the Great Lakes, they were gradually pushed west until in the 1860s they were finally settled in Kansas under the Dawes Allotment Act, the turning point for the Indians between their earlier expulsion to 'Indian Territory' beyond the frontier and their confinement to reservations. The land on theirs was mainly poor and at the best a world away from their previous lives as forest Indians, then as Plains buffalo hunters. Once even powerful enough to defeat the warrior Sioux in battle, they have since been depleted and scattered by land fragmentation, aversion to farming and the endlessly changing policies foisted on them from Washington. Only a few hundred of them now live on the reservation, but Ralph suggests that this is no measure of their sense of identity. They tend to use, rather than assimilate the outside world, partly because it conflicts with traditions but mainly because of its contradictions; while the Indians' mythical status is high, in practice they're as exploited and discriminated against as any other minority group. In old age many of those born on the reservation return, having often left their children to be brought up there as Indians. Others, unable to work outside it, are reduced to living on welfare – a situation Ralph describes as fairly representative of a large proportion of the Indian population of roughly half a million.

The Potowotami dancing ground, where the drum ceremony's due to be held, is rather like a gipsy scene, a few old cars under the trees and everyone seated round in a circle, women with dark braided hair and coloured blankets over their shoulders, bead ornaments and moccasins combining with cheap, bright clothes. The men are less colourful except for one with more beads than the women and even a touch of rouge on his cheeks – a formal transvestite, Ralph explains, a status accepted and even respected in traditional Indian society, though he's one of the last of his kind and got roughly handled, as well as wounded, on military service. (Though it's hard to conceive of a sharper subjection to the crossfire of history, he's surprisingly extrovert and later talks to us quite a bit.) A few teenagers in the background, flashily dressed and sporting shades, stand out from the others: but in five or ten years, according to Ralph, when the glamour of off-reservation life and higher wages has worn off, they'll probably be part of the crowd again. And he seems to be right – there are several people there in their late twenties or thirties who blend with the rest in the same remoteness, as if they don't do things as individuals so much as from a sense of belonging to a people living overtime, existing mainly for reflection. Far from resenting outsiders, they take little notice of us. Just advice when it's called for and occasionally a greeting ('bojo' – the remains of 'bonjour', acquired on the French Canadian frontier some three centuries ago). They appear to be too far away to count us even as intruders, let alone as reminders of what our world's afforded them. They make us feel strangely immature, or awkward at least, suddenly conscious of the absurdity of our involvement with time, ambitions and possessions. Even Ralph gives the impression, though he must be used to it, of sometimes feeling the same thing.

It's only as the four days unfold that we glimpse the positive meaning of it all. The humble, improvised quality of their material possessions – eating things, cars, everyday clothes and the two drab houses near by – soon seems irrelevant as consciousness centres more and more deeply on things created on a symbolic, aesthetic level and obviously with consummate care; the carved pipe of peace passed round as each ceremonial day begins, the bead-belts, belled anklets and moccasins later put on by the men, and the focus of it all: the drum. Three or four feet across, large enough for the four players to sit around it easily and divided by yellow lines: one side quartered blue and black, the other completely scarlet, and ringed with blue and white beads in the same geometrical pattern as on the moccasins and belts, with multi-coloured tassels and bells and fastened at each of the four directions with a sacred eagle-feather staff. Gradually, as the drummers play in a taut ceaseless monotone with a matching chant, 'aiya-aiya', every object and action gets woven into its orbit, in which time and space intersect as it moves on each ceremonial day to the next of the four directions within the same dancing circle, taking every ritual with it – the passing of the peace pipe, the communal meal at midday, the men beating with bowed heads, the dancers' far-removed style of jigging and gliding across the earth, looking down with faces set as if they're somehow dancing to it, as more and more young people join in where only old people danced at first. So that there's a mounting sense of balance and continuity in defiance of this dying setting. A child takes the name of an old man whose funeral was held recently. A man and a girl who've both lost their parents receive ritual substitutes under the aegis of the drum. Their adopters bring them new clothes as they sit in the centre of the circle on ceremonial blankets: screened by assistants, they put them on (moccasins, bead-belt, silver ear-rings) and emerge reborn. The crowd claps: then everyone brings a symbolic gift – fruit, cloth, a bead bracelet. And finally a very old man gives a brief speech in praise of the dead, apparently for us too, as at one point he breaks into

English. 'Our people says, the drum religion, how a man dies and goes in the earth is like how a man is born. Born and he lies in a cradle and his mother lifts him up. Dead and he lies in a cradle again and his new mother earth carries him. Spirit takes him and makes him new. Born again.'

As they reveal this cosmic balance of integration with self and family, tribe and time, earth, life and death, whether still attained or just ideal, their manner with us gradually relaxes. From the outset, for all the distance, it's been strictly egalitarian. It's clearly assumed, as we're there each day and perhaps because we've come with Ralph, that we take part in everything. The food (and we must bring our token), the dancing, the exchange of gifts: and once an old lady, Pnokwe, famed for her hundred and six years and needing a helping hand to the ring, simply gestures to me as the nearest young man available. Beyond this at first there's little more than polite answers and tactful instructions (take a single draft at the peace pipe, always enter the circle at the west door and leave by the east). By the third day, though, big George and Johnny Crick, the transvestite, are starting to take us under their wing, explaining the speeches and rituals and joking with us occasionally. George, a leading disciple of the drum, is a different man here from the one who sits in the schoolhouse gazing silent at the skyline: his heavy face has come alert and he's often the first to dance, dramatic in a dark blue shirt with a ruffle front and red and green streamers, an eagle feather in his hat, moccasins and bell anklets, feet tap-tapping the earth with a lightness his figure seemed to have lost – gliding through the braves' dance (bending to search the earth for tracks, leaping, pausing, stalking forward) and then with a friendly wink at us putting on the paleface dance, his big face in a bluff grin as he goes through its satirical movements, pulling on trousers and stumbling, cutting himself as he shaves, drinking and dancing rock, the follies of the paleface world.

By the fourth and last day the dancing ground is almost full, perhaps a couple hundred people, almost all Indians but many from off the reservation and often more tourist-like than us, with new cars and cameras and their children different beings from the reservation ones, who are far less importunate and more reserved, little adults. Two more drums are out today and half the adult men crouch round them, backs turned on the outer world, as if sculpted from a single stone. The beat is slower and more insistent and the singing's risen like a tidal wave, 'aiya-aiya' against the heat, as if the strength of sound and movement are a conscious reversal of their outward passiveness. The peace pipe is filled again, turned towards the four directions and passed ceremoniously round the circle. Speeches are made between the dances. Big George, very slowly, silhouetted against the sunlight, points to the earth, then to the sky and a sweeping gesture over the drum. He relates its power (as he tells us later) to control the lightning and thunder and the panther in the underground lake whose sudden temper causes floods. Describes how the drum's goodness has pacified a hostile world.

After his speech the food is shared – lemon juice, cornbread and corned beef, watermelon and blackberries fresh from the reservation hedges. The pipe repasses. As the dancing picks up again hands are raised towards the drum and there's no sense of it drawing to an end, the rhythm seems eternal now and the song still mounting. The light's already begun to fade. Movement ends. The last drumbeat. Most of the visitors have gone and it's like the first day, just the reservation people piling into ancient cars and walking off down the narrow tracks in quiet knots, the children behind. Big George is one of the last left, leaning on his own on the fence and looking at the empty dancing circle.

Out on Route 70 the old cars hug the shoulders as this year's model bullets past; and their drivers never look up , not even for the huge billboard a mile or two further west

INDIAN VALLEY ESTATE
LOTS FOR SALE

with its mocking ad-man's picture of a multi-storey wigwam.

The peyote ceremony a few days later varies the drum's theme of retreat with intimations of the cross-currents between the Indians and the outside. Produced in Mexico and the Southwest, the revered peyote button is the dried top of a cactus with hallucinogenic effects similar to mescalin's. Its ritual use by a large number of North American Indian tribes dates from after the white conquest and seems in part a response to it. It's sometimes described as a healing agent; or as a source of strength, or vision, leading to a self-knowledge and adjustment to the world like that of the old vision quest, when a young brave went out alone to find out his role in life from the Great Spirit. The peyote songs suggest this in being learnt 'from peyote' (that is, under its influence), with words usually intelligible only to their individual 'owner' or singer. Until quite recently its use was forbidden in most states, so peyotists incorporated as the Native American Church in order to claim immunity on the basis of freedom of religion; since then it's usually been tolerated, though repression still occurs and the formal incorporation combines rather uneasily with its theme of lone perception (almost the opposite of the drum's, solitude as against community). One result of this history is an annual peyotists' convention and this year it's in Kansas, on the Potowotami Reservation.

They're holding it at the pow-wow ground, a few fenced acres of land round a community building where thirty or forty cars are drawn up; everything from rusty old Fords to brand new Chevrolets and licence plates from as far afield as Wisconsin and New Mexico, the delegates from other tribes. The faces in the crowd range from near white to full Indian: the clothes from suits and bead pendants to women with shawls and moccasins. Inside the building there's a dishevelled formality: men on one side, women on the other, the older ones with tanned faces and bright kerchiefs around their heads. Children running in and out; old men dozing in patches of sunlight and younger ones chattering seriously. And in the middle the delegates. Several tribes are represented, including most of the bigger ones: a well-to-do, stocky Navajo who keeps jumping up to speak, round face and a crew cut, with gold-rimmed glasses, a dark suit and a silver Navajo pendant. A big, bull-shouldered Sioux and beside him a frail old man, spare frame and thin white hair, listening intently but silently. Two Winnebagos from Wisconsin, slighter and sharper-featured, apparently nervous, when they speak, at the formality of the occasion. An Omaha, face like an old vole, who mutters an occasional approval but says nothing publicly. Paul, a round-faced Potowotami, roughly dressed and extrovert, with a quiet sense of humour; and another Potowotami beside us (we've come with Fred, Ralph's assistant, who knows the local peyotists well), a veteran of the Normandy landings, he tells us, when Fred introduces him. As he mentions his memories of London it's a sharp reminder of the often neglected fact that American Indians are American as well as Indian; a complex combination, as the convention soon suggests. Up on the platform are the officials, with tape recorder and microphone: a girl secretary, almost white, with an authoritative voice and a young man, the treasurer, whose radio-announcer's style has a somewhat glib effect. Between them sits the president, an older, wary-faced man who lets the others direct the proceedings.

As the topics emerge – renewed police persecution, the problems caused by students getting illegal peyote shipments – fewer and fewer people take part. The old people seem a bit lost, usually just nodding assent when a motion ends. The white world is blamed roundly for almost every problem mentioned; when one old man observes that Indians as well as students sometimes discredit the use of peyote, it's obviously not the kind of thing that the leading figures want to hear and passes without acknowledgement. There's an increasing bizarreness about their control of the discussion: Peter James, the Navajo, jumping up at every point to launch an anti-white tirade full of legalistic and military jargon; the young treasurer congratulating him and also phrasing everything in terms of Indian versus white, though they themselves have little that's traditionally Indian about them and short shrift for those who have. Audience comments are rarely invited and generally brushed aside, especially the older people's. When there is a break and they file out into the sunlight, they make little disguise of their relief.

The afternoon audience is thinner. The main issue is whether non-Indians should attend peyote meetings – one that's long been topical, due no doubt to white persecution but somewhat in disregard of the help from non-Indian lawyers and especially of peyotism's universalistic nature. The first speaker is an oldish lady, slightly nervous but insistent. 'I don't believe we should make this distinction. One time I was outside a church and I saw this little Negro boy, he was standing outside and crying, so I asked him why he was crying and he said it was a white man's church and he couldn't go inside. I believe that's wrong, we shouldn't do that. We shouldn't make these distinctions.'

Peter James, the Navajo, jumps up indignantly. 'Mr Chairman – my opinion is that this is a truly native Indian religion, perhaps the last. We should keep it that way. The objects we use, they are Indian. The beating the water-drum, shaking the gourd, singing the songs and blowing the whistle – these are the native American ways of praying to the Great Spirit. White people take everything from us' – one or two people glance at us and his pause suggests he was waiting for this – 'and now we offer them our religion to steal in the same way. No, Mr Chairman, I cannot agree. I therefore entertain the motion that people attending peyote ceremonies must be bona fide members of an organized Indian tribe. Only these groups should be allowed to practise peyote in our Church.' He sits down adamantly.

The frail old Sioux gets to his feet for the first time (he's somewhat deaf and the proceedings are relayed to him by his younger neighbour). The treasurer introduces him. 'Mr Silas Yellowboy, the Oglala Sioux representative from Pine Ridge, South Dakota.' The old man looks around. They're quiet – there's suddenly a presence in the room. 'Members of our church and brothers from distant tribes. I know myself for a member of this noble race of the continent. We was living here before our brothers the white people. We claim the right and privilege of our Native American Church.' His stiff figure sways slightly, hands moving slowly to fashion the words of his old style Indian oratory. 'The principal reason of our worshipping God, which is our own Great Spirit, through this divine peyote is that God created the world and its various types of nations, white, black, yellow, red. He gave them various languages and the knowledge of God in their different ways. So we create our own Church which is the Native American Church. The white people have their book: we have this sacred cactus button. But when the Great Spirit made this world with all this diverse peoples, he blessed them all with the same hand. So we want all peoples to know how we're moving in our Native American Church. Not only full-blooded Indians – but we should open the gates of peyote for the fellowship of all nations. They should see what we are doing, if they come in the right way – that is all we should ask of them.'

'Iyu, iyu' from all the old people, the first time they've seemed aroused. One or two others voice their assent, if not without a grumble, and the day is clearly Yellowboy's. Though a vote isn't taken, the others' polemics seem forgotten. But their atmosphere lingers on amongst the younger, more urban-looking of the tribal delegates. They're ostentatiously cool to us and some pass mildly racist comments which we're meant to hear. Fred says he's often found it like this. It's usually the better-off Indians, many with professional jobs, who talk anti-white (often anti-black too), although in relation to other Indians they tend to imply their superiority in terms of essentially white values; whereas in reality they themselves have sometimes been pampered and it is the reservation Indians who have suffered most and still do, from economic exploitation and bad educational services, without reacting in racial terms. It's as if the guilt of white society, its patronage and contradictions as much as its straight prejudice, impinging most on the urban Indians, has fostered an exaggerated, mildly paranoid ethnicism of a rather non-Indian kind. Eventually it's getting unpleasant and we're toying with the idea of leaving, until the two Potowotamis with whom we're sitting ask us to stay, aware of what's going on and obviously embarassed by it. As we eat together under the trees, there's less sign of the younger group, who seem to keep very much to themselves; the atmosphere returns to normal, as if it was all a ritual gesture rather than a sustained conviction.

Figures weave slowly through the dusk, carrying the long beaded boxes in which the peyote objects are kept. The ceremony was to have been in a traditional tepee, but as so many people are here and a storm's brewing on the low horizon, they're holding it in the community building. Already the chairs have been removed and bright coloured blankets spread round the walls. For a while people wander in and out; all night we see nothing more of the hostile clique. Perhaps they're upset by the others' acceptance of us, though Paul, the Potowotami, suggests that the prospect of the night-long ritual has dimmed their enthusiasm – 'motel peyotists', he comments wryly.

The old president, who is songleader, appears through the door which faces east. The room is almost full now, sixty or seventy people, men of all ages, a few elder women and a scattering of children. The silent vole-faced Omaha is on one side of us, Paul on the other. It's just after ten o'clock. The song-leader sits in the centre of the western wall, an assistant on either side. He takes out his staff, carved in the form of light-ning with a small cross on top, representing the four directions; a gourd rattle, with beaded handle, and a sacred black and white eagle feather. Silence, apart from occasional murmurs or a whisper from the children. Heads bow as the songleader intones; the others join in with a low hum. Water is put in the kettle-drum, then coals, to give it the voice of thunder. When its skin is back on, the assistant tilts the drum to wet it, then taps lightly, a low thrup thrup swelling liquid resonant into a fast, unbroken beat, as the songleader's eyes close and his brows knit in concentration; a high-pitched complaining note, then his voice deepens and expands, words rising and falling until they mount in rending enquiry. Staff in one hand and gourd in the other, a quick-running accompaniment to the single pulsing of the drum. After a while his voice recedes and the drum drops to a low mutter, tilted to wet the skin again and then the beat surges back speeding into a single flow and the old man's face is clenched, eyes closed, four songs before the drumbeat fades. A pause. The assistant brings out a small leather pouch and scatters incense on the fire: fans it with the sacred feather, then leans across to the songleader and wafts the purifying smoke at him, tap-tapping him all over. Then he walks right around the room offering little dabbing movements to bless all the partici-pants. The songleader dips in his box and brings out a bag of peyote which is carefully handed round, a ritual four buttons to each person, tough little yellow-brown discs, bitter as coffee beans yet sickly-sweet smelling like fresh hay. The faces are unmoved as they chew, but the stillness already suggests a withdrawal. Paul leans across to us. 'It's a hard thing to take, this peyote – that's why they say it's like the old vision, like travelling far out in the plains. First time I take it I was sick. Take it piece by piece, real slow.' Drops his voice. 'Some of them fellers was saying white people can't take peyote. No trouble – just eat slow.' And he nods confidingly, expression receding into self.

The drum and rattle and staff pass round to the next pair of men. The drumbeat again, more and more fevered, until beat and resonance part and the resonance lifts you like big wings, heads and eagle feather flickering in time to the drum and figures shimmering, floor shimmers and words shimmer, nervous, imploring. Four songs to each couple and then the falling away of the drum, the tilting to bring the water up glinting in tiny bright cascades, the drum rings, an enquiring phrase and then the full singer's pitch.

Hour after hour it passes round, peyote too, till the slow-sweet stench of it seems to envelop everything. An hour perhaps, or two or three, as if you've been away for a while and then suddenly returned, though everything is still remote but the distance is gentle, soothes, even the song is far away and the figures too, yet very precise: crystal-bright leaning forward sideways back, scarlet shirts and jet black hair a single frieze rising and falling; only the drum whirl is close, all enclosing tunnel of sound, and you're floating up it, hung between songs until they lift you back away to where everything's so far below it's like looking back in time. And still, everything's very still, even the singer statue-frozen even the song

dropping down, floating. A pause. Heads rise. The songleader brings out a pipe and blows a shrill, rising note that doesn't seem to end so much as fly off into the darkness. The midnight whistle. Crosses the water, burns incense and fans the sacred fire softly. He prays again and the others murmur, the words floating away like gauze. The drum moves on: a Hamlet-like young Winnebago, scarlet and blue sash at his waist, head thrown back and body taut. Then the big Sioux, crouched forward, high-pitched hum dropping to a bellydeep cry, gourd twirling, eyes closed in a concentration of searching the peyote road as the gourd shivers and drum rings and body seems way below with the figures a single rhythm of lines in the distance, is dying this moving off alone, only the noise is a little strange and the going upwards into the light falling round and everything lit – Paul's hand way down is a continent a forest plateau broken gullies purple shadows – blanket folds el Greco grey – the stones on the walls a thousand colours never having known before that so many greys greens browns existed and all with the same inner light as the song comes back a river of sound deep with islands suspended out of space and time – outside the darkness is thinning. The humped outline of the trees is edged with purple, now with grey. Cool. Over the deadflat horizon a slow rose beginning of light with violet clouds scudding across it and a sliver of a moon, a mobile between sky and fields. The old Omaha's face has sagged into gleaming crags and crevasses. The song-leader is very still: the young Winnebago taut and alight. Suddenly sunlight breaks through the door and a splash of it hangs on the wall behind the song-leader's head. The drum dies obediently and he raises the whistle to his lips, head rising and thrown right back as the pipe shrills its narrow note into the fresh morning air.

Brahmin-like he sets it down. As he does so the dawn woman comes in through the door from the east, a pale blue shawl over her shoulders. She sits in the centre of the floor, legs folded under her. The sacred food is brought in, corn meal, fruit, meat and water. She prays to the life-giving dawn as the light spreads, then slips away. After the blessing with the eagle feather the four bowls are passed around, each person taking a mouthful. The solemn Omaha stands up. 'I thank you all, brothers and sisters. I feel good now, feel lighter, something lifted from my shoulders. I travelled far, seen very far. All of you and the herb helped me in the road tonight. I pray for your safe journey to your distant homes in other nations and I thank you for the goodness from the songs and the sacred drum.' One by one the men speak, answered with a soft 'iyu' and a brief pause of respect. Then as the day's warmth begins, the songleader takes the gourd again. A final quartet of songs reverberates into the young sunlight, no longer in the faraway but still retaining the peace from it, the end of the peyote road, where everything else is very remote, time, place, all limits of being. The drum dies for the last time. The children are waking, sharp-eyed. The songleader opens his box and puts away the sacred objects. Blankets are shaken out and figures stand murmuring outside, watching the huge globe of the sun suspended wham on the flat fields like a resounding swipe at a gong.

Over in Horton, the little village where Fred has a room, a few minutes away, old ladies are going to church through a Sunday morning bright with leaves.

CHAPTER 9

MANSCAPE THREE:
Kansas – Washington State

After daylong Kansas flatscape, bronze Nebraska rolls faintly under the summer lightning flickering several miles away. Even Middle America looks frail when the storm lashes down, erasing the skyline, then the road, and driving the cattle into the gullies, ('Had a mean one last year,' the proprietor of the rooming-house at railroad-side Anselmo tells us, 'bust up the cattle, bashed in the houses, picked up cars in Main Street and just wrapped em round the trees'). Then as we reach cattle country, varied only by rodeo posters and deepening Western pleasantries like the notice in a store – 'The hurrier I go, the behinder I get' – Indian faces are back again: the Sioux of South Dakota, grandchildren of the leaders of the Indians' final stand against the USA's expansion.

Their faces are heavy and sculpted, sombre still under black Stetsons: women in shawls and ankle-length skirts, with long, carefully braided hair. Their passiveness is different from the Potowotamis': not just a withdrawal – it's a watchfulness that seems compulsively attached to the absurdly colonialist fringe of the enveloping white world. Pine Ridge, the centre of the reservation, looks like a refugee encampment, very much as it must have done when the tribe was rounded up after the battle of Wounded Knee, just a few miles away, where their defeat in 1890 spelt the end of Indian resistance. Straggling out in all directions from a single intersection, almost its only solid buildings are the Indian Bureau offices and one or two stores and a gas station, all white-managed and owned, as well as predominantly white-staffed: most of the neighbouring Indians' homes are shanty-boxes of timber and zinc, joined by muddy little paths. There's hardly a sign of activity: it's as if they specialize not just in being motionless, but in making the

world aware of it, especially round the little white strongholds
of stores, gas stations and bars, where they lean on the walls and
sit on the steps, their big heroic features accentuating their air
of defeat. Their eyes follow our every movement. They're
not hostile exactly, just mutely accusing, dramatizing the
contrast between their displacement and their good looks.
The whites play a corresponding role – the proprietress of the
one hotel, the barman, a magistrate we talk to – in pronouncing
explicitly on the Indians' backwardness, their drunkenness and
dishonesty. ('What you have to understand with these people is
that they're still in the stone age,' says the magistrate we meet
in the diner, who sees them in the dock every day.) Incredibly,
when they say these things, there's apparently little attempt
to avoid the Indians' hearing: they listen without a flicker of
reaction, as if it matches the expectations suggested by the
mask they wear.

Whenever one of them talks to us it's in much the same terms
– a soliloquy on how the whites have broken every promise to
them, whittling the reservation away and providing few opportunities. True as this is – Government policy has always swung
between reservations and integration, in effect Democratic
neglect or Republican exploitation – they speak as if nothing
has happened on their side for two or more generations.
Occasionally they even refer to the Battle of Wounded Knee,
though there are few Sioux left who were alive at the time.
Not implausibly, their version of it differs from that of the
history books, which attribute it to resistance to a peaceful
Government round-up when revolt was in the air in the mes-
sianic form of the Ghost Dance, inspired by Sitting Bull's
prediction of the return of the ancestors and the end of white
rule. The Sioux allege that when it happened – the mowing
down of a whole encampment by two big Hotchkiss guns – the
troops responsible were drunk and shouting 'Remember Custer'.
Whatever the truth, the distrust involved is still stamped on
every detail, in movements, expressions, conversations, and
above all in the silence with which they ring everything round.

The rest of the reservation is similar, dotted with drab settlements where the only substantial buildings are stores and bars

or a mission church. Again there's nearly always a crowd hanging round them silently, watching the white attendants and members of white farming families who've leased reservation land. Such as it is. Further north it erodes into a bleached waste where only a few cattle browse, culminating suddenly in the towering moonscape of the Badlands.

Below them by the thruway another West is celebrating this Fourth of July weekend with a wild little rodeo all loose walks and high boots, men and women dressed alike, and big, dust-covered station wagons gunned off by teenagers riding bareback a moment before. We're adopted by a group at the bar who regale us with beers, disdain of the East and the exploits of local heroes: the cowboy turned Hollywood stunt-rider who came back to his home town, took its only corner at eighty then won the world bucking-horse championship with his back in a plaster cast; and another one at a recent rodeo who drank so much he jumped in the ice bath where the beers were keeping cool and held the cops off with a gun until he'd finished the last can. 'Ruined a nice new pair of boots, hundred bucks, so they didn't charge him,' the barman observes philosophically. 'Fellers there paid for the beers.' Whoops and stamping and horns blare as bareback riders lap the ring, steers are roped and dust flies. Once a tier of seats collapses in a chaos of cokes and stetsons but no one's hurt, just roars of laughter and it's soon up again. There are a few Indians present, but in the audience they're mostly together, intent, but showing little reaction: and when they're competing in the ring it's with a silent determination and disproportionate success which reduce the white West's booted and spurred masculinity to something of a caricature.

The Sioux's holiday celebrations don't begin until after dark – dancing at Wounded Knee, on the very spot where the massacre occurred. They have the same gliding style as the Potowotami, executed with rapt care; and all night long the same singing fills the warm summer darkness, 'yaia, yaia, yaia.' Wilder by far than in Kansas, it has exactly the same tone of being the one thing that rouses them deeply, a ritual reversal of their silence, hauntingly suggestive here of some defiant recollection of the Ghost Dance.

By daylight the silence is back. Pine Ridge is deathly still. Even the motionless figures are missing, as the bars and stores are Sunday shut; just a middle-aged man and woman arguing tipsily at the corner as we stop to check the map. The only other sound is a radio blasting out a revivalist sermon full of anti-communist hate, like the voice of some hidden Big Brother who rules this hopeless vacancy. The man sees us and comes across. 'Gimme dollar. Need a drink.' As if he's not quite sure of success for his mocking implication of our duty to patronize him, he points at the woman: 'She need a drink too.' But as he points she leans forward and retches slowly, almost theatrically, with the preacher's voice in the background flinging out its hysterical taunts like some lunatic commentary.

Beyond the magical Black Hills with their green slopes and tight valleys where buffalo browse like wise old men and the grave-stones of Calamity Jane, Potato Johnny and Wild Bill Hickock neighbour under the pines at Deadwood, it comes as a shock to re-emerge and find the plains still there in front, a dancing ground for the silver sun, deep in cattle country silence. Gas stations bawl their prices at the unanswering emptiness, bones of farm machinery drown in the flat, quivering stillness

MILES CITY 171

and the rhythm of the dead flat road loping on, teasing us with its liquid-shimmering sameness, the doubt of whether it leads anywhere, never changes, never turns, nothing new, nothing exists, just the silk-smooth prairie grass and the railroad track and a few tail-switching ponies. The Black Hills dwindle and vanish leaving only the heat haze, always near, always receding, pirouettes, belly-dances, always there, never closer, catch it but it's gone again, dancing, mocking, pirouetting.

YOU ARE ENTERING WYOMING
LAST GREAT FRONTIER STATE OF THE LAND
FAMOUS FOR ITS CATTLE RANCHES THAT SUPPLY
THE CORN BELT
ITS PEOPLE ARE HIGH WIDE AND HANDSOME

Cattle stand and moon at nothing, iridescent black on green, strop of a car, bleached trees

MILES CITY 130

four little dots, two and two, dancers of the empty prairie, still now, waiting, whap

HAMMOND POP. 40

gas station, OK CAFE, two shacks bang gone, a blip on the blankness, fencing reels

BROADUS 30

grazing lands split and gulch and now it's just possible no one exists, ever existed, it was illusion, is illusion (moving?), grain elevator and rodeo sign, but didn't we see them yesterday and the same road dusk after dawn, sunrise behind, sunset in front, days and nights going round like a wheel and still the road zing in front through the big just fly-buzzing stillness.

BROADUS

jumps up out of the flatness and limps along aimlessly, its only excuse a bend in the road. Gas station, store and a café where the truck-driver perched at the counter swings round and back, round and back, as if he's pushing time along. Two tables, a juke box and a girl like a dusty sparrow. Smiles at us, 'Hi folks,' but her face goes back to nothing. The trucker's making a pass at her, he's mildly bugged by our arrival, chicken dinner shrimp dinner beefburger love dinner fishwich and Seven Up, 'Thanks come back again' (back again?).

Big trucks mammoth by hot-breathed, driver perched way up, face set, hands and eyes unmoving. Busby, next spot on the map, is marked as a town but it's just a store and gas station with Indians lounging in the porch. Cheyennes, slighter than the Sioux, with thinner, more foxy faces: keep their eyes to themselves. Inside, a white man is leaning on the coke machine. Watches me in curiosity, until I ask the distance to the Custer battlefield.

'The Little Bighorn?' He raises his head, a humorously

wrinkled face and now he's got his cue he's away. 'Around twenty-six miles. There's a sign on the crest of a hill, can't miss it.' Pauses. 'Sound like you come from England.'

'That's right.'

'Knew by the accent. My dad was English, came from Cornwall. Which part d'you come from? Oxford – is that right? My old man was goin there. His folks was only fisher-folks, but he had this scholarship for Oxford University. Then his buddies wrote to him, they were tin miners from Cornwall, and they told him things was boomin right here in Butte, Montana. So he came out to make a million. Like all the others.' He laughs. 'Didn't work out that way, though, he died without a copper cent. There was a few millions there but you had to have a bit to start with – guys that got it didn't reckon on sharing out.' Swigs his coke. 'Butte was a pretty rough town. Lynching and shooting, he told me about it. The big guys was tough on the little guy, but the little guys hit right back. Had some rough strikes there – bosses had to call the troops, they even had martial law one time. Ain't so different now, either. State's still owned by the copper men.'

Like many historical sites in the States, the nearby Custer battlefield has its essence almost smothered by the image thrust at you; by the souvenirs and dioramas, postcards, folders and footnotes and illuminating statistics. 'This monument contains 765.34 acres and fourteen rest rooms.' After these preliminaries it's hard to imagine the same spot as nothing but an open frontier where men like Custer and Sitting Bull confronted each other a century ago. A bleak memorial to Custer's troop, the 7th Cavalry, tops the hill. Beyond it prairie green and yellow slope down to the Little Bighorn Valley, where the Indians were camped when the 7th appeared.

No one quite knows what then happened to give them their biggest victory against the advancing USA; the secret died with Custer's men. It was the climax of Indian resistance. By the late 1860s the Southern Plains tribes were pacified; the Indian frontier moved north towards the Cheyennes and Sioux, who soon accepted a large reservation in the Dakota Territory, including the vital Black Hills, where the buffalo grazed in the summer. A few years later the 7th Cavalry explored the area. Gold was found and the news leaked. Miners began pouring in, contravening the Indian treaties. The Sioux and Cheyennes, starved of their buffalo and embittered by broken promises, moved out on the warpath, attacking prospectors. The Government ordered them to disperse, but in February 1876, almost before they could do so, a battle-eager Custer advanced against them from Fort Bismarck. When his scouts saw the Indian camp he decided to attack at once instead of waiting for reinforcements. The sun and the smoke from campfires may have concealed the Indians' numbers, but more probably Custer disliked sharing his glory and hardly believed that an Indian force could constitute a real danger. If so, he was wrong. The Indians were ready and led by some of the most skilled tacticians that Plains warfare had produced. As Custer advanced, Chiefs Crazy Horse, Gall and Sitting Bull apparently formed a pincer movement and attacked across the river, trapping the 7th Cavalry on the rise where the monument now stands. By the time the reinforcements arrived, only to be beaten back, all they could see was the Indians milling about the battlefield, apparently shooting at the ground. The next day, as they vanished, only a horse was found alive. (It was zealously preserved in alcohol at the University of Kansas.)

The reaction was violent. The Bismarck *Tribune* reported the news in a special issue, alleging that Indian squaws had mutilated the dead soldiers after they had been tortured to death. Apparently no one thought to enquire how the reporters came by such details. In a language foreshadowing future wars, revenge on the 'red devils' was called for, as if, as empire began, its one-sided vision was coming inevitably into being, to mould and serve as apology for the Indians' oppressed status right down to the present day. The myth makers had their way and Congress responded smartly. Shortly afterwards the Indians were finally split up and defeated. Sitting Bull fled to Canada and the Sioux were confined once and for all. Their land was steadily reduced and divided as more prospectors and settlers poured in, isolating the Indians in mainly worthless areas to subsist, as many still do, on slender rations from Washington.

Later conflicts were massacres rather than sustained wars: Wounded Knee amongst the Sioux; the heroic Nez Percés retreat under Chief Joseph in the north-west; weekend hunting parties to shoot the California Indians in their caves up in the hills.

It's in Hardin, a few miles on, that this past does make a living impact: another flat little prairie town with Indian faces everywhere, in the bars, on every corner, half sheltering, half just present. The solid-looking citizens in the respectable coffee house might be in a different country from the next-door bar with its frieze of slumped figures, a startling inverted reminder (alive there, numb here) of those at the peyote meeting. One of them, just coming out, apparently registers that we're strangers and latches on to us doggedly as we make for the coffee house. The people inside pretend not to notice – or perhaps they don't anyway, perhaps they're too used to it – as he totters after us. Puts his arms around our shoulders, his face between us, very close: a shipwrecked, finished little face. He tries to laugh but stops halfway in a reek of liquor. 'How're y'doin? Tha's good. I'm Indian – you know? We people, Indians, here before white men. Excuse English. Don't speak good, only Indian. This Hardin, white man's town. Cross river, Crow Indian reservation –.but white man buy, steal it all, got us poor.'

We stave him off by mentioning the Potowotami and Sioux. He seems surprised at our knowing about them. 'Little Smoke my name, Crow Indian, you nice, I gonna get you my picture, you remember Little Smoke, Crow Indian. No time? You wait.' He sways and belches. The waitresses watch dead-pan. 'I jump in my friend car, get my picture. Little Smoke. Crow Indian.' He staggers out earnestly, waving aside our advice that we're leaving. What did he want? Not money, apparently. To register that the proverbial figure, the drunken Indian, is a being, I, Little Smoke, a person? Or the opposite – just an audience for the same role that mocks both himself as actor and us as spectators of it? We slip out, justifying ourselves with the thought that we'd never see him again, even if we sat there all evening.

Beyond Hardin the land's undulations slowly break into sandstone ridges, first note of the end of the plains. Round a bluff the Yellowstone valley sprawls below us sleepy-blue and points at a purplish silhouette, it could be just a trick of the dusk and the wisps above it just clouds until suddenly they collect into snowcaps catching the last fling of light: first glimpse of the Rockies, sixty or eighty miles away, not a part of the land yet, just an echo in the sky, suspended, drowning in the dusk, inching closer then retreating, another mirage in the morning brightness beyond the long swerves of hay. The valley farms are slowly contracting; sheep dot the easy slopes. A train toots, fades and toots, the Northern Pacific, a hundred freight cars. Its last note circles and dies, leaving the valley hushed and empty, such space that even silence echoes until the traffic hurls by again; the idiom of the big land, a thousand, two thousand miles to go, for the sun-polished silver trucks with their California, Arizona, New York licence plates.

Manscape recedes as the bluffs hunch in on either side of the Yellowstone River, farms gone, pinetop lonely (seventy still where a century ago the pioneer wagoners heaved and strained) and the foothills are under us, wind whacks steeples butt at the sky road slashed in the shadow-purple riding at clefts way ahead until White Hall, 'population 800', its single street plateau-flat and the cottonwood trees on either side dropping their green pools of shade beside the Northern Pacific freight cars. An old man in faded levis trims a proud strip of grass between the siding and the road, excuse for a handful of picnic tables. Blue-grey wave of the Rocky peaks still hangs on the skyline. Traffic smoothes by, pace checked by the dozing town. Two boys on horseback cross the street. The old man puts down his shears and nods in greeting as he sees us. Seats himself in a tree's dappled shadow, leaning back against the trunk, pulls out a cigar and lights it. Its blue smoke is the only movement.

Pass and plateau, bluffs spin

WELCOME TO BUTTE
MILE-HI CITY

where the Cornish father of the man we met yesterday sought his luck. A sudden smoke and chimneyscape, founded by Marcus

Daley, just an Irish grubstaker until he sold his claim for a
fortune to the Anaconda Company, a prince among the robber
barons, producing multi-millionaires, a quarter of the world's
copper and violent strikes by its underpaid workers. Butte
shows the scars. An ugly little shanty-town dribbles out along
the road and the hills are gouged into red-brown ruin, still the
near-feudal domain of the Anaconda Company, arbiter of half
the power and resources in Montana.

Riding the shelf of the Rockies now, cattle perched against the
sky and not a sign of habitation, just

MISSOULA 87

MOBIL – ESSO

TRUCKERS WELCOME

GAS FOR LESS – EAT BEEF

fifteen, twenty miles apart and the pine-topped pinnacles with
the shadows in their thighs.

WELCOME TO MISSOULA

VISIT MISSOULA COPPER SHOP

LEVIS AND LEATHER BOOTS

LEFT FOR LEWIS AND CLARK HIGHWAY

THANKS FOR COMING TO MISSOULA

SAFE TRIP

COME BACK AGAIN

Rain shafts the lonely hills. Horses browse on the upland
pastures. The sun breaks out in a last salute, pitching pine
shadows down the slopes. Lolo Pass: walls of spruce, wild
lupins in the dusk. Thunder breaks behind us on the backbone
of the USA – the Locksa River, crystal stream that bubbles and
spits at the foot of the pines, is running west towards the
Pacific

catching the young sunlight as it pushes the valley walls
apart with just the occasional fisherman to vary the green, pine-
needle stillness. Rapids and spindle waterfalls wedge their way
between the trees, falling in suspended motion; it's over an
hour's drive to Lowell, the next roadside lumber village, two log

cabins and a café. Inside it are penny candies, coloured postcards and wooden Indians. Handwritten notices on the wall:
Home made Cake / Home made Pie Blueberry Gooseberry or
Cherry / If you want to kill time Try working it to death /Danc-
ing nitely / Selway Trading post 3 miles up Selway river.
At one table two holiday couples sit pink and out of place, a different race from the locals, plump hands and awkward thighs
protruding from vacation shorts. Another two men who obviously live here have a leathery look to them; check shirts and
lumber jackets and that woodman's silence, won't talk for the
sake of it, only if it's necessary.

It was good prospecting country once, part of the mountain
silver belt that ran northwards from Nevada: no sign of it now,
though, just an isolated sawmill or a cluster of wooden cabins,
until the valley opens out and the Locksa River runs wide and
placid. At Lewiston the Rockies are over. Freight cars of the
Northern Pacific are backed up to the lumber yards where the
red pines are jammed together pellmell from up the river. Beyond them the farmlands are there again, Washington State's
rich wheat bowl.

The long hills turn shadow velvet. Small fruit farms line the
road, their orchards heavy with apples and peaches. A green
sea of alfalfa nibbles at the open horizon. Fields seem strangely
empty after the Rockies' pine and crag line.

Walla Walla, heart of the wheat lands. Max's grandparents
expect us, the first familiar name since Kansas, a couple
thousand miles away. Figures stroll at Western pace down the
wide, open streets and between the rectangular buildings there's
always the open, quilted land. New England quiet and Western
casual: the first person whom we ask knows the way to the
Hendersons and obviously makes a mental note that they have
exotic visitors.

The driveway's concealed and overgrown, but beyond it the
garden's neatly kept. Lavender and hollyhocks almost hide the
weathered notice at the edge of the flowerbed: 'Drive Carefully,
Children at Play'. A diminutive figure in a faded green dress
looks up from a raspberry patch and waves as if she already
knows us. Dusts her hands hastily and bustles towards us

through the shadows. 'You're here at last – why it's almost as good as if Max himself was here.' Laughs sadly, a high trill. 'We don't see much of them now, you know. Donald.'

The reply comes slowly from behind venetian blinds. 'Yes, Helen?'

'Here they are.'

'Well, that's good.'

The old man appears, a heavy, patriarchal figure on the elegant wooden porch. Silver-haired and he moves carefully: but you can see that not long ago his figure was still powerful and firm.

CHAPTER 10

DEPARTURES:
The Northwest

Though their house is only just out of town, its day is summer-still and quiet: the garden deepens it, trim lawn and a linden tree, its olive-green oval cutting the hills. There's an English quality in its lavender-scented ramblings. It's fresher, though, newer than English, new world, but leisurely. Sound of the cars out on the road is an infinity away.

The house itself has the same balance; an unmistakably Western home, frontier-simple and wooden built, it also has an elegant touch, broad stairway, books behind glass and high-backed colonial chairs round the long dining-room table. Cool shadows fill the hallway behind the careful venetian blinds. A grandfather clock taps at the silence; and the faces watch from silver frames – children, grandchildren, weddings and picnics, teenagers in party dresses. (Max: 'We all lived there at one time, it was a great place for kids, the garden, my grandmother's preserves . . .'.) We recognize them from his descriptions. His mother, remarried now and living in the South-west. Her blonde daughters. More grandchildren, Max's cousins. One of Max in a sailor suit, very serious, aged four. Their youthfulness seems emphatic.

The old man's waiting for us outside, sitting up straight-backed on one of the wooden chairs on the lawn. They were made in Vermont, he tells us. 'We had them made and brought out here specially. That's where you get the reg'lar craftsmen, up there in Vermont. Helen's people, her grandparents, they came from there.'

Two sprays turn on the lawn, swinging the last of the sunlight round. A scurrying in the undergrowth and the hoarse, fluting call of a bird. Quails, he says. The blue spruce settle slowly into the dusk. Between them the long wheat fields reach at the low slope of the hills.

He follows our gaze. 'The Blue Mountains. I wouldn't mind betting they've not thawed yet. That's how we get these cool evenings, breeze coming right off the mountains. Sit out here almost every night.' (Max: 'He just takes off sometimes, took me with him once or twice, goes to the coast and walks by the sea, miles from anywhere, no one in sight – he still does it occasionally . . .'.)

His face is strong and dogged, suggests he's always made his own way. 'You'd never get evenings like this down in the Southwest, say, where Max's mother lives. That's why we came here. Thirty-five years ago – seems longer. It was just wild grass here then, had to clear it all ourselves. We built the house, myself and Helen, and planted all those trees there. Those blue spruce – they were just bushes when we started.' He stands up rather heavily. 'Like to look around? I usually stroll around in the evenings.'

He moves stiffly, his body held carefully erect. The tall beech tree behind the house is already joining the shadows, its branches reaching out towards a rambling second-floor balcony. Maples, sentinel in the corner, recede into the hideaway garden; you can sense that children have played in it. The squat, blue-berried juniper trees mingle with the tall grass. Their dry scent hangs on the dusk.

'The children loved that balcony, used to have barbecue parties there – our own and then the grandchildren. That's why we built the house so big. We were a good-sized family by the time we'd finished it, we were glad of all those rooms.'

He speaks slowly and firmly, as if everything he says comes from a distance, carefully weighed. 'Reg'lar time we used to have when they were all here summers. Course we hoped they'd stay around, but that doesn't happen. People get scattered, young people specially, they don't want to live in a small town. I was hoping Max would take over the paper when I got too old for it, but it's too small for him here. Doesn't say so, mind, but I know what he's thinking. Course, it was all right for us, wasn't anything here when we came, we built it all, it suited us. But the young folks, they want to move on, want to make their own way.'

By the time she comes out to join us, a full moon is lifting slowly. The old man braces himself against the cool hint of a breeze. 'If you look close at the moon, you know, there's a profile down on the right-hand side – not the old man in the moon, it's a girl's face with a high ruffle collar, see, just like a cameo.' His white hair lifts slightly. 'You know who told me that, Helen?'

'No, Donald.'

'Old Henry Breton. Moonlight made me think of him. He lived in Walla Walla, died just a few years back. Came over here right from Russia, before the Russian revolution. His folks were serfs on a Russian manor and he used to tell me about it, how they harvested by moonlight. Midday they'd get black bread with some salt on it. Evening the same and midnight they had the day's treat – some lard on the bread. That's how it was. I'd ask him about it, if they never thought of rebelling, but he said no, they were used to it. He ran away, though. He was just a boy then, in his early twenties I guess, when he came over here. Way back – how old was he, Helen?'

'Old Henry Breton? Ninety-two.'

'Ninety-two when he died, that's right. He arrived in New York with thirty-five cents. Didn't speak any English but he'd heard about the West, so he jumped a freight train – lot of good men came west that way. Ended up clear over here. Remember how loyal he was, Helen?'

'My, yes, he was loyal to us. Hadn't a thing but the land he worked, but he really loved that piece of land. Said he'd never expected it, to work on his own land, you see. He used to come and help us here. It was sad, all his children had gone away and he didn't have much support, so he had to go out to work, doing odd jobs for people. And people didn't consider him, just told him to do this and that. He felt he'd lost his independence. Think of it, after that life he'd led, and nobody to listen to him, even look after him. I don't know what happened to his children. You know what happened to his children, Donald?'

'No, Helen. But they went away, I know they didn't stay

here. Of course their lives would be so different, a long way from all that. I doubt if they'd even remember his stories about the girl's face on the moon and that midnight harvesting.'

He leans forward into the darkness. 'Course, we had plenty of characters here. Those days you had to be one to be living this far west. If they weren't a little bit crazy, them or their parents, they wouldn't have come. There's a few here still, it looks pretty quiet, but they're characters all right.'

His wife gives her high-pitched, mischievous laugh. 'Some of the ladies here, oh my! Like Mrs Cooper – she goes travelling. One day she was out in Egypt and you know what really struck her? Not sphinxes or camels – refrigerators, remember, Donald? She was always talking about it – pink refrigerators they were, sitting clear out in the desert. When she first saw them she thought it was an ancient city, hundreds of them, all piled up. US Aid had sent them to a place with no electricity, so they dumped them in the desert. That's what Mrs Cooper said, she even wrote her Senator about it.'

The old man raises his head, far removed when he's not talking, his figure always held very straight and face turned towards the moonlight. 'Did you tell them about your folks, Helen? Her grandfather, he was one of the first to come across the Oregon Trail. Mighty interesting folks.'

'Yes, he was a fine man. Scottish, he was, my grandmother too. They both had those blue-grey Scottish eyes, came from some place around Glasgow. They'd started up in northern Vermont, mining granite for a living. Then he got malaria down South in the Civil War, him and a friend of his, Captain Max, so they decided to come out west, the climate was better. It took four months in those days with the wagon trains on the Oregon Trail, starting from Independence, Missouri. Somehow their two families got split off from the rest of the train and met up with Indians. Well, Captain Max had this blonde daughter and the Indians promised to guide them out west on condition he gave them his daughter afterwards – she had this long blonde hair stretching right-a-ways down to her knees. They couldn't say no, or they'd all have been killed. So on they went – but when they got to the other side they hid the girl inside the wagon and blacked her hair and cut it short – the Indians were mad, but by then it was settler country, so they got away with it, paid the Indians instead. That's how they reached the West.

'They were still alive when I was a girl. My grandmother, I remember the way she held her teacup, so delicate, she always drank green tea, that's why I went right out this morning and got a packet for you specially, I remembered how you folks like it. Eventually my grandpa became a Quaker missionary, one of the first in the Northwest. But he never seemed a pious man, except on the Sabbath, then he'd be different. We kids, we couldn't believe it was him standing up there in the pulpit with his black frock coat and high collar. We had to sit still as mice in the front pew, we didn't dare move, even if we had pins and needles. But weekdays he was a real person. He used to find pets for us out in the woods – coons, squirrels, porcupines even. And one day he came back with a bear cub and raised it for us. Must have been in his sixties by then, but when it got big he'd wrestle with it and throw it right down. Even in those pioneer days folks didn't quite hold with that, not for a Quaker minister. He was real devoted, though, used to travel about on a pony through wind and snow to reach people. It wasn't so long since the Indians had massacred the first mission – the Whitman mission, right near here – but he kept on going. He took me with him a few times to see the Indians, the Nez Percés. The Wallowa Valley, where we lived, was the greenest valley in Oregon, it had been their favourite hunting ground. The settlers treated those people so bad – but they didn't resent us personally, even after their Chief Joseph was killed. We used to see a lot of them – they were real poor people but they made me a present of a pony. Some relatives of Chief Joseph even gave me the head-dress his daughter had worn. I'll never forget that.'

'Tell them about your father, Helen, how he met up with your mother.'

'That was right around the time of the Chief Joseph massacre. He was on his way to college at Stanford, in California, by buggy and railroad, and he happened to stop at this little station, it was the Wallowa Valley, just to get a bite to eat. While he was standing in the store, in came this beautiful girl.

188

So he decided to stop there a while.' She laughs. 'He was like that – mind you, if he'd known the girl was the minister's daughter, maybe he wouldn't have been so hopeful. But he stopped there. And when he got to know her, he just forgot all about college. Started his own little business and two years later he married her, and of course she was my mother. He never did get to Stanford. We all grew up there – nine children we were, in the end – in a village in the Wallowa Valley. Then I met Donald and came up here. My parents felt the same way, I guess, about my leaving home and the valley, same as we felt about our children – never did expect us to leave. But that's how it is, isn't it?'

He takes us to the mission one day, a few flat miles out of town, past the orange bunches of onions up for sale by the road. Tells us about it on the way with an almost personal note – we often notice this in references to Walla Walla. It's the same with the cashier in the bank as he tells us how many types of wheat are grown by the local farmers; and with the Whitman mission brochure when it states reproachfully that the pioneers of Walla Walla were 'killed by the Indians they sought to help'. Almost everyone seems to have it – a quiet pride in the origins and the near-idyllic tone of their life in this rich lap of the hills.

It's hard to be stirred by the mission site, where the present obscures the past again with its trimness and over-documentation. Or perhaps it's just that missionaries are the least dramatic pioneers, bending a frontier to their values, rather than exposing themselves to its Dionysiac potential. Bibles, yokes, pots and pans are the Whitmans' only relics. Not that they were lacking in pluck. When they crossed the Oregon Trail into Indian and fur-trapping country in the mid-1830s they were the first settlers to bring their wives and wagons with them, trail-blazers for the thousands who followed. The Indians, bewildered and wracked by diseases, blamed and cut them down in broad daylight. Their portraits show stern, black-bearded men and steely-eyed, puritan women with none of that usually romantic look of the migrant USA. It comes as no surprise to learn that they were from upstate New York and Boston.

Walla Walla town grew up roughly a generation later. In western terms it's an old community: a century ago its population was still bigger than that of Seattle, boom city of Washington. You sense it even on the streets. Time has a particular gait, a different element from the East's; greetings too, yet the style's not quite Western. It's too solid, too finished for that. There's nothing raw about the ambling figures, the 'howdies' of the citizens who sit on the windowsill of the First National, panama hats rather than stetsons, puffing cigars and nodding affably. A parking ticket seems unlikely: the meters are for leaning on when people stop for a sidewalk chat, which is remarkably frequently. Strangers acknowledge us with a quiet curiosity: they know that we're from out of town. The talk in the bars is a sleepy buzz, swing doors open to the street; if the television's on, it seems pretty much ignored.

Inside the First National, between the Gothic marble pillars, they keep a proud harvest display of the different kinds of wheat and barley grown in the Walla Walla region – Gold Coin, Zimmerman and Surprise, wheat that's made millionaires in half a dozen seasons. But the affluence is unobtrusive, perhaps because it was hard won – the farmers of the Northwest were heavily hit by the Depression and long before that they were pioneers in the movement for farmers' unions. And the friendliness is spontaneous, not just Yankee salesmanship or the closed good-chummery of much of small town USA, which doesn't usually extend to strangers. Unlike most Midwesterners, the cashier's too sophisticated to doubt a New York traveller's cheque: instead, it's an excuse to chat, to advise us what to see, find out where we're from, whom we're staying with, how we like it. He knows just the place to go for the new primus stove we need and even phones ahead for us. 'Ed, couple of folks here I'm just sending along to you, reckon you can help em out – they're staying up at the Hendersons.' The next customer seems unoffended at having waited; she says goodbye, along with the cashier. The same with Ed: knocks two bucks off the price of the stove and then gets down to the real business of a long, leisurely chat, calling me by my first name as soon as he's learnt it from the receipt. He never travelled much, he tells

us, except just to Seattle, of course. Says Walla Walla suits him
too well. The directness of these encounters compared to those
farther east reminds us both of differences between the north
and south of England.

The old man agrees. 'It's Western, but it's not the yip-yip,
ride-em cowboy kind of town with a saloon on every corner –
that's cattle country, over the mountains. Just easy-going and
friendly. Nobody hustles unless he has to. They like to know
about other folks, how they're feeling, what they're thinking.
In the old days, of course, we felt it was bigger. Folks didn't
travel so much then, though we did have a passenger line on
the railroad – that's gone now, everyone flies. People don't get
together so much, they don't seem quite so close as they were.
Those days you couldn't just live here, you had to belong. That
old building on the corner – it's a tyre company now – it used to
be the town theatre and folks'd come down there dressed up
swell in tuxedos and long dresses. Henry Irving acted there
once, all the big names were there. Then it became a movie
house. But after television, even that couldn't last.'

Its flavour has, though, in people and building, even if they're
not as he knew them. The Dawes Hotel is disused now, a huge,
brownstone edifice with balconies round its elaborate windows;
but it still commands the skyline on the eastern side of town.
The billboards are big all right, but a lot of them advertise events
already over. And beyond them, whichever way you look
through the broad gulch of the streets, the pastel haze of the
farmlands is still a thinly-peopled Eden.

Long summer days revolve slowly round the big, peaceful house.
The wheat fields are only clear in the morning. Afternoon heat
shimmers and drowns them; sundown fires them out of existence
until they float back chiffon blue through the sensual summer
dusk.

Inside it's always cool; the blinds trellis the day-long stillness
with their splinters of sunlight and shadow. The grandfather
clock strikes discreetly. Helen laughs. 'Max used to say goodnight to it, solemn as a little owl, every night, as he went to
bed: "Goodnight Mr Clock"! The grand piano hasn't been

played since the children left,' she adds. There's a map of Spain spread on it, Max's, with a route traced out. 'It's the only way we can follow their travels. We sometimes get to wondering why they always have to be travelling – but they've got their own lives, we can't tell them what to do.'

The old man spends most of his time in the garden, reading under the beech tree or tending the fruit and vegetables. The rich black Washington soil pitches them up in a lush green, sweet corn, raspberries, grapes; there's even an old apricot tree dropping its shadow on the wheat field that jostles up against the fence. She's inside most of the day, preparing her large, homely meals – including, for our English benefit, tea instead of coffee (after her Scottish grandmother) and a huge roast beef on Sunday (because she's heard how Churchill liked it). Between times, she's still busy, setting out her Spode china or making preserves, grape jelly, apricot and raspberry jam, to line the cupboards in the basement. 'I make my own soap, too – just for the fun of it, you know. When the old folks came out here, they had to do everything themselves, weren't any stores about then unless you chanced to meet a pedlar. And they brought us up the same way – my daughter Jenny, she thinks it's nonsense, she tells me I should buy these things.' Laughs. 'She doesn't understand. This basement is where the boys used to be, a dozen sometimes, Max and his school friends, they used to come up here and work at the harvest. They camped down here – my, those boys' appetites! We'd be feeding them all day, ate like reg'lar little tigers, out in the fields picking peas, back in the shower, round the garden, parties up on that balcony – there's nothing like having young folks around.'

They listen to the news occasionally, but it seems far removed here. 'I turn it off soon as I can, Donald gets so upset by it. He used to listen to it every day, but now, oh dear – he gets so upset over this terrible Vietnam war.' ('Veetnam', she pronounces it, emphasising her anxiety.) 'He goes outside soon as they raise it, right-a-ways down the garden, I can't get him in for meals. My, it's a terrible thing we're doing, we feel so bad about it. Those poor people over there, they don't want this war we're making. And all those boys going into it – Max's cousin,

Steven, I'm afraid of him getting his draft card and they'll send him out there – can you imagine it, he's such a sensitive boy, only twenty, always painting. That's not the kind of thing we've lived for, brought our children up for. We don't agree with it at all. And it's not the same any more, you can't talk about these things. Soon as you speak your mind now, people call you a leftist, a sympathizer, fellow-traveller. If you've got a business in town, you'd be finished, they'd boycott you. Even the churches can't speak out and it's the same with the papers. They don't dare say what they think any more. People'd stop buying them.'

Her voice can be startlingly firm when she's roused. 'We've written our Senator about it – but you know what politicians are, you just get a polite answer, it doesn't mean anything. Wasn't like that a while back. You knew what was going on then and you didn't have to agree with people so's to remain friends with them – these last few years it's changed.' Furrows her brow: until now it was difficult to imagine her angry, but once she is it's remarkable how much energy seems compressed into her small, insistent figure. 'I'm not anti-Washington, but the big organizations, they control everything these days. Just money, money and double-talk – soon as they hear that Dow Jones average coming out of Wall Street there, they don't mind if a hundred boys has gone and died in Veetnam. It's Wall Street is pushing this war, just to keep the economy booming. You know' – she stops and looks at us firmly – 'you mightn't know it now, coming here for the first time, but when we were young this country was liberal. We believed in everybody's freedom, not just our own – that's how it was. But now you can't say anything. You just have to sit and listen while those Washington folks have cocktail parties and play their footsie with dictators, so's we can keep our bases down in Latin America and send boys to Veetnam. It's all wrong and people know it – but the people don't govern any more.'

The old man passes the window and moves the spray across the lawn. The rough-hewn chairs from Vermont pitch their shadows on the paving stones. A baby rabbit is browsing quietly a few feet from the junipers, cocking his head every now and then to check up on the tabby cat. Two doves flutter down into the top of the blue spruces, tilting their heads forward and churring. He's sitting down now on one of the chairs: his stillness, as often with older people in this sometimes crudely youthful society, suggests a constant remoteness from it – perhaps the only alternative to the fantasy of septuagenarians dancing to the latest hits in expensive 'Senior Citizens' homes.

He gets up as we come out. 'Just going for a stroll down the back there. You coming?'

Behind the house the stillness is deeper. The grass stands almost knee-high beyond a flight of overgrown steps. 'You mightn't believe it, but that's the tennis court – made it ourselves, like the rest, but nobody plays there now of course.' He seems uneasy in this wilderness of rambling grass and juniper bushes. There's been a gale since we arrived. It's split the apricot tree down the middle, showing a decayed inside that its summer green had hidden. A little stream at the back of the garden is shadowed by overhanging branches. In one corner the ground has been cleared and partly concreted over.

He tests the concrete to see if it's dry. 'Building a little patio here, do it myself, I prefer it that way, just needs a bit of rubble and cement.' He glances at us. 'I was thinking they might like to sit and read here when they're back, the young folks – a feller could sit and read here, they could have barbecues, couldn't they?'

The sun's dying between the branches in a last wheat-burning flare. He points across to a little shed on the far side of the stream. 'That was the boys' play-house, Max and Steven used to play there. Might take a look inside – I haven't been in there for a while.'

It's fixed up in homesteader style, with an ancient stove and a pair of bunks. A few flags are pinned on the wall, the kind you get at tourist spots with the names written across them – Gettysburg, Pennsylvania; Hartford, Connecticut; Seattle. 'Those flags, they used to collect them whenever they went travelling. Took them to some of those places myself. Seattle – we went there together, that was one of the best days, on the waterfront at Seattle. Used to be lots more than that, the whole

7

wall was covered with them. I'd just come down here and look at them sometimes. The neighbours' kids must have taken the others.'

He mentions it to her later that evening, as we're sitting outside again. 'Helen, those boys have been in the play-house and taken Max's flags away, most of them.'

'Oh.' But she doesn't comment. 'You took them down there? The other children play in it now, we hear them, but we don't see them so often. This house used to be full of them. Those boys' appetites' – and she gives her bird-like tinkle of laughter. 'Well, they've gone their different ways – Max in South America and Steven over at Harvard and I'm always worrying, case they get drafted for that terrible Veetnam war.' Pauses. 'That Steven, Donald – I've been wondering. You think he'll marry an Eastern girl? He's over there so much now and I know he's got a girl. But I don't reckon he fancies them' – laughs in her young, mischievous way. 'He says Eastern girls are cold. It's true, you know, they're different people from us folks that live out West. My daughter Jenny, she went over there recently – I never have been myself – and she said there were so many people, all rushing here and there, she wanted to come clear on back without even stopping there a day. But an Eastern girl' – she shakes her head, if only half seriously – 'I don't believe it would suit him.'

The old man breaks in without looking at us. He's in his distant mood. 'He's a philosopher, you know, Steven, a Harvard philosopher. I've asked him – asked him questions, what life's about and all that, but he tells me philosophy doesn't answer questions these days. He just tells me: "Grandpa, you aren't asking things correctly."'

A long pause. Then he murmurs, but it's only half to us. It's the lines from Omar Khayyam about how the poet's grown tired of politics and philosophy. 'You folks ever read that, the Rubaiyat of Omar Khayyam? I suppose it's old hat these days? It was my book of philosophy – well, it still is, I guess. When I was just a young feller, cub reporter I was then, that poem had just come out in the little pocket edition – bound in leather, an inch square, one stanza on each page, little things you carried in your pocket. I was up in Spokane then and a friend and I, we'd gotten hold of it. Well, we were so took by that poem that we went back to my place one evening and sat up I don't know how long, just reading it out to each other. Used to know a good bit of it:

> *There was the door to which I found no key,*
> *There was the veil through which I might not see,*
> *Some little talk awhile of me and thee*
> *There was – and then no more of thee and me.'*

The moon's up again, spectre-thin, swinging round behind the spruce trees. 'Always makes me think of it, sitting out here evenings, watching that moon come up so reg'lar – like old Henry Breton used to watch it.

> *Yon rising moon that looks for us again,*
> *How oft hereafter will she wax and wane.*

You know that bit? How does it carry on, now?' He slows, searching for the words. Fingertips meet under his chin.

> *'How oft hereafter rising look for us*
> *Through this same garden – and for one, in vain.'*

Colder tonight. The hoot of an owl, answered by a screech from another. She leans across. 'If you folks are going to reach Seattle tomorrow, you ought to be getting some sleep. I'm going to wake you at six, you know. It's sad you couldn't stay a while longer – a week doesn't seem so long to us. But Jerry and his folks are expecting you – he's a good friend of Max's.'

He joins in quietly. 'Going to meet Max and Diane, aren't you? I guess you'll see them before we do. In Mexico City, isn't that right?' And he nods, knowing already, just confirming it to himself.

She looks at us. 'Tell them to come and see us. And you tell them we want a great-grandchild to run around this garden of ours. Tell them if we don't get one soon, why, I'll put them over my knee and wallop them, that's for sure now.'

She laughs. But the old man hasn't heard. Watches the darkness, bolt upright.

*

Pine-big green of the Cascade Mountains that we cross on the
following day encourages the fantasy that here at least there's
still a frontier unseized by neon and Las Vegas baroque: but
Seattle's outskirts kill it

WELCOME TO SEATTLE
POPULATION 564000
TURFERS SURFERS AND QUEENIES IN BIKINIS
WELCOME
FROM PEPSI-COLA

pulsing sleazily through the dusk. Six-lane freeway parabolas
up at a Manhattanese-and-Venetian outline hung between the
inland lake and the Puget Sound's Pacific sundown.

The side-road for Jerry's address slips into hillside suburbia
and here it's more like Walla Walla, half demure and half casual.
Homes and gardens are trim and discreet and their owners
relax in wide porches; old ladies water their lawns. At Jerry's
it's the same. A big, bluff character, he takes us into the garden
for a drink, where his father, insurance agent, shows us 'what
I like to call my wilderness area. Makes a difference when you're
a city-dweller to have somewhere you can potter and remind
yourself of a frontier life.' It's a despairing gesture, though, after
Walla Walla's preservation of the world he hankers for; a six-
by-four-foot rock-garden with a handful of shrubs and creepers.
'I named it after an area in the Cascades – my brother and I
used to wander there, used to go hunting when we were boys, we
wouldn't see a soul for days. All these things came from there, the
ferns and brambles, even the rocks.'

His restlessness, it soon turns out, is a family characteristic.
Jerry's equally prey to it. A student at the State university, he
sees the world through different eyes since his spell of military
service: it was all out of *Catch-22*, he says, which isn't a satire so
much as a documentary account of it. Now, having been wrung
through it, he sees the same system everywhere. Including the
university. 'I'm just waiting for graduation next year – get my
campus discharge papers and then I'm heading straight for
Europe. After that, I don't know. Used to think I'd stay there

– now I'm not sure. Things are moving, not here maybe, but in the East and California. Maybe Europe will just be a break.'

His mother we don't see much of, as she's busy attending summer courses, getting a belated BA, about which Jerry is sceptical. 'It's become an obsession with her. It's all the commercials she's listened to, telling her she's a non-person unless she's a college graduate. She's brainwashed, I've told her so – next thing she'll be turning hippie, she's trying so hard to keep up with them all.' He gestures at the patch of woods immediately behind their fence. 'We need another frontier again – this was bare fifty years ago, there was hardly a house on it. You could dance in the woods or build your own house. Now you're a cipher – you have to be one. That's why I want to quit while I can.'

His grandmother's the only one who seems contented with her lot. Tints her hair silver-blue and wanders in and out of the garden picking lavender and roses and dusting the antiques on the shelves. Always addresses us as 'honey', with a Southern lilt – she was born in Louisiana, she tells us. She's reserved about it at first – so much so that we get the impression she's been taught to avoid the subject; but eventually she comes out of her shell. 'My folks were in sugar-cane down there – we moved up to Missoura when I wasn't much more'n a girl, but it still seems like I just left. Folks talk harsh about it now and some ways they're right, of course – but there's lots they don't know less they lived down there themselves. There was good and bad, like anywheres.' Certainly, if we make her nervous, which would hardly be strange, she makes a brave effort to conceal it during the week or so we're there.

It's the more surprising, this seeming uneasiness of theirs at their frontier's reduction to middle-class norms, in that Seattle seems to reflect them. The city's outline's a modest one, with spire-topped brownstone, creamcake marble and silver-grey thrusts of lake and canal: houseboats squat under sweeping bridges. There's a rugged sedateness to it, pioneer but without California's far-western glitter of Dionysiac experimentation, as if this receded long ago, despite Seattle's being a centre of the aircraft industry. Even the towering space needle of the '58 World's Fair, out of date in itself, looks futuristic beside the rest. The terminus of the Union Pacific is more like a historical monument than a modern railroad station. The traffic, crowds and shop-windows have little urgency of dazzle; the atmosphere is quietly restrained, subtler than the Midwest's, but with the same concern for the present rather than a dizzy future.

Perhaps it's the way the Northwest began, with Western intentions but Eastern style. The wagoners of the Oregon Trail had little in common with the heroes of the gold rush and cattle frontiers. Many were from New England, merchants, professionals and artisans, God-fearing and family-minded; and their successors were similar. The immigrants among them were almost entirely North European, British, German and Scandinavian: with their Irish and Latin and Eastern European contemporaries only able to make it to the Eastern ports, or at best Chicago, the myth of the melting pot had a limited truth even at source.

Such little eccentricity as the city's founders did display lay precisely in the un-Western sobriety with which they grasped their destiny. Arriving in 1851, they surveyed the Puget Sound with a washing-line and some horseshoes to find the most favourable harbour. This done, one Henry Yester set the pace by building a sawmill which linked the hillside with the bay along the 'skid road' for his lumber. Until it became the gateway to the Klondike goldrush in Alaska in the 1890s, the city grew at a modest pace; but after this it mushroomed. When the Northern Pacific Railroad declined the Seattle citizens' request for a branch line, they picked up their shovels and built their own to connect with the Canadian Pacific. It was to pay handsomely; their drive so impressed Jim Hill, the baron of the Great Northern, that he made Seattle his terminus, opening up a direct route east for its fish and lumber products.

The city was made, but even then its people didn't wait for their chances: delegates in '94 to Japan, making Seattle the main port for American-Japanese trade; delegates in '97 to all the major Eastern cities to advertise Seattle's assets as the stepping-stone to the Klondike. The strongest impression their history conveys isn't just utopianism – it's their conviction that it would work exactly as anticipated. And it did, inexorably. At the turn of the century half the city was razed and rebuilt, to lower its gradients and widen its layout. Next, the Union Canal was cut, linking the Puget Sound with the inland Washington Lake to provide a second waterfront; typically it had long since been started by Henry Pike, a local worthy with even more foresight than his peers, who'd set about it personally with wheelbarrow, pick and shovel. Its completion made Seattle the pivot of US-Pacific trade. By the end of the First World War, the city was second only to New York. It was exactly sixty-five years since the pioneers had arrived to launch their hyperbole of US and especially West Coast history.

The men behind it were Paul Bunyans – for all their touch of Horatio Alger – as big as the landscape they adopted. The Benny brothers, Arthur and Dave, who built the first two log cabins, followed them up with public buildings, electricity lines and canals, and at one time or another held almost every local office. Dexter Horton, one of the workers in the original Yester sawmill, set up a store where he safeguarded wages in meal-sacks and coffee bags; it became Seattle's first bank and gave him one of the Northwest's biggest fortunes. Jim Hill of the Great Northern broke his every competitor by re-surveying the route west and also investing in freighters which extended his private highway from the East Coast to Hong Kong. His irritation in old age was attributed to his failure to encircle the whole world with it.

The USA's boom time, to which these men contributed, was Seattle's too; the Pacific trade, the fisheries, lumber to Australia and Central America, grain to Europe. The city's population increase was one of the rapidest in the States and new industries maintained it into the mid-twentieth century. Yet Seattle retained its original style, vested in a waterfront that was rarely modernized, and wealthy but discreet suburbs. Beat Frisco, neon Vegas and megalopolizing Los Angeles belong to a different far West. There isn't a single hint of them in this damp, slightly English air, where archetypal pioneering has given way to an undeniable, however bourgeois, composure.

(Though even this carries a hint of the seeming uncertainty of Jerry's family. The middle-aged here look at us strangely, not exactly as if they object, but as if our novelty disturbs them. As if they too are troubled by the question of where the Algers' children turn, now that their elders' building is done and even a flaw or two apparent in its design and execution.)

Nine eyes watch us unflickeringly as we park at the edge of another Seattle, only slightly more concealed and no less persistent than that of the hilltop. The ninth belongs to an old black figure whose whole crippled side, face leg and shoulder blend into the narrow doorway as if it's the setting that's broken him, this skidrow cobbled crack of a street pitching down at the waterfront, at the flat roofs, black cranes, trucks backed up to the warehouses. Washington Street. The name's irony has the same mocking bravado as the men round the doorway (old black man wears his cap at a jaunty swaggering angle over the relic of his face), same as the high-rearing building, grandiose under its grime: ST CHA LES OTEL ROOMS $1.00.

One of the men shambles over. Watches us solemnly, his skidrow stance a calculated contrast to our locking of the Chevrolet doors. Sways a little and catches himself. Then peers at our licence plate and looks up at us long and hard as if he's not just assessing us for pickings – challenging us to get out of it.

'Scuse me, mister, where're you from?'

'England.'

'Limeys? Bless my rotten old soul.' Belches like a ripsaw. 'Well, mister, glad to meet you, Paul Donoghue's the name, born over in bonnie green Ireland, don't hold nothin against a Limey . . .'

A loud hoot interrupts him. One of his cronies has followed him over, a smaller man, clown-like and half aswim in a baggy old suit. He doubles up in mocking laughter, flapping his loose sleeves grotesquely. 'Bonnie green Ireland. Say, mister, if he was born in bonnie green Ireland you can git there in five minutes, aint no more'n a block from here. Now I was born in Denmark, mister' – ferrets in his cramful pocket and pulls out a plastic identity card: 'US Merchant Marine, David Linsted, Seaman. Merchant seamen, that's us.'

Paul Donoghue sees a cue and recovers his lost poise, converting a momentary lurch into a queenly pirouette, thanks to the parking meter. 'Yessir, merchant seamen, just waiting for a boat to Frisco.' Waves his arms expansively. 'China, India, bonnie green Ireland. A bird a passage on the tide a fortune, that's what my old lady called me, she was born in Ireland, mister, aint no place like bonnie green Ireland. Mister John F. Kennedy' – lowers his voice, slows it down and brings his face very close, pallid skin under his stubble, wrinkled remains of a girlie tattoo through the open front of his shirt – 'President John F. Kennedy, mister' –

'Your cousin President Kennedy, Pat' – his friend breaks in again, twisting with laughter, ghoulishly spiteful, spoiling his style. Donoghue curses him quietly, rewraps himself in his pirate's smile and tries a more direct line.

'Well, sir, you're a gen'leman – aint that right, he's a gen'leman, missus – and we're waiting for a boat, barrel's getting a little low, I was wonderin – why, thanks a million mister, we'll meet in Frisco, ask for Donoghue and we'll spread a table for you.' Arm round my shoulder, dead weight. 'Bonnie Prince Charlie, you know him, mister? A fine Irish gen'leman he was, in the name a Bonnie Prince Charlie God bless you,' and he pockets the quarter and lurches back, act over, jauntiness gone. Stops, bends down and spits on the cobbles.

Broken windows and fire-escapes snake up to 1st Avenue. Choked little alleyways lead off, ending in under-tenement darkness. There's the same shore-leave, out-of-work slouch in every corner and doorstep group. Japanese, Indians and Blacks dissect us with the scepticism of eyes that never made the dream with which we're identified by our trappings, camera and Chevrolet. This back of Seattle's waterfront used to be known as 'down on the sawdust', built out on the slopes and mudflats by dust from pioneer Yester's sawmill, with Skid Road leading down to it. Soon it was a hotspot: shortly after the city was founded, its first dance-hall went up, an upstate lumbermen's Mecca famed for its oriental beauties imported from China and Japan by the rough-house queen who ran it – 'Mother Damnable' they called her. The men who ended up there were the flotsam of the westward tide: Indians from the reservations; Scandinavian and Mexican fishermen, Swedish lumbermen, Chinese labourers left workless after the railroads were built; and then the mining camp veterans, when the Klondike gold rush completed a fifty-year trail of dreams stretching from California back to Nevada and the Black Hills and ending up in Alaska. Saloons, hotels and dance-halls multiplied, Billy the Mug's and the Baronof, some of them, for a brief while, with daily turnovers of thousands. But most of the prospectors were still unlucky and in Alaska they'd played their last hand. Many of them drifted back to Seattle, swelling the human underbelly of the spent-out Western dream, the men forgotten by the myths, the millions, workers, loners and hobos, overshadowed and ground under by the colossus – Jim Hill or the Weyerhausers, who inherited half the Northwest's lumber without even knowing the smell of sawdust. Seattle has somehow preserved them, these men who did the real building, still tied to the hockshops and flophouses that their fathers must have used, as if these at least have been claimed for theirs from a history that brought them no dividends.

Their outpost is Pioneer Square at the junction with 1st Avenue: skidrow faces are suddenly set against a downtown skyscraper canyon. In the centre a Tlingit totem pole raises its colourful thunderbird crown against the glimmering outline of office blocks and modern hotels. Old men sit in a shadowed arcade. Two Indians shuffle over for a drink at the water fountain, then go back to squatting at the feet of the totem pole (strange combination, its superbness and their vacancy, is this what they're saying?), watching the traffic with dulled curiosity. Washington, true to its blend of the roughneck and the puritan, still restricts its public drinking: round the corner are the speakeasies where the Indians sit unsmilingly in the wooden drinking booths, No talk: just frozen figures, the new world's absinthe drinkers. Outside in the sidewalk shadows the Indian women sit stoney-eyed with their children sleeping beside them, waiting for the men to emerge.

Up on 1st Avenue the frontier lingers. Menus in the rough restaurants offer squaw candy instead of smoked salmon: they serve it in chunks rather than slices for those who still prefer it that way. The little notices ROOMS FOR RENT have a militantly footloose note. Shoeshine sits in an alleyway and rolls himself a cigarette and four girls lounge on the sidewalk, bare arms linked and laughing under a notice: AL'S PLACE ROOMS. Japanese, black, and white – discrimination only belongs to a purer, more fastidious world: the waterfront's clip-joints have been closed several times by local reformers, but always bounced back again. In this setting they look as irrepressible as Montgomery Ward elsewhere.

An old Chinese behind a window, eyes hidden by sunglasses, dilates his thin, flabby lips like a fish in an aquarium, in and out, very slowly. Heads in the long, narrow bars turn round occasionally to watch the outside world go by as if they're total strangers to it. The tight little stores, for all their dust, are as lusty as supermarkets:

SURPLUS STORE
USED CLOTHES
SEATTLE'S GREATEST HARDTIME BARGAINS

Denims, ropes and pressure lamps piled high behind cruddy windows, boots, knives and crumpled suits, elk heads and sharks' teeth, handless clocks, battered flasks and ancient sepia-toned photographs taken at the mining camps; (solemn faces stare at the camera, emphasized by that incongruous gear, white shirts and dark waistcoats, as if they'd been sitting in the office and rushed straight off at the news of the strike).

All pell-mell piled together, the anarchic real estate of the lone hobos and roadsters who are vanishing from the USA, or at least losing the independence which allowed them more than their poverty. Right along 1st Avenue it feels like their last concerted stand, on the country's westernmost street, against the new world that's fought them back with Floral Heights and a Chevrolet. Yet there's more to its defiance than just a

wilful nostalgic pride: more than just a spit in the eye for
Floral Heights society – a knowledge perhaps that it's closer
to something which this society's beginning to miss, those
girls' laugh, Donoghue's challenge. Something which Floral
Heights children are crossing the tracks to rediscover, especially
here on the West Coast, the USA's frontier again: turning back
to the travelling life; to the carefully forgotten, underbelly's
bits of history; to the folk-songs this history produced, whose
anti-heroes are still echoed in Seattle's waterfront figures. Just
an alienated few at first but now enough and no longer children
to tilt the balance and looking back in new picket-line forma-
tion at Floral Heights. The tie-up's apparent on the shelves and
in the window of a bookstore which looks as if, until recently,
it sold only the comic books which have now been overshadowed:

HOW MANY SOUTH VIETNAMESE FOUGHT IN OUR CIVIL
WAR? HOW MANY AMERICANS HAVE DIED IN THEIRS?
WHY ARE WE THERE, BROTHER? WHAT CAN WE DO ABOUT
IT?

(And underneath other
hands have added their
answers to the final
question. Someone
wrote 'Screw'; another
'TURN ON'. But a third
hand has crossed them both
out: written
'BURN – MAKE REVO-
LUTION')

Out in the narrow
side-street leading back
up to 1st Avenue figures
drowse in doorways, faces
are black against wall
peeling, cranes cross
street slash of light but
it's dark in the doorways
and alleyways and

Down on the waterfront itself it's the same antithesis to the
prosperous hillside city. Pike Street market's the underside of
its Anglo upper crust:

Chow mein, Japanese lanterns, heads bow Chinese murmur
Indian women in saris with the scarlet caste-mark on their
foreheads and in the Filipino stall an old man shuffles in the
background soft-faced whispering in Tagalog, the old gods

ranged behind him; bamboo-bell note follows him around, dove soft. And in Vi's Used Clothes, with its skidrow and Indian faces, suspicious hands rummage their way through crumpled shirts, skirts, coats: from 30 cents to $1.00. The quayside's visible through the windows and down the pinched alleyways. Old men line the railings, baggy trousers and stooped shoulders. Cheap saloons, Chinese laundries and the once famous hotels, the Grand Pacific and the Baronof

ROOMS $1.00 AND UP
MOTHPROOF LOCKERS RENTED BY MONTH

with their dates inset in the grey brickwork: 1889, 1897, gold rush days.

There's a connection of a kind between this waterfront atmosphere of a place suspended in time and the other Seattle's old-fashioned flavour. It was partly the waterfront, fighting back at the hilltop bosses, which ended the city's original boom. For a generation and more it was a stronghold of the Wobblies, the Industrial Workers of the World, who soapboxed the USA to the brink of revolution in days recorded by novelist Dos Passos. The turn of the century: a new dream was stirring the chaff of the West Coast, including the men whom the robber barons had threshed to build their private empires. 'Big Bill' Hayward and Wesley Everest, Wobbly leaders, were moving among the out-of-work dockers, underpaid lumberjacks, hungry miners. Teamster's strikes on the West Coast, riots in the lumber-camps, protest meetings in Nevada and Gene Debs for a Socialist President (though his speeches got him jailed, he won several million votes). When Hayward founded the Wobblies for a workers' commonwealth 'to end the capitalist wage system, monopolies and robber barons,' he made Seattle his headquarters. Washington labour had always been strong ('the soviet of the USA,' people were calling it). As the Wobblies won their victories from New England to Nevada, it was the mainstay of a movement unique in the challenge it presented to the course of US history, until World War I, when patriotism suspended any earlier restraints; along with pacifists and Germans, the Wobblies, who'd always been met with violence, were mobbed, lynched and pitched into jail. When the war ended, the establishment had regained its balance. Wesley Everest was seized at an IWW meeting, driven off in a large limousine, castrated and dropped from a bridge with a rope round his neck; and when Big Bill, given twenty years, jumped his bail, fled to Russia and died there shortly afterwards (his autobiography, 'Bill Hayward's Book', a buried classic) the movement all but died with him. (Was it ever more than a dream, disorganized as it always was, in a continent still so lone-man open?) Though the Wobblies carried on for a while in corners of New York, Chicago and especially Seattle, even playing an important part in one or two subsequent big strikes, business unionism was in. The hilltop had won; the Wobblies were almost written out of US history.

Signs of the struggle remain, though; the stillness on the waterfront and the old men leaning on the railings, gazing at the quay-slapping water and the bleak, littered wharves of the Alaska Steam Boat Line where a huge crane loads the SS *Tonsina*, ALASKA written rough and bold on the crates that swing at its prow. Further along by a smaller jetty the hulk of an old paddle-steamer reclines in a chog of greenstink garbage old crates old rope green slime. One of the old men stationed above it tells us where it was made, up the coast, and how it carried passengers up and down the Puget Sound. 'She was still runnin pretty nice when I first come down to work here – this whole front, godammit, whole place was pretty fine. Until the Depression cleaned her out – she was down before that, though, rough times, the bosses was rough, the men wouldn't stand for it, there was a lot of hard feelings.' Purses his lips reflectively and spits in the water with rare precision. 'Times we was pretty near civil war right here on this waterfront. But you couldn't beat em, they closed down on us. Come the war she picked up a bit, but since then it's been the same. Trade going off, work hard to get. Still get a big day now and then, but she's nothin to what she was. When I was a young feller, your age, they'd be in and out of here, boats from India, China, Japan – they'd be in and out of here like peas jumpin out of a pod.'

Down in the Olde Curiosity Shop, stuffed with relics of the

seven seas hocked there by vanished seamen, a barrel organ plays hurdy-gurdy. Kids and mothers on evening walks jostle at Ivan's seafood stand; the world of the freeway overhead, set on tall concrete pillars and whistling by at seventy, makes no impression on the waterfront with its tenement-shouldered alleys and truck-rambling and railroad tracks. Clang-clang of a handbell and the puff of an engine towing the Union Pacific freight cars and they all jump up on the benches and pull skirts so mother looks, the little boys with ice-cream noses, the girls with their hair in curlers, and jump and wave at the engine driver who waves back and clangs goodbye. The old men just watch quietly.

Pacific dusk creeps up the inlets: darkens the lakes, wipes out the bridges and turns on the lights up on the hill. It's dim, though, back in Washington Street where the same figures sit slumped silent under the weakly lit sign ST CHA LES OTEL ROOMS $1.00. On the corner of an alley a middle-aged Indian woman is trying to persuade a man to come home. Pulls at his sleeve and whispers to him in a low, urgent voice, but he leans back, laughing helplessly, slipping slowly down the wall and throws her hand away with a curse. She stands over him pleading.

Eyes watch from across the street as we unlock the car door.

Jerry takes us out one weekend to the family beach cottage by the Sound, where some of his friends join us. It's built in Scandinavian cabin style, wood-grain mellowed by the sea, prints of clipper ships on the wall, a big open fireplace and creepers drowning the balcony: old paperbacks everywhere and its furniture has the imprint of a generation of summer weekends. Most of the friends are at college with him and from much the same background. Pete, big and fair and goodlooking, whose father is a successful lawyer, and his sylph-like wife, Wendy. Dave, who's been working as a woodsman and writing lonesome poetry somewhere up in the Cascades. Ricky, son of an academic who's been doing what Jerry plans, tramping Europe for nearly a year and sleeping mainly under the stars. They're all strikingly unpretentious, none of them what they might have been with

life falling so plumb at their feet – neither ostentatiously hippie
nor sports-car nor career minded. Like Jerry, they're disen-
chanted with the university, but they haven't gone for the
standard alternatives – without being cynical or indifferent,
they're inclined to be sceptical of the motives and reasoning
behind much student activism: grass and similar trends appear
to play little part in their lives. Despite their closeness as a group
– they've known each other from childhood and it's obviously
intense, if relaxed – they make us feel easily at home. With this
and the old family cabin, the day has a gentleness that removes
it out of time, matched by the soft lap of the sea only a few feet
away. Now and then somebody swims or collects driftwood for
the fire. The Sunday papers pass round.

Yet when anyone does talk, they seem to share Jerry's restlessness. It's almost always of going places, mainly Europe or
California, as if our arrival as birds of passage has articulated
a feeling never very far from their minds – increased by their
general depression at most of what's in the newspapers, Vietnam
and the country's general return to the ideological limbo of
before the early and mid-sixties. And it has a more personal
aspect: the implication that everything is just too predictable
for them, overloaded with tacit assumptions as to the roles
they're going to play in their prosperous slice of society.

Jerry says as much as we lounge on the beach, watching a
lonely steamer picking its way across the Sound. He's been asking us about Cornell: our account of it matches his expectations.
'Max told me what it's like, he feels much the same as you. It's
different here, but only in degree – the result's the same.
Squaring you up for the blue suit, the blue views, the blue
job – to play your part in the same scheme that's produced
it all, from Vietnam to pollution. And with only one way of
looking at things – it may be all quite liberal sometimes, but
always with the same horizons – there's only one world, it's
made our way and you have to step right into it. Until one day
you cease to believe in it – then you're really in the dark,
because it's all that's ever taught, so that no debate is possible.
I think that's partly why the States has become more creative,
ironically. In rock music, novels, things like that. It's about the

only way for people to speak with their own voice. Even liberal parents seem unable to grasp this – they built the place, so they just can't see why we don't pick it up without question. So where do we go from there? I guess we've all come to the same point – and we don't want to run off to Greenwich Village, that wouldn't do anything for us, we'd only be more spoilt than before. So' – digs his toes in the sand – 'that's why this summer's been kind of quiet. And it's come to a head for Pete – he didn't get into graduate school and now he's got his draft card. Has to report next week. It's damped everyone down a bit. I still don't know what they've decided – he doesn't know whether to object, what his real motives would be if he did. But he says he'd refuse if he was assigned to Vietnam. He's been thinking of leaving the country – but that's tricky. You can't come back. Now I don't know. They've been quiet about it the last few days.'

Soft Pacific lap and sigh (opposite of the Atlantic's pounding), lapping at a journey's end but ceaselessly, marking no conclusion, as if the end's just a re-beginning; a subtler re-phrasing of the questions. The day drifts by, other-worldly serene: sun burning on the water, making crystal silhouettes out of the rowing boats and driftwood. Smoke from a beach fire, snatches of conversation, sleep, book and newspaper pages turning, Jerry and Dave spilling dice. Pete stands at the water's edge, big and thoughtful, flipping stones so that the light and water dance. Wendy rowing on her own, silhouette oars rising and dipping.

The lights of Seattle wink on again, sloping down into the Sound. The ghostly Pacific spills and sighs along the narrow arc of the shore, phosphorous-flashing on the darkness, pulling and pushing at the driftwood. Jerry's lit the fire in the cabin. Pete and Wendy reappear. They must have been gone nearly an hour, disappeared down the beach together. Wendy rouses Jerry from his reading to make him light the charcoal broiler out on the balcony. She cooks a huge dish of hamburgers. Ricky puts on a record, Bach, but it seems too solemn and by general agreement it's changed for some rinky-tink country music. Jerry and Dave make mad poetry, each alternating a line, the only rule being to rhyme. The wood-grain glows in the yellow firelight. Foghorns enquire.

At Jerry's next morning the phone rings early. It's Ricky. Pete's mother just rang him. She found a note under the door from Pete and Wendy. It was short. Just said they'd left and she'd hear from them soon.

She asked him: 'Ricky, where are they?' (Ricky doesn't know.) 'Where did they go?'

Sara Parkin, 29

PARKIN, *Sara, 29, slight, attractive, blonde, reserved,* b. *small East Texas town where her family still lives. First came to Austin, state capital, as college student. Since then has taught for several years in the city's East side ghettoes. Now back at college as graduate student.*

I somehow always knew I wouldn't stay in Jericho, even when I was still quite young – never quite fitted in – partly that I was solitary because I was an only child – the social attitudes too, they were very rigid, even as a child you were trapped in them – had your social category as black or white, wealthy or poor, they were the basic categories, and you stayed in your own or you got into trouble – trapped because I think I did become aware of this early on – school was segregated and even the poorer white kids, they were called 'the cowboy group' and kept apart – dominated by the kids from the wealthier families – even as a child your relationships were stifled by it – experienced this bitterly once or twice – half detached myself. In a way I was always waiting to leave.

(Not that her family was extreme. Father was influential and in local terms fairly liberal, even had Negroes come to the front porch instead of the back. Yet that upset them, they were afraid of crossing traditional boundaries. As a child she became aware of such fears. And as fundamentalist Baptists and solid Southern Democrats her parents shared basic local views on integration, religion and politics. Growing older, she found herself reduced to near silence.)

Apart from the way it narrowed relationships there was always this contradiction, hypocrisy I guess I should call it –

very Texan – a virtue to be plain-speaking, as long as it's plain conservatism. But liberal topics like integration are just taboo – left you powerless and not just that, you were dragged into it step by step – still go back – love the countryside, I was close to it as a kid, I used to get back from school and go riding. But I can't be myself there –

imagine how it was for me getting to a biggish place with a university – yet Austin's not that different – personally it is, of course, friendships are more free here, but socially – strictly divided on race and class lines and demanding your complicity as a member of the white middle class – people in city government referring publicly to 'niggers' – the controlling interests, banks, insurance, real estate groups, all buying up minority leaders as soon as they show some ability – the whole set-up works that way – not something I'm inclined to think, as I'm just a plain liberal by nature, but it's true – always made aware of it all through my contact with the other side – an old man in East Austin, a cobbler, the grandfather of one of my pupils – talking to him about all this – as I was leaving he looked at me very directly – miss, us blacks over here got the fever, but the sickness is the other side of town –

hardly apparent to me at first, especially in the university – seemed extremely liberal and a completely wonderful place after growing up in East Texas – yet the social blindness of some intellectuals – even the political groups, including most liberals and radicals – knowing very little either about what they're up against or the people they're fighting for in East Austin – hardly consult or take account of them – personal more than a social crusade – find I can't align myself with any radical group here – feel hypocritical, having these views and yet taking no position – not because I haven't spent a whole lot of time thinking about it – inevitably some real upheaval in American society – see no alternative –

partly why I went into teaching – getting away from all this to something I could get a hold of, and some human contact – six years at a junior high in East Austin – mainly Chicano students, with a large black minority and some poorish whites – kids themselves split up, in the lunchroom for example, into separate ethnic groups – what can you expect when the whole community's shaped that way, from the top down? Including the school principal – very few teachers, as middle-class whites, are equipped to make any difference – brings you right up against all this – a game of wits – I'd even wonder how much the average teacher has to offer in such a set-up – standards alien to the students and often very dishonest too –

feel I did make some headway. If you can make the break-through, it's a very rich experience. What's striking, though far from obvious, is that most of them really want this – hoping you're the sort of person who'll get to see them as individuals – prove this, they open up and the cynicism and withdrawal lessen – one student of mine – in my remedial reading class – problems lay in not getting on with teachers, rather than in reading – one day writing quietly on his own – all the fashionable names that have been applied to minority groups. It said: 'First I was called a Mexican. Then I was a poverty case. Then under-privileged. Now I'm disadvantaged.' It ended up: 'So who am I?' –

classroom's a sheltered place – whatever you and they've achieved can be blown apart – so many of the brightest students – often the hardest ones at first – got into fights – usually dismissed – so much bitterness that I'm often afraid they'll kill someone or at least end up in jail – few who have gone on to college have eventually dropped out – less because of intellectual than because of social problems – Benny, one of my brightest students – state university – bummed ever since, ending up in Mexico, where I think he may well stay – it all began with his problems with another student, a white boy he was put to room with – unhappy about rooming with a Chicano – parents made a fuss – that really began it – rejected the system, out of distrust and disgust – or that it rejected him. The result's the same –

finally I left – I no longer wanted to work with a system that's rejecting kids with that potential – very little chance of myself being able to influence this or even avoid its frustrations – great admiration for them, they're the few students I've encountered on any level who could criticize what they're taught – far more

214

sympathy for them than for the system I was employed by. But the system's stronger –

that's what I mean by predicting some major upheaval, countrywide – no guarantee as to what it's going to produce, given the power of the vested interests – thought of leaving Texas, of going to live in Mexico – some place you can at least kid yourself you're free of it all – though I doubt in the end if I would leave – at least the countryside, it's my first and only homeplace – perhaps I'd come back too because, for all I've said, I want to see changes in Texas and can't finally despair of them and do still want to work for them. When I know how. That's the question.

CHAPTER 11

SCENES:
San Francisco

Backdrop

Celluloid real it glides by through the big Chevrolet window, the bluer than blue and greener than green (only the image is true now) of the pinestill Olympic Peninsula with lime-coloured shadows and nuggets of light as the big road rides through it all and leaves it remote and untouchable and the sudden Pacific drops below making its music, whoosh and spill (opposite of the Atlantic's. . . . 'Ricky, where are they?') along the long swings of surf then sunlit redwood and sea flaring · *and now the news headlines brought to you by courtesy of your new Pontiac dealer at · two Negroes reported shot both believed to be in their teens · five hundred tons of explosives on suspected Vietcong* · and a lone voice, the gas pump attendant grizzled and leaning on the door for his taken-for-granted chat (in case we'd not realized it was entailed, that you can't just grab your gas and go buzzing on to distant cities): 'Just caught me, I was about closin up to go back there and catch my supper, git me a nice steel-head trout. San Francisco, is that right? Folks sure git about these days. You'll just catch that last ferry over the Columbia River, she generally goes around sundown' . . . WELCOME TO OREGON stars slung low, little lace curtains in trailer windows and portable TV shots and screams and washes whiter and Perry Mason and

THINGS GO
BETTER WITH
COCA
COLA

whoosh and spill hushed

(where are they?) through the fresh morning mist mysterious trees birds in the quiet FANTASEA CAFE SURFSIDEMOTEL MARINE WONDERS 8 MILES cedargreen down in ravines and the sun-up sea Kodachrome blue. Cormorants plummet and seals mooch WORLD'S LARGEST UNDERGROUND CAVE SEE SEALS IN NATURAL HABITAT GET THERE BY ELEVATOR mist WELCOME TO CALIFORNIA muffles the redwoods, yellow ghosts lumbering headless out of its silence, not until night and a clear patch of sky (and little lace curtains . . .) that they tower in full black flight, mocking man

WITH

COCA

COLA

reduced to real again next morning, their last night's giant earthness erased by their picture postcard familiarity and the everywhere redwood stores for mementos of only a memory already thanks to Redwood Postcards Inc · *that the USA will not tolerate any escalation of the war* · ♫ *she was twenty-one* ♫ *when I left Galveston* ♫ *Galveston oh Galveston* ♫ *I can hear your sea waves crashing* ♫ *whilst I watch the cannons flashing* ♫ *and I clean my gun* ♫ *and dream of Galveston* · a last raped red sea of stumps as 101 swings arrowstraight south SAN FRANCISCO 227 rockdotted surf through the tail of the mist and battled farms on the bare hills · *described by the city's chief of police as a bunch of unwashed Communist dupes* · *killed one Red attacker by smashing a hand grenade into his face* · *which means that your investments will yield you more than ever before if* · ♫ *I clean my gun* ♫ *and dream of Galveston* ♫ *Galveston oh Galveston* ♫ *I am so afraid of dying* ♫ *before I dry the tears she's crying* · and suddenly it's California (Steinbeck's Granma in *The Grapes of Wrath*: 'Pu-raise Gawd fur vittory!' and even the sun's a new one washing the hills sloping down to slivers of orchards in the valleys, pinched but already a promised land look for the slow figures that should have been Granpa in faded overalls tending their green and place names FORTUNA SANTA ROSA SAN FRANCISCO 113. Dusty one street pick-up towns with dappled eucalyptus shadows and distilled light like the light of Greece ·

*charged with defacing his draft card by placing tomato catsup on it
and subsequently eating it* · *shot his wife after an argument over
which television program to watch* · bouncing off the bronze hills
lumping trees into jet silhouette and burnishing grapefields
horizonwide below the pale blue burning sky · *que la huelga va
continuar* · *bebe Coca Cola el primeiro en todo el mundo* · California,
convertibles, platinum hair in the wind at eighty · *it was the same
in ancient Rome when they were losing their empire, the same
symptoms of moral downfall as in our modern USA, they had
hippies too, you know, stripping in the streets like ours and people
sitting in the restaurants naked from the waist up eating nothing
but imported foods, you just look around you, isn't that the same as
today? If you want to learn more about the way America's going,
write The Voice of Freedom* · a child's face straggle-blonde
(though most are darker, Mexicans or US-born Chicanos) peering
through the slats of a truck, whole families herded home from
the long Saturday's harvesting, SAN FRANCISCO 24 · ♫
Galveston oh Galveston ♫ *I am so afraid of dying* · Spanish tiles
and white colonnades then suddenly it's there: the hazy way
below blue of the bay and the fairy-tale finger of San Francisco
floats up skyscrapers eggshell pale and the little white sailboats
hang like toys (but Granpa left on Oklahoma's Route 66 with
his dreams of grape juice running over him) and the steamers
toot and the Golden Gate flies up in filigree · ♫ *before I watch the
seagulls flying* ♫ *in the sky at Galveston* ·

Cash

A supermarket in downtown Berkeley, branch of a big West
Coast chain, on the edge of a black neighbourhood where old
cars take regular at a dollar's worth a time and kids play on the
railroad tracks. The usual stock for a supermarket in a poor area
– the only thing in the whole wide States (along with the higher
prices than in your better districts) that seems to differentiate
them: cheap bacon cuts, all fat, cheap low-grade brands of
liquor and tired women who fill their trolleys with almost
nothing but bread and eggs. And single apples and oranges. And

single sticks of margarine. There's no piped music even, as if it's
not worth the management's while where there's no spare cash
to be charmed away. We've brought a few dollars' worth of food
and it's on the cashier's counter. Two women are standing
behind us, frowzy, middle-aged and white – as are most of the
cashiers, though ours is younger, twenty maybe, poor com-
plexion and patchy rinse, but not unpretty behind her make-up.

CH: (taking out travellers' cheques, American Express, $10
each) 'Can you cash a travellers' cheque?'

Cashier: (eyes fixed hard on June, clickety-ping like her
machine) 'We don't take cheques' (still staring at June). 'They're
not worth much around here. They'll cash it at the liquor store
right around the corner there,' (catsmiles at June now, almost a
wink, though we're both meant to see) 'you know where it is,
you show him, uh, honey?'

The women behind us take their cue, sniggering softly.

Black

Ashley's apartment. It's in an oldish sector of Berkeley, part
black, part Chicano, part student. Ashley is a Ph.D. student,
engaged to a friend of ours at Cornell: a scientist, quiet-spoken,
late twenties, spindly, bespectacled, black. A warm Saturday
afternoon. The street below the window could be part of a
Mexican suburb – trees on the sidewalk, kids roller-skating, pink
and white Spanish style houses and a branch of the Santa Fé
line rusting into quiet decay.

Ashley: 'It's pleasant to live in – but it's changing, the usual
cycle. An average middle-class district and then a few blacks
move in and the real estate agents get busy – buy up all the
houses cheap as the whites panic and move out. Then they cram
them with blacks and Mexicans, anyone who can't afford better.
Sometimes they even subsidize the first black families to move
in, to get prices moving their way. Then with the overcrowding
and no maintenance and poor tenants everything starts going
down. The better teachers quit the schools, public expenditure
drops, prices and unemployment rise and next time round it's

a riot area. And so it goes on. The ghetto process, all part of the
system. Have you seen that side of things as you've travelled?
Is it easy as a mixed couple?'

June: 'Not as hard as some people warned us, I think it's
because we're hard to place and obviously not American. That's
provided a sort of screen. But it's confining. Often Colin's gone
out on his own – because even being on the edge of it as a
foreigner gets you down. It makes me bad company – the
endless stares and silences from all those good, god-fearing
people. I can't even go into a public washroom in a campground,
for instance, without the conversation freezing. It's not worth
the price, in the end. I can't imagine how so many West Indians
have settled here. Nowhere's perfect – but can you imagine
stepping off a plane or a boat and finding you're suddenly this
thing, this weird idea, a Negro or whatever? In the first pair of
eyes you confront.'

Ashley: 'But you've still seen a lot, more than most Americans. The States must be the world's hardest place for someone
from one social group to make contact with the others. Especially if you're black and not foreign, it's just not practical to
travel any more than you have to. And when you do, you don't
see the same things. Half the things you've described to me could
be from a foreign country. Except the supermarket incident –
people often imply a mixed couple's a pick-up, if only to
reassure themselves. I've found it's not worth poking around,
you get hurt every time. And I've got advantages – I'm a
graduate and I'm not that poor. For most blacks, white USA is
pretty much like outer space.'

CH: 'You sense that, there are so few around in places like
campgrounds, even diners – maybe that's why people seem
plain confused by us. As if they're bothered by where we are
rather than whatever they take us to be. They do often stop
what they're doing and just watch us till we leave. In tourist
spots especially – as if they feel that at least we shouldn't take
vacations.'

Ashley: 'That's it and there are good reasons for it – even
when they can afford it, blacks don't do the things you've been
doing. Especially with whites. Travel's exposure. If you have

to travel, you look for shelter, not adventure. That's another unwritten black code – you're part of a network soon as you reach another city. Even if you don't know people there, someone's going to fix you up soon as you're in the black part of town. But it means all you see is black ghettoes. And they look much the same anywhere.'

June: 'Were you born in California?

Ashley: 'No, in Maryland. So that's really my USA, the border South, and the cities. And I hardly feel interested in the rest. Why should I? I've little to do with it personally, socially, historically. I guess it's hard for you to imagine – the business of knowing the States as just ghettoes. It's simple, yet it's beyond the grasp of anyone who hasn't lived it. It colours everything. Take riots – riots are something that occur in your own society. But if the society isn't yours, which is what I've been saying, then you're not rioting, you're at war. To talk of 'black riots', as the media do, is a logical contradiction. That's self-evident, but not from outside it. Like the rest – the insignificance of poverty programmes or civil rights laws. They're gestures, not changes. That's partly why I became a scientist. I think I'd rather have been in the arts but there you're more exposed to it – to contradictions and to wondering if you're just a token black. And personally I just don't want to be bugged. As a scientist your qualifications are clear, you know exactly where you stand.'

CH: 'When did you decide to be one?'

Ashley: 'In high school, I guess. But the roots are way back. You learn these things from when you're a kid. For instance I remember quite clearly crossing the state line from the North – we had relatives there we visited by train – how they'd bundle the blacks out into segregated cars. That's how I knew we were nearly home. Once they pushed a pregnant woman and she fell, but no one complained. Only afterwards. They were too scared. You see these things and learn you have to look after yourself. Qualifying as a scientist is one of the few available ways. It puts you in the scientists' carriage. The nearest thing to immunity.'

CH: 'But is that where it ends? Are you that detached?'

Ashley: 'Yes and no – no, I'm not, because if you're black you're an obligatory activist unless you really bury your head. But personally I still feel withdrawn because I just don't see it changing, not inside a hundred years. And that's not a conclusion I'd jump to, I've felt forced into it. Here for instance – and here it's quite mild – schools get worse every year, people get poorer all the time, half the kids can't get jobs, washing cars if they're lucky. Welfare's given like a kick in the groin. And all the talk of fair employment, opportunity training, etcetera – all that just increases frustration, it's so small-scale and full of lies. And what's the common denominator? Almost everyone is black. It's just a fact that if you're black the cops will bother you more often, that your job prospects are lower. It's a state of mind I can sometimes suppress, being in middle-class surroundings – but you can't break away from it. Because it's not just race, it's deeper, the way the whole society works. It's built on antagonisms – race is just the most obvious and permanent. I used not to feel that way, I thought it was changing or at least avoidable. But it isn't. Race is the States. It's a national language. Civil rights hasn't helped, it's confirmed it. Black power talk bugs me sometimes, but it's achieved ten times as much. Everyone feels that – I've seen it in every friend of mine who's become an activist. They really have drawn their own conclusions, not just been swung by clichés. And they've either withdrawn or they're ready for violence. It's depressing. But I can't see it any other way.'

Saturday San Francisco seems to corroborate what he's said. We're with Mac and Maureen, close friends of Ashley's; he's a post office worker and she a primary school teacher. At the Bay Bridge the toll gate attendant, young and perfectly pleasant-looking, eyes us strangely and stares after us, literally shaking his head as we go. Presumably (though on the Bay Bridge he must see stranger sights than us) it's because we're such assorted colours, Mac black and Maureen white and all of us with arms round shoulders (which space compels in Ashley's car); except that is for Ashley, alone at the wheel like the evil genius of an ethnic wife-swapping party, or so it must seem to the attendant, who's still gazing after us open-mouthed as the next car awaits him. He talks to its occupants, still shaking his head. Sure enough, as Ashley hugs the slow lane (also obligatory in his car) they sweep past us and slow for a stare, a prosperous-looking middle-aged couple. Their eyes pop. Mac pulls a face and they speed on indignantly, their worst suspicions clearly confirmed.

Mac's hard to fathom. Exuberant one moment, silent the next, an opposite to Ashley's objectivity and to Maureen's reserve. Maybe it's this contrast that makes the three of them apparently so close, with a suggestion that both Ashley and Maureen are afraid for Mac in some way. His mood tends to dominate as we eat down on Mission Street and then go on to the Jazz Workshop and the Both And, Frisco's rhythm and blues shrines. When we're talking again about travelling, he's a lot more curt than Ashley: 'The best way to see this country is from the air, that's enough for me. It wasn't so bad when I'd just quit the military and usually had a bit of bread – when I was a fifty dollar bill nigger. That's the only thing matters more than race. But now we're broke and there's the two of us to travel – you can keep it all, brother.' Silence. But then he'll revive to ask us about the Caribbean, say, and react like a kid hearing *Gulliver's Travels*, as if anywhere with race relations different from the USA's must belong to another planet. It's a topic he won't let rest, in that he constantly role-plays black with 'baby' and 'brother' all the time and confidential communications always with other blacks in the Both And and the Workshop. Yet even here he's ambivalent; alternately vivacious, as if he means it, then jaded, as if it's just a ritual that he feels obliged to perform amongst the shades and Afro-styles of an ostentatiously ethnic setting. And not just there. Even outside on the seething sidewalks it's hard to tell, when he 'hi-brothers' yet another black passer-by, whether he knows him personally or just through this same stifling image.

Perhaps San Francisco influences him, as the whole city's a bit like that: so deliberately different and doubly so on a Saturday night that everywhere it's hard to know where performance ends and real begins. From Haight Ashbury hippieville to the tourist delight of Fishermen's Wharf, anti-image seems so contrived that it's an image in itself, an ironic reflection of the establishment it disclaims – as if the latter can't but consume such spontaneity as it allows, to regurgitate it standard and dated. The City Lights bookshop, where the beat of a new USA began, is already an ancient monument subsisting on paperback Kerouacs adorned with every fusty cliché – 'hip, crazy, fantastic' – and psychedelic posters of Ginsberg looking now like any other well-established radical guru. Even strippers are advertised like varieties of hamburgers: 'topless' and 'bottomless' and in one case 'double topless', as if drive-in imagery has acquired anthropomorphic powers. Almost everything shares the castration of the latest now meaningless words on the latest lapel buttons, sold at a cut price per thousand. Like encounter groups, California's current prescription for self-discovery; priced and publicized to death, they already sound like package holidays (one group markets souvenirs, pictures, pencils and little notebooks). Buy your self in Palo Alto. Selected for your income group.

Maybe only music escapes, too deep to be touched by it, keeps its uniqueness. It's Art Blakey at the Jazz Workshop and here even Mac appears to relax, though there's still a conspicuous difference between the all-absorption of older members of the audience and the exclusive in-group style, black to black, of the younger people: self now taking precedence where music took precedence before, an inevitable part of alienation's turning to anger. No doubt where Art Blakey's at, though, lost to the world, lost in the drums that he's been conjuring for thirty years. Plays with his mouth slightly open and eyes closed and the mood is still trad, timeless, gut-melting, comical, and Art opens up to talk as he plays, talks to the audience, to the group (to the horn player: 'You flyin', baby'), cajoling the cymbals throwing his shoulders at the drums laughing like a king then lost (like the bowed heads listening, the older ones) and after one number that ends with his drum sticks flying through the air to land in the audience: 'That lil number was completely unrehearsed, a spontaneous combustion you might say – me an' my friends here might never play it that way again. . . .'

(Ashley, back at the apartment that night: 'Mac's in some sort of down-spin, I can hardly reach him any more. When he came to San Francisco he felt it was really the place for him and it seemed that way for a time. He got a job with a big drugstore chain as a trainee manager and he was doing real well – until one day the branch got a new boss and he happened to come from Alabama. In three days Mac was fired – allegedly for not implementing some new accounting system that he hadn't even been told about. Well, he complained, did all he could – he even went to Chicago to the company's head office. But this guy had been with them for years and they backed him. So Mac lost his job. And once he'd lost it, that was it. Every employer he went to asked about his previous work and checked with the drug company, who described him as "difficult". So he had to take this post office job. And he hates it. Since then he's just slid downhill. He used to be one of the cheeriest, most extroverted people I've known . . .')

Peace

A Sunday night at the Fillmore, one of the shrines of rock music. A converted thirties ballroom, it's kept the features of its past: a huge, cavernous dance floor with big columns and a balcony, a golden ceiling like sagging drapes and a broad stairway with faded red carpets and dim-lighting baroque chandeliers. Strangely enough they go with its present, which seems to have chosen and preserved them in some unconscious folk recollection of lost and redesired emotions – it's probably no coincidence that the Fillmore's rival, the Avalon, has exactly the same history, also a downtown ballroom just saved from demolition by rock's renaissance of the live, communal music once rooted in spots like these. It's converted but not distorted by the psychedelic lighting, with its suggestion of a world half hideaway and half fantasy in rejection of the one outside. All-engulfing, it's not a trend but a norm, as is the style of the audience – not hippies so much as themselves in their own way, no longer obliged to present an image as in smouldering Haight

Ashbury, where we've spent most of the day. Ashley, Mac and Maureen seem much more relaxed than before and the feeling's infectious, as if here at least there's a temporary freedom from the undercurrents of the previous evening.

There are no physical barriers, apart from the ornate old columns posted with outline photos of girls whose contrasting nakedness is simple and genuine; and it's through this emptiness that the audience make it belong to themselves as their own chosen place. Figures sit and lounge on the floor and the legless sofas and chairs round the walls, like magic carpets in the shadows. Others stroll in a free-moving pageant, the long hair seeming near priestly and hats with an Amish look, also holy. The stage is less of a boundary than a focus where groups can be watched from all sides and followers can sit at their feet or drown in the electronic canyon of amplifiers ten feet high – the whole like a temple, Zen or Buddhist in the trailing and scantness of dress alike, which conveys tenderness rather than flesh, and the dry everywhere scent of grass burning by the altarstage round which everything revolves.

This night around the Grateful Dead, the Bay people's oldest rock group and loved as their own poets and legend (they live together in one large house, which is like the Fillmore itself with its feeling of everyone having come home): Jerry Garcia on lead guitar, who always seems to be leaping to sound having just appeared from underground and peering forward through small glasses set in a ring of black hair and beard; Pigpen on Congo drums, mocking chunky face and headband; Bob Weir on second guitar clean-cut as a farm boy on Sunday and then a blond ponytail; Phil Lesh on third guitar very thin-faced also ponytailed but more withdrawn; and a small dark percussion player, Afro-jack and headband with a scraper and bottles and spoons, an attendant sprite who moves in and out choosing his particular sound (sometimes going behind the amps to do his own experiments, once it's thunder and another time he lets off a cracker with a bang and pink flash then spiders back to see what effect) – these are the ones that front the stage while drummers and pianist are a hidden centre, a ring of headbands and ponytails, one with the figures drifting round them, with everyone, listeners, technicians and stagehands. A new folk of a new time needing their own new Lautrec, woven together by lights and shadows and plugging in amps like underground genies using electronics (as the poor in other lands use the West's material leavings, steel drums or old cans, to conjure a new art into being) with an ingenuity that mocks their source and makes them their own. (The use of the hall has the same intonation, pointed in its re-construction of something the present had cast aside.)

Jerry Garcia: 'Come on let's go' and he jumps to the mike, 'Hello everybody' and twangs and already everyone's with them as they move off into the sound that seems to come not just from them but the tender sea of figures too, like a bus ride for a picnic, say, with Jerry Garcia at the wheel and the Dead the Bay's own so that as they drive off there's no performance, too busy with sound, and everyone knowing the allusions and words so it's not players and audience but one as the lights pound man-gut pulsing – they're gentle at first even with the volume and as sitting figures start to sway Jerry Garcia comes forward at moments to sing not exactly a song just lines like pretty stones he's discovered meanwhile from peering into some blue beyond and as it collects and the temple shudders and sound goes through you the group huddles up (percussion figure a little doom-bird hopping between them in and out) looking inwards a single mould like the Potowotami drummers (same quest?) then drifting out and in – no pause for perhaps an hour and the whole hall rocks and drifts and sways, travelling on a sea of sound, one girl leaning back hair floating – Bob Weir out front (Phil Lesh comes forward, comments and retreats) standing in rock-steady silhouette and playing very straight and Jerry Garcia laughing singing 'like diamonds', 'while we can', turning back to sound collecting crashing dropping down to a little jig that keeps coming back, a familiar junction where people regather (some clap in time) before travelling again – Pigpen chants 'Turn on your light, turn on your light on me,' Jerry Garcia peers forward and the movement's the whole room now, not dancing, it's too concentrated, reverent, no individual dancers but everyone part of the single movement to reach where all belong in one through a subtly-growing smash of sound, exploding lights, a holy one (rock past protest into vision – as hardly numbers any more, just trips, nor dancing just this movement and looking in) and then as half the group comes forward the floor rises and comes towards them moulded single as them and with them – one – just Pigpen at the mike now telling them to love each other well – behind him two little girls are dancing, they've been at it non-stop like rubber bands (children of the group and always there, always dancing, Maureen tells us, must be as long as they can remember). And when it's ended they mix with the crowd and the two little girls with the other kids who are there with parents (no longer just one generation's sound).

And figures are still swaying and it's strangely quiet, deep quiet (which it always was and always deeper), strollers move gently, it's another place.

On one of the columns in thumb tacks:

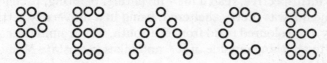

Clifford Newton, 26

NEWTON, *Clifford, 26, eyes that fix on you as he talks, blue-grey, and sandy hair. Grew up in quiet New England suburb, locally prominent upper class family, old house, nursemaid etc. Liberal parents, Democrats since Roosevelt; father a biochemistry professor, mother a painter, allowing children an independence indulged more on books than on teenybopping. Private school, then as long intended, Harvard.*

I was introspective, read a lot – inventing, painting, psychology – home life was pretty sheltered, being in a university setting – Jenny, our coloured maid from the South, was around the closest I got to anything outside of it – and hikes in upstate Maine and New Hampshire –

even Harvard wasn't that different except as my first time away from home. Also for this guy that I roomed with, a lapsed Mormon, he loved painting, you could sense the freedom it gave him, especially after Mormonism – in a way my life was like his, even the liberalism in my family had always controlled – we bust out together – drugs, just grass mostly, talked a lot, went to the movies – avoided my parents, then bang – at the end of my first year of college, I'd flunked –

should have shaken me, but it didn't – not much value in the things I'd had to do – confirmed when I went down to Baltimore, where my father was now working – the dullest, most conservative, dollar-minded city in the country – but it's the States – fell out with my parents but I stayed in Baltimore, as I had to work for a year before reapplying for college – my father – mad because I'd flunked. Also because we disagreed over the work that he was doing – connected with germ warfare – that good men could deceive themselves. Everything I'd grown up with began to feel kind of hollow, sold out to the USA I was getting to see in Baltimore – then civil rights – '62, demonstrations were beginning and I was taking part – they disagreed – world was too small, my taking part was a threat to his job – so we fell out completely –

most of my time in civil rights – under SNCC, the Students' National Coordinating Committee – wasn't one eating place in the whole city that was integrated – picketing – early days – hadn't much experience, especially people like myself – didn't see how deep it went, not the whites among us – thought everything would be for the best – I see it differently now, good intentions aren't enough – things got rough – beaten up a lot, more or less every night in the end, especially the whites among us, disloyal to the race, I guess – then the real blow – blacks among us turned on the whites – working with whites was a contradiction – group broke up – same thing as happened to the whole civil rights movement after 1964 – cut me up, people I'd been living and working with suddenly calling me a blue-eyed devil – now I guess I understand – hit me hard – I quit – nothing else I could do –

went back to college – had to keep on until I could see things more clearly – straight through college, still looking like a clean-cut American boy, though I hadn't much contact with my parents and I still turned on a lot, just grass and acid occasionally – graduated with honours. Mainly as a biochemist – graduate school, Johns Hopkins, back in Baltimore – when I came back for my second year and saw my desk space waiting for me I just turned round and walked right out, went back to my room and packed my bags. I couldn't go back. The experiments I was doing, the work, it had its own logic, but nothing more. I was tired of killing rats and maybe it would help kill people. And I was bored – more concerned with the workings of the mind. So I just walked out. I've never been back.

Not that I knew what I wanted – turned out it was mostly drugs – New York on the Lower East Side working as a bookbinder, living alone, just counting how many books I'd bound. And turning on. I hadn't gone beyond grass and a bit of acid before, but now I used everything, grass, acid, speed, cocaine, anything I could get a hold of. Then I found I was talking to myself on the subway and getting terrified of cops. And of being alone – snapped out and came here to San Francisco – friends here, I wouldn't have to get high alone – the fall of two years ago – lived up in the mountains with them and then on the coast, inventing things, watching the birds, things I'd not done since I was a kid, working a bit when I had to. And turning on, by now I was high nearly all the time, on grass at least – some good experiences with drugs, especially at this period, with friends, group experiences – kept journals and saw things going on in my life that I hadn't seen before. And things outside it, the way they were. All the time it's been like this except at real bad moments, things have been getting clearer to me, leading up to my present position as a Scientologist.

Our place on the coast – a real community, turning on, eating, living together. But people moved on, it broke up – I moved into San Francisco, Haight-Ashbury. For the same reason as most people – a pattern of relationships, a community that didn't exist elsewhere – people from all over and mostly, in their different ways, with the same intentions and values. Wanting to live their own way, free to create and work things out, or let them work themselves out. And then move on with whatever they'd learnt, wherever it took them. Whether through drugs or art. Or just through each other. But it didn't work out – became an institution, the media were eating it up, the cops were itching to beat it up, we became the alien group, the hippies. People used us for something to hate, to make money out of, news, commercials, anything they needed. That poisoned – into a different gear with hard drugs and more and more violence. And less and less understanding – went bad, it could still be controlled by the people who control everything, people I'd now call suppressive persons, now I'm a Scientologist. The hidden controllers –

set up a pillow-fighting emporium – might open people up, take out their up-tightness by shedding their aggression in play, pillow-fighting. But it went bad. Like the Haight – by then there was violence all the time, even killings – police put in hippie undercovers to plant drugs and start confrontations so's they could move in. People got bitter and endlessly high – one guy on speed all the time, once I asked him what he did and he said: I think about killing people. I asked him who and he said: well anyone – pillow-fighting emporium flopped – an aspirin for pneumonia. People would slash the pillows, pull knives, fill the pillows with scrap and stones – I'd had the Haight – wanted to get off drugs too, I was high almost non-stop, acid three or four times a week, and cocaine. I was scared –

got out with some friends – went to British Columbia – good for a while. Thirty miles from the nearest town, very quiet, I cut right down on drugs. Like the others. But that was the problem, it was like a mental ward, there were creative vibrations between us but they all got kind of tangled – broke up too. They're thinking of starting it again but it's not for me at the moment, I've quit retreating, I see things more clearly now and know what I have to do about them. Through Scientology.

Of course I can talk about it, communication's the thing we stress – certain beliefs, like reincarnation and the goodness of man, but more of what you might call technology – perceiving things and controlling our perceptions – process people with a simple auditing to remove the pictures, accumulated misconceptions – successively higher conditions of awareness until finally they're clear – the big word: clear – in control of their perceptions and free of communication barriers, which is the way to solve any problem – soon as we have clears instead of repressive persons in power, problems will fade away. That's why they're persecuting us. They're afraid, the repressive persons who control the system, they're afraid because we see through them – something I don't know too much about, I'm not that close to my clear yet and that's the only way to know, as Ron says, Ron Hubbard, our founder – world is that way and to me this is how we can solve it: through the mind. After all, everything's been tried, therapy, drugs, protest, community living, encounter groups, I used to go to encounter groups. But they're just for comfort – got to save things. Before destruction. I know it'll happen, we have people working our way on high levels in government, everywhere. Yes, Scientologists. You should see something happen this year as a result of this, something on a world level –

friends don't accept it yet. But this doesn't worry me, personally I know it's right, so I know they'll eventually follow – friendship's a fragile thing – communication barriers – Scientology's the only way – don't correspond with my parents either, my mother writes me occasionally, but my father hasn't in several years. Refuses to hear of me – doesn't bother me – too much to think about – the social and personal things, they'll be solved together. If we're in time –

if we only open our minds to its possibilities – like what Ron Hubbard said about how he'd come from another planet. Of course people are sceptical – narrow-minded – if your cosmology's open to it, you understand the possibility of solving pretty well anything – Scientology groups are happy – people coming in – good vibrations – before they push the button – all the lies – out of his clear – contamination – the system – repressives – non-clears – know myself and my friends know it, you need a clear environment to think in, like a floating community or what we were looking for in the Haight. Some place where people and things can't reach you until you're ready –

isolation doesn't matter, I know my friends will join pretty soon. It's the only way. I mean look at the world. Can you see any other?

CHAPTER 12

STRIKE:
The Central Valley

South from San Francisco hints of the lush Central Valley begin long before crossing the Coastal Range, as if its fertility's burst its bounds. The hills recede and the land levels, every inch of it croprich in geometrical lines and squares, lettuce and emerald alfalfa; orchards fat with nectarines, pears, avocados, peaches and plums. And in an instant the faces have changed: suddenly half are Mexican-looking, migrants and their descendants, heirs to the Okies' hungry dreams, their smaller than American figures crowding the dusty farming towns – shacks, dead-straight railroad, Main Street, fruit stalls, more shacks and then in a flash the fields again.

Even up on the bare Coastal Range the well-ordered olive groves and arrowstraight irrigation canals are omens of the valley's approach until suddenly it fans out below, dismissing the last gestures – stalls, motels and wine-tasting ads – to anything but the business of growing. For it's not, as its green suggests, an opposite to coastal megalopolis, but a billion dollar counterpart, with ownership of its biggest tracts deeply embroiled in California's ultra-conservative politics and overlapping with interests ranging from steel to chemicals; even this one-time utopia, now turned agribusiness, is linked with the military-industrial complex. Relics of a beaten alternative persist in a few small family farms, the type for which the irrigation, dating from the New Deal, was intended; but they're rickety and declining, cramped on to the valley's edge. Beyond them, apart from sentinel date palms, a lone plane and striding pylons, nothing breaks the varied green of orange groves, cabbages by the mile, beans, alfalfa and glittering grapevines in the dancing, pounding heat; hardly a human note obtrudes, apart from the non-stop traffic north and south on Route 99.

And the figures in the fields; men, women and children whose smallness is accentuated by the bare horizons round them. But they hardly seem to belong to it; they occupy rather the edge of existence, too remote from the affluence of neighbouring agri-business and thruway to register on the same plane. The disingenuous folksiness of the billboards advertising fruit in 1930s pop style, in counterpoint to its modern mass-production, rebounds when it comes to these figures, because they have the same quality; they too could be straight from films of the thirties recording the Okies' roadside subsistence. They echo every Okie image, whether stooped in the fields under battered hats big enough to shade half a body, especially if only a child's, or camped by the road in dusty lay-bys with nothing but the bare bones of living, raggedy clotheslines and little stoves and maybe an old folding chair round a battered pickup, their home, with the children asleep in the back. When we pass them on the move, overladen low on their springs and so slow that they appear to be limping, the humility of their hugging the side, to avoid the faster traffic, reiterates this remoteness. True, if our eyes happen to meet, they sometimes wave, but it's tentative, as if in surprise at this contradiction of their living outside the world they serve.

The contrast is even sharper in the lonely roadside settlements, each re-duplicating the last, just another standard link in the mass production process – railroad junction, elevator, silver refrigeration plant and then the crude, huddled shacks of the workers' camps and shanty-towns, hardly as big as the huge letters of the company names on the warehouses, DEL MONTE, DI GIORGIO. At best they're converted trailers or rows of one room wooden cabins crammed together as if the growers can't bear to lose a foot of soil; but many of them look homemade, built of anything to hand, tar paper, planks and old zinc, stepless and windowless and sharing a single tottering privy. Women bend over washtubs round a communal central tap; kids play in the dust. The only green is that of the crops thrusting right up to them, a reminder that they're on sufferance, privileged compared to some of their neighbours squatting in the narrow gap between the highway and railroad. If there are other buildings, bungalows and maybe a store, they only deepen the effect, as they're usually across the road from the straggling fieldworkers' quarter. Even in the bigger towns right by Route 99 the difference is only one of degree. On their outskirts patches of shacks cling to the highway's edge as if trying to register their existence. And then in town the same two worlds: the poorer one looks more settled here, with genuine houses, but they're still small and rundown and the roads between them unmaintained and the whole often cut off by the highway from the Anglo business section. When the fieldworker/Chicano half does intrude on the other, it's with the same quality of forays by another people: the massed faces peering out from the work-trucks returning from the fields; the figures in the supermarkets searching out the cheapest bargains and struggling back with them on foot, helped by their quiet, serious children, adults before their time.

It's no surface image, this look of the thirties. The faces may have changed and the details softened, but in effect they're the same people, for all the New Deal and *The Grapes of Wrath*, heirs to the age-old exploitation of the US farm worker, migrants especially; underpaid, unemployed for half the year and specifically excluded from the Labour Relations Act, which gives the right to unionise. The unsung half of the valley's history, they've always been part of it: first the Chinese, surplus after they'd built the railroads; then the Japanese; then Jack London's bindlestiffs, some of them Klondike veterans via Seattle and San Francisco and briefly organised by the Wobblies, but beaten apart as everywhere else; Filipinos in the twenties and then the Okies in the Depression. It's only since then that the Mexicans came, originally to fill the gap caused by the Second World War; but the movement continued, often illegal, but connived at by the authorities. For a hungry northern Mexico, it was a welcome employment outlet; for the growers a source of pliant labour, defenceless when illegal and always too weak to organise; for the authorities a handy way of keeping the growers politically content and ensuring a stable and low price fruit and vegetable market. Though many of the migrants settled,

California still called them Mexicans and kept them second class citizens, whether in Los Angeles' ghettoes or their miniatures in the valley – powerless, generally segregated and with little chance of improvement in housing, employment or education. Ignored by the big business unions, threatened by vigilante groups and faced with their employers' power to dismiss them penniless and manipulate local police and courts and even state and federal bodies, the 'Mexicans' had nowhere to turn. Such was the human background to California's main industry and the leading canned fruit labels in the supermarkets of the Western world.

Until 1962 – the year in which Cesar Chavez, son of migrant Mexicans and already experienced in social work, decided to build a farmworkers' union. The only one in the valley at the time was small and very narrowly based, covering mainly Filipinos and affiliated to the AFL, the American Federation of Labour, with its traditionally limited aims. What Chavez envisaged was very different – a return to an old style social union, reminiscent of the Wobblies, to challenge the whole status quo of the valley; a movement as much as an organization, run by the workers themselves and concerned with civil rights as well as wages and working conditions. If this was like turning history around, Chavez at least knew the valley well and in the climate of civil rights and the Kennedy era, time appeared to be on his side, especially in California, with more than its share of radical as well as reactionary forces. Basing himself on Delano, a fairly typical valley town of some 14,000 people, roughly half of Mexican origin, in a grape-growing area, he began canvassing patiently. The test came sooner than he'd expected. Three years after he'd founded his group, the Filipino Union struck at the big Schenley estate and Chavez amalgamated with them to prevent the usual defeat by scab labour from Mexico. Aware of the balance of power in the valley, he accepted AFL membership and began looking further afield for help. He was dramatically successful: 'la causa', as it came to be called, became a point of reintegration for much of the civil rights movement, temporarily set back in the South. Supplies for the strikers immediately arrived from liberal and radical organizations whose members joined in the picket lines to share the beatings and sprayings with insecticide long familiar to the workers. Outwitted by this new alliance, Schenley was finally obliged to accept a union election and recognize the Chavez amalgam (UFWOC – The United Farmworkers Organizing Committee), when it won against the big, employer-backed Teamsters. The resulting contract, which went beyond wages to unemployment and medical security, was a revolution for farmworkers. Immediately the movement spread: marches on State capitals from Texas to Michigan, as well as in California; strikes over in Florida (the West Indian migrant workers), in southern Texas (Rio Grande County, hourly wage fifty cents), even in the Mississippi cotton fields. But the other growers in the valley held out. A long deadlock set in, paring the conflict down to a microcosmic USA – on the one hand the vested interests seemingly local but in fact influential right up to federal level: on the other the strikers and a handful of full-time union workers, many of them volunteers, hoping to build the organisation on which full victory would depend. Amongst them a couple – Chet and Anna, friends of friends of ours in New York – who've been there almost since it began as members of the union staff, and suggested that we visit.

Delano's first impact is that of other valley towns, checkerboard functional and unvaried, more like a sprawling farm depot than a living community and faithfully divided by Route 99 into an Anglo-commerical and a mainly Mexican-American section. The union office isn't hard to find, a bungalow right on the corner of the Mexican-American half. The cars outside announce it with a pageant of 'causa' stickers, HUELGA – STRIKE and BOYCOTT GRAPES, only a few yards away from a well-fenced field across the road where the vines confront them symbolically.

The office is a catching combination of banter and intensity. Chet, dark and stocky, is busy on the phone, but manages to introduce us to the others whilst still maintaining a discussion with Chicago. No one there looks over thirty and most of them are nearer twenty, in many cases students who stayed on to work full time at the five dollars a week plus keep which the

238

union pays its staff. At first glance it's this youngness which makes them seem so intimate, though only at first, as they're equally easy with the older people who come in, whether field-workers or other officials from Chavez's office next door. But certainly it's conspicuous in comparison with the norms of US labour politics – from the banter and mini-skirts to the cartoons mocking the growers and posters of the movement's heroes: King, Ghandi, the Kennedys, Chavez (round and gentle-faced) and even one of Zapata, under which someone has added 'tierra y liberdad', the cry of the Mexican Revolution. Yet even more striking than their youngness is their equal professionalism, anything but starry-eyed, so that the sparkle seems merely a way of avoiding any pretentiousness or over-institutionalisa-tion. Almost everybody is bilingual and some are also Tagalog speakers. Legal documents are much in evidence and maps on the wall show the distribution-of-labour statistics and strike committees. At first it's unimaginable that such a new and small group with so few material resources should have the ambitions the maps suggest: a challenge on a nationwide scale to what in the last analysis is a slice of the total power structure. Yet it's obviously not a conceit nor just an act of faith. Everything that they discuss – statistics, queries, court cases – is handled with a cool hard-headedness that involves little idealizing or simple liberal indignation. And as if conviction creates its own logic, the hard facts do justify it: nationwide grape sales, for example, are down since they instituted a boycott, despite the Pentagon's weighing in against them by exporting much of the consequent surplus to the troops in Vietnam.*

It's the same in the Filipino hall, not far from the union office, where everybody gathers for meals – old Filipino bachelors, the union staff and striking workers whom the union feeds and shelters until they can find fresh employment. The matter-of-fact detachment, rarely without a touch of humour, with which strike issues are discussed: topics for the union's fortnightly paper which is set on two letterpresses nearly a

* 1971. With the current decline of this market and the maintenance of the boycott, grape surpluses are now being bought by the Federal government for distribution under the anti-poverty program!

century old between them and taken to Fresno for printing, no local printer being willing to do it; a current court case against growers who send workers back to fields just sprayed with insecticides liable to cause skin cancer weeks after their application. Advice is sought and information given with no apparent awkwardness or patronage on either side; as if it's not the least surprising, this identity of purpose between a young Jewish lawyer, say, so well placed, if inexperienced, and an old Filipino fieldhand who must have seen too much in his time really to expect many changes now. Perhaps the possibility is something very American, however remote from American norms; remote too from the common conception of the radical politics of the young USA as something rhetorical and naïve. And maybe there's also a tacit sense of mutual needs on either side. In this setting it's hard to believe that the fieldworkers are the same withdrawn figures to be seen by the road or even in Delano – any more than the young union workers fit the image of middle-class rebels. For all their light-heartedness, their dedication is almost daunting and though it's clearly not intended, they occasionally give us the feeling that our lives as non *'causa'* workers verge on the frivolous. One dazzling-looking girl, about twenty and of Mexican origin, reproaches us whenever we smoke. Quite apart from the health hazard, the brand we're using – didn't we know? – is blacklisted; its tobacco is picked in the South by scab labour. And with a worldly genius for getting the best return on her looks, she manages to make us feel not unflattered that she's noticed. As if, in addition to everything else, they're a talented team of actors, knowing that neither side in the conflict can afford to show a crack– in which respect they're well on top, having kept cool through everything from veiled assassination threats to having their toes stamped on by infuriated growers' cronies while on the picket lines.

Later, back at their apartment, Chet and Anna bring us up to date on recent developments in the valley. Since the first major strike, which won the union recognition by the bigger wine grape producers, others, especially the table grape growers, still haven't accepted it. Though pickets have kept production down, the union lacks the resources to force the issue to a head in the face of opposition not just from the growers, but from the local police and courts and Anglo community generally. So they've moved into a new phase; in addition to strikes and further recruitment, a nationwide boycott of table grapes, since most of them come from California.

Curiously, though it is in keeping with their movement's reasoned style, they've few hard feelings for the growers – even a note of sympathy. Chet: 'It's not like the South here – oh, there are beatings and threats of worse and the police do their best to unnerve us by photographing the licence plates of every car that stops by the office, things like that. But there isn't quite that Southern feeling of hatred. People here have met us with violence, but they're genuinely bewildered, especially the big family concerns that we're up against right now. They control the valley politically and even have federal level influence on farm labour legislation, for instance. Yet what they're defending isn't just economic, they've spent as much fighting the strike as concessions would have cost them. They're defending a very American myth – that they're modest, self-made men who've won the right to control things here and are now faced with conspiracy. And that is a myth. Their holdings are huge and far from self-made and were mostly illegal in the first place – the Allotment Act limited each family to a hundred and sixty acres, but they amassed huge holdings by registering them in employees' names. And what made them wealthy was irrigation – the Central Valley Project – but it's still on the books that growers can't use it unless they cut their holdings back to a hundred and sixty acres. They're so powerful locally that it was never implemented. So the image is false – yet even they to some extent believe in it. Which means that to question one aspect of it – the feudal way they handle labour – is sacrilegious, un-American.'

Anna: 'What really upsets them is the social aspect, the very idea of bargaining with their Mexican fieldworkers. They don't mind talking to us much because we're white, college-educated – although they know we work under Cesar. Maybe they'd accept an orthodox union with a façade of middle-class lawyers. But one like ours, with workers' committees and Mexican-Americans

at that – it's too much for them, they've told us so, though
previously they always alleged that the reason for not having
unions was that the Mexicans couldn't produce their own
leaders.'

Chet: 'They really stake their status on their traditional
patronage system and its racial overtones. That's why founding
the union is in effect revolutionary when it could be just progressive. Even today most growers still have segregated camps,
Mexican fieldworkers in one, whites in another, Filipinos, etc –
that's how they keep it all so feudal and stop them bargaining
together. Everyone's so tied to this that it was pretty hard for
us to get the white workers involved. Although they're also
underpaid, as semi-skilled workers mainly, they identify with
the growers – although most of their parents were fieldworkers
and treated as harshly as today's.'

CH: 'Is this generally true in the white community?'

Anna: 'Yes – especially with smaller people, I guess because
they're more insecure. It's funny, because many of them stand
to gain by what we're doing – business people especially, if the
workers' buying power went up. But no – they organize Citizen's
Groups, identify violently with the growers and see us in good
old style as "reds". You remember the red phone in the office?
It's the standard type they issue for unlimited inter-state calls
at a fixed monthly rate. But the electrician was in today and
looking at it real oddly. I guess he hadn't seen one before. So I
said jokingly: "That's just our hot line to Moscow." And he
really looked upset – I had to explain I was kidding and even
then I'm not sure he believed me. The myths go deep.'

Chet: 'And wide too, they're powerful. You know there's a
special report on us by the Un-American Activities Committee
of the California Senate? That's what I mean when I say we
aren't just fighting something local. For instance, if they need it,
the growers can always get money from some of the biggest concerns in the country – the Bircher type, based mainly on oil.
And in Texas, where our one strike so far was a pretty nasty
failure, landowners just couldn't lose under LBJ as President –
their support was vital to him, so they had Washington right
behind them.'

Anna: 'That's why we had to branch out and get nationwide support. First by involving the whole movement – student, church and political groups – which Cesar did, right from the start. And now with the boycott – it's the only possible way.'

CH: 'And can you really manage something that extensive?'

Anna: 'It seemed impossible when we began – but with only a hundred representatives, fieldworkers mainly, we've now got a boycott committee in nearly every major city. And it's working. Take Boston – it's been virtually sealed off to grapes by one fieldworker who can just read, helped by a single student. Or Chicago – there it's a high school dropout who worked as a field-hand, he's twenty – his committee's now affiliated with nearly every city institution. Even in England and Sweden it's just one girl – she's cute, I admit – who's almost closed off grape imports.'

Chet: 'That hurts the growers' pride too – that all this can come from a small office on the wrong side of the tracks which doesn't even get advice from a public relations firm.'

Anna: 'It's only a start though. The wine growers, who've accepted the union, are just part of the grape industry. And the grape industry's only a fraction of California agribusiness. And California's the tip of the iceberg – the situation's much worse in Texas and Arizona, say. But few people would have believed we'd get this far – so why not further?'

Chet: 'After all, what are we asking for? Immediately, just the rights that other labour groups have got. And even if we pressed for land reform, it's only what was recommended as part of the Central Valley project over thirty years ago. Smallholdings are economic and some of the land could be used for urban renewal – a logical step, as the present set-up helps swell the urban ghettoes.'

CH: 'Is this the origin of the Mexican-Americans in LA, for example? Were they once migrant workers?'

Chet: 'Yes, or their parents. That's typical in that so many of these problems are interdependent. That's why you're up against so much. But it also means that things like the strike can have really far-reaching effects. For instance it's easy to laugh off a lot of student radicalism – but people wouldn't be so concerned if it were all just play-acting. Students are a privileged group, so when they reject a system, what's in it? That's why people get hysterical about the SDS – the Students for a Democratic Society. And the fact that they're a minority, which people stress, doesn't mean a thing. Innovators always are. I don't think it's exaggerated to think that something new is happening in American society and that this is part of it. Even high school kids – when I left school, my head was full of ballgames, I didn't know right from left politically. But now a lot of our boycott depends on local high school groups – that would have been unthinkable only a few years ago. So what will the next few years produce? If activism is already changing Vietnam policy, I don't think we're hoping for too much here.'

CH: 'How long will you stay?'

Chet: 'As long as we're wanted.'

Reading the report on the union by the Un-American Activities Committee proves a strange experience – I hadn't known such investigations existed on a state level. But if this one's typical – a string of vague 'subversion' charges against union activists, full of insinuation and almost devoid of facts – they must be an industry of latter-day McCarthyism. All in all, a chilling reflection on Californian 'democracy'.

Chet meanwhile strums a guitar. (♪ Come mothers and fathers throughout the land ♪ And don't criticise what you can't understand ♪ Your sons and daughters are beyond your command ♪ Your old road is rapidly ageing.) But not for long. And even now his rugged face doesn't really relax, nor Anna's, slighter and finer-featured. Five minutes later they're back to work. Boycott leaflets and statistics, boycott committees, tomorrow's meeting. . . .

The Town: doesn't hint outwardly that it's the focus of what could be the valley's social revolution and a detail of the USA's. Broken in two halves by the thruway, physically and socially, it lacks any signs of a central identity. Slow-paced, but never utopian in the style of Walla Walla, its exchanges are very matter-of-fact and few people just pass time on its streets: those that do are lone and poor-looking, whether Anglo or Mexican,

and seem to be there less for the town than for want of anywhere else to go. So too it's sometimes hard to imagine where the
people on foot are going, generally Mexican origin or occasionally black or Filipino, when you see them vanishing down one
of the three or four central streets; wide, straight and dead-flat
streets, central only in their trappings, parking meters, un-
memorable stores – clothes apparently immune to fashion, not
a single bookshop, monsters at the movie theatre and finally in
every direction the gas stations and machinery depots, buildings
all so squarebuilt as to seem devoid of the details or idiosyncracies of human existence. It's not formally segregated, though
apparently it used to be – there are better-off looking Mexican-
Americans at lunch counters and on the sidewalks, if generally
on their own. Yet this prosperous half, east of the freeway, gives
you the feeling that it's the freeway which bounds and defines it
absolutely; that the far side's existence is tacitly denied by the
division. (In a recent local publication on the community's
history, almost the only allusion to the Mexican-American population was a brief paragraph on the Spanish-American Society;
as if it were only and for ever a temporary, alien group.) Though
in fact the other half begins even this side of the freeway where
the streets peter out in a welt of potholes by the proverbial,
rusting tracks: crouched by the big warehouses and bright Shell
and Texaco banners six or eight times their height, there are the
same fieldworkers' cabins, patched and re-patched, cellophane
windows, perhaps two rooms, washtubs and privies outside and
sometimes a small front-yard with a defiantly gay hibiscus.
Images so juxtaposed with the thruway and the planes overhead
that the whole seems like an overstatement, an intended hyperbole of the two halves of the Western world.

It's only on the west side and after we've been there a little
while (long enough to have been carefully identified with the
union office and so receive a nod or a wave) that what's going on
is apparent. The same houses as in other Mexican-American
sectors, ranging from modest to decrepit; the same old cars,
windowless, rattling, that save the growers' charges for transport to the fields and back; the same un-American sight of
figures walking and overburdened. But there's a faint new

vibrancy too, the cars driven without that humility, clusters of people talking, waving to passers-by; even the guard at Chavez's gate, though singularly unmenacing, is proudly defiant, as if pride is nine-tenths of the art of defence. After which we sense it slightly even on the east side – in the not un-friendly curiosity of the young white waitresses at the counter, for all their knowing that there's only one thing that brings strangers to Delano; in the barrage of questions about the world from a Mexican-American schoolboy who is sitting next to us. A sense (subtle yet encroaching hard on the black and white surface images) that even obdurate Delano, middletown of its time and region, of the USA maybe, can't long remain what it's previously been.

The next morning Chet and Anna hand us over to Marcello, a veteran Filipino who's been in the fields half his life and is now a union worker. As he's got the morning free, he offers to show us round. Small and crouched, with greying hair, ancient horn-rimmed spectacles and pencils stuck in his jersey top; face very soft and grandfatherly. The only counterpoint to his mildness is the alsatian he brings with him – something they've learnt from the growers, he explains, who use them against the picket lines. The inside of his small car has a flavour like so much else in the union and fieldworkers' world, one of complete detachment from the General Motors USA, old and carefully preserved, with his personality imprinted on it, so that it's rather like a home.

He was born in the Philippines, he says, as we drive to the site where the union is building new premises; came to the West Coast at eighteen and worked as a waiter in Seattle, sending most of his wages home to educate his brother and sister and going to night school himself. Then, when the Depression came, his own education went by the board as he had to work double shifts to keep up his remittances home. In the end it was only the brother and sister who went to college as he'd also hoped to. After the Depression he came south to the valley, where he's worked ever since, ending up as a foreman before he became a union official.

Meanwhile the bigger cars streak by, their inmates looking

back in surprise and sometimes open hostility at his BOYCOTT GRAPES sticker. At the new union site, with its handful of temporary buildings, another car draws up behind us, a family with a sick child who've come for treatment at the clinic. A wave to Marcello, as so often in this intimate world where everyone seems to know each other in a quiet community of purpose. He points out the various buildings to us. The clinic's just a trailer as yet, but they're planning a hospital, cooperatives, a social centre, the national headquarters, the local.

Marcello watches the family waiting at the clinic door. 'That clinic makes a real big difference. Before, we were treated like animals – worse. Animals they take care of, but fieldhands, no – you get sick, you get fired. The growers don't worry – there's plenty of people waiting for your job. So when people get sick, they don't say, they just try to keep on working. And then maybe your neighbours can help, but to get into the hospital in Delano, that cost a hundred dollars down, because they knew people were poor, that they couldn't pay their bills. Now the growers that signed the contract, they have to pay sickness benefits. And people can come to the clinic too. The doctor there, he works free – the people here don't like that, professional people especially. They tried to stop the first one. He was a young fellow like this one, the medical association told him it was illegal to help us. But he wouldn't stop. So the local draft board stopped him by sending him to Vietnam. But they can't stop us. We got another one. That's the difference these days, that could never have happened before. The workers here, we were kept right apart from the rest of the world – even from each other. But now it's all changing – these young people, the lawyers and students, we couldn't have done all this without them.'

CH: 'But was it difficult at first, their getting together with the fieldworkers?'

Marcello: 'Not so difficult. Sometimes they're new, they say things that hurt, mistakes, but not very often. And we understand why – we've been kept apart, they couldn't know how we lived, what we think. But they learn, like we learn from them. And we admire them. They don't talk about it, but we know they don't have to come – but they come. That's enough for us.'

CH: 'It was a very new experience, this contact between fieldworkers and students?'

Marcello: 'That's right. Before this everyone was separate, separated by money, it was just the survival of the fittest. Even the workers, the big unions, they didn't bother with us. Professionals too and the churches – they all had their own separate interests. Even our people, Filipinos and Mexicans, the ones that got an education, they forgot the rest of us. We were alone. That's why we couldn't do anything. We saw how people were against each other – even against the Jews, and we thought, well the Jews are white, they're Americans – if people are against them, how can we expect anything? Even the Church had Catholics against Protestants, Protestants against Jews – you think they were going to help us when they were all against each other? But now it's different – the church people are with us, they don't mind if we're Catholics or not, and there are Jewish people here, rabbis, students. It's all changed. People see things differently, they don't want that old, private set-up. We don't feel alone today. The students, they've got education, their parents have money, life's easy for them. But they don't want that any more. And the Church. They don't come to preach at us now, they come to help – that's all new.'

CH: 'Do you think they'll last, this confidence, these new attitudes to each other?'

Marcello: 'I believe so, I believe they have to. You see, these people, what they're doing is not just helping us. Because helping us – I can't explain too well, I never had much school – but choosing us means they move away from everything, from supporting the way things are. They can't just go back and be like other lawyers, other students, not after this. What they're doing is against the whole system – it means the system has to change. And that's where our problems came from, the system – the way it kept us isolated, powerless, minority groups. Raise our heads, bang, we were finished. But we're not minorities any more, because now the others are with us. And I think I know why. Because they're not so different from us, not now – they're like a minority too, because they're outside the system, they won't accept it. You know, I lived here most of my life and maybe when you live at the bottom you see things clearer, how people feel, why they're unhappy, things they don't see themselves. I see it too because here it's so different from how I grew up, in the Philippines. The fight to survive here, always do better, I've seen how it makes people insecure. How it destroys relations like between a husband and wife and between parents and children – the parents force them, then they lose them. People say it's a modern society, but no, that's very traditional. And young people don't want it now, they say relationships matter more. So they want some changes, like us, we learn from them, they learn from us. That's how we all understand each other, the people working at the union. But what do you think – you believe it is changing? You think our non-violence is right?'

We talk on in his car, like some anchorite's retreat in its independence of everything outside it. It's strange how this oldish man, who's seen and mulled over so much, has drawn conclusions so similar to Chet's about the situation they share and its potentialities. This perhaps more than anything else lessens the look of frailty in their challenge to these bland surroundings: the green waste of organised wealth stretching unvaried in every direction and the radio station across the road – the Voice of America ('but not our America', Marcello remarks) with its towering pylons and barbed fence, fortifications against the new message that neighbours it in the union site.

We've been talking all morning. Marcello drives on a bit before turning back to Delano, past the mile on mile of vines with the figures stooping between them or walking at the roadside; sometimes a wave, sometimes perhaps they're too nervous. He points out the different types of vine, describing the ways they're cultivated. It's ironic how much more he must know than most of the growers who profit by them, many of whom are absentee – one a banker, he tells us, another the head of a law firm. At times the atmosphere's almost that of the Caribbean or Central America – the palm-lined avenues leading to the growers' houses, the rows of box-car workers' shacks like the lingering slave ranges of a Caribbean plantation, the NO TRESPASSING notices and guard dogs at gateways reflecting the rule of a private law. Even the place names have a flavour of speaking only for a chosen few, like Richgrove (for whom?) where Marcello lives – hardly a town, just the usual campment that seems to have outlived its time. A few square blocks of crude houses, from shacks to peeling clapboard, with old cars and dusty lanes and yards dotted with derelict possessions. The blank fields envelop it all and over the road a stone's throw away are the huge, solid storage sheds. No attempt to dull the contrast or conceal its wider links; modern California's garden with its neighbouring railroad leading straight to suburbia's supermarkets.

Back in Delano Chavez's house-guard raises a hand as we pass. The house is as humble as any other, the open porch small and peeling, BOYCOTT GRAPES notices its only distinguishing feature. Marcello: 'You know what they tell the workers? They say the union's robbing them, that Cesar takes all their money and lives in a big luxury house. That's the level they've always dealt on. They think they can still win that way. But they're wrong. At last. It won't work any more.'

The figures in the Filipino Hall: which is hung with decorations of handmade tinsel and coloured paper that could be from a bygone Christmas or some traditional holiday, but not so much tinselly as bearing the signs of patient making, each a private work of art and together asserting a communal claim to the being of their own which the whole hall suggests; a being wrested from life in the fields, cut off from the other USA and existing in spite, not because of it. As if here at least it's been said: this is ours, the terms are ours. They're always there, the old ones at least, and not just Filipinos but Mexicans as well these days since the strike; they nod and smile or just let us pass, even silence an acceptance in a dimension as private as this (a note you sense immediately, as if you've crossed a drawbridge between the hall and the street outside with its over-generous police patrols). So you wonder how they see it – having preserved this privacy – the sudden eruption of churchmen, journalists and organisers, promising a new world too late for them (most are in their fifties or sixties), unable to give them back the past and maybe even endangering this being that the hall conveys. How do they see these newcomers' claims to understand what is hinted at in the lines of their own faces, in their hands and in their tired if strong sitting postures? Are they sceptical? Or too far removed? The older women are especially quiet in their colourful but very old clothes with only eyes kindled bright as if independent of the tiredness their bodies suggest: the men more talkative but very much amongst themselves, except for extroverts like Marcello, and often in Tagalog, which few of the newcomers understand. This too perhaps preserved from life like the hall, a fortified uniqueness. The depth of this privacy being a hint of the unfathomable distance (every bunch of grapes picked and every grain of soil turned) between the equally alienated heirs and victims of exploitation: and the hall, in its new, shared aspect, a first intimation of revolt, a drop in the sea of imagination which must begin somewhere to span that distance, maybe here. . . .

Chet and Anna have a meeting in Cutler, a small farmworkers' town some fifty or sixty miles up the valley. We leave around dusk, together with Irene, a big determined cheerful woman (Mexican-American and a long-time '*causa*' worker in Chicano civil rights in LA as well as the valley) who looks young to have a son in Vietnam; but then the son is only twenty. Route 99, six-lane highway, flickering neon-lit seventy with hardly an old car in sight and no suggestion of the world just yards away on either side. Cutler's a few miles east of it, a dimly lit straggling town which looks much the same as all the others housing mainly field workers; a frontage of small wooden houses with rough stoops, cleanly kept but unpainted in what looks like a generation.

We're ushered into one of them by Raul, the local boycott leader, a youngish man, Mexican born, but living here for several years. Inside it's just one main room, part kitchen and part living, with two small bedrooms to the side, the whole miraculously trim, given the five young children who greet us: a handful of pictures on the wall – the Virgin, a wedding photo and Cutler School, Grade II, nearly all Mexican-American; an old television and a shelf of books, mainly children's – the two eldest are soon back to reading once our novelty's worn off. Raul's wife is in the kitchen, pretty and slight for a mother of five, preparing supper for all of us. There's not much time and it's soon ready – a spread of tacos and enchiladas, beans and salad and hot chilli which she replenishes like a magician while the children eat in the living-room section, as there's only just space for us in the kitchen. Raul tells us a bit about himself, quiet but very self-possessed – their early years in the valley, when the first two children were babies; living in shacks provided by the growers, who could sack and leave them homeless the moment they protested at wages or working conditions or the breaking of promises which had brought them there in the first place. Often the camps had private guards and the workers weren't allowed out except under supervision, for fear that they'd quit to avoid their 'debts' for transport and rations. But most of the talk is about the boycott; in addition to the major campaign stretching right across the country, they're launching a consumers' petition to Safeway, the big supermarket chain, to abandon the scab grapes of which they're a major marketer. That same all-pervasive image: the incredibility, especially in this modest setting and with Raul's limited English, of their calmly challenging the citadels of the status quo. Yet again it's taking form. In four days Raul has obtained a hundred and fifty signatures, by no means all from fieldworkers. Anna tells him if he rings the office to ask for her, to leave no messages, not to be too explicit – they're pretty sure the phones are tapped. Raul nods. No surprise.

A hurried goodbye to his wife and children and down the road to the meeting in a neighbour's slightly bigger house. Forty or fifty people are there, nearly all of Mexican origin, sitting round in a quiet circle, straight-backed and faces intent. The older men have that same air of having seen so much that you wonder how they can still believe in change; heavy Zapatista faces, showing little outward reaction, that might belong to a Mexican village. But this isn't true of the younger people, including a fair sprinkling of women, several of whom have their say before the evening's over. A handmade banner sets the tone: a background of scarlet silk and on it in black the union's initials, UFW-AFLCIO, and the Aztec Thunderbird, their symbol. The family who live here seem progressive. The fair number of books on the shelves include a well-thumbed encyclopaedia: a snap of a sharp-looking high school daughter and classical music scores on the piano. Though far from prosperous, it's hardly in keeping with the alleged resignation of the 'culture of poverty', whereby all is explained and excused.

First an introduction from Raul: then Chet speaks – a greeting from the union office, then he describes the progress of the national grape boycott. He tells how it has spread to Baltimore, Boston, New York, Chicago, even Atlanta. The listeners clap, enthusiastic yet curiously matter-of-fact, though they know that most of the people who've done it are fieldworkers like themselves, who'd hardly been beyond California when the boycott began. Then Anna. (What do they make of her, the girl with the sharp Jewish features, fluent Spanish and pert figure, far from unfeminine, despite the tomboy haircut and a punch that belies her physical slightness?) She explains the special Safeway boycott. The chain buys an annual million dollars worth of grapes from the blacklisted growers; if it can be persuaded to drop them, victory will be almost certain. 'We don't have the money or the equipment, but here in the Southwest we do have the people. The farmworkers are one now and that's where our real strength lies – already on Wall Street Safeway shares are looking shaky.' She reads out the petition to Safeway to stop selling grapes or face picketing. They must get everyone to sign, even the children who go there for bubblegum, whilst people with credit cards should be asked to turn them in. Already a number of Safeway branches are unofficially doing as they've asked. All they need is more signatures and the management will start to talk. *'Viva la causa!'* More clapping. A few of the older men can't help smiling at her diminutive strength, but it isn't scepticism. After Anna, Raul; quiet and sharp, none of the abstract rhetoric of old style Spanish-American oratory. He describes the response to his local petition and asks them all to help him by soliciting more signatures – he hands out the forms, which include a space for addresses, no half commitment. Then questions; one of the younger men asks about the union's medical coverage. A woman sitting at the back: what are the plans for cooperatives and when are they scheduled to take effect? And though the women sit together, there's no taking second place, they make as much running as the men, discussing, questioning, criticizing.

Finally an old man gets up to thank Anna and Chet and Irene. He praises Cesar Chavez and mentions the name of Bolivar. More clapping. But in fact the atmosphere's far from traditional or ethnic, rooted much more in their common concerns than their common origin. Furthermore it seems different from its predecessors of the mid-sixties, from civil rights or Vietnam protests, with their flavour, for different reasons, of events as much as grass-roots movements. Here it's the latter that really emerges. A people speaking out for themselves, each a mind as well as a life, conceiving the possibility of action with an individuality which belies the common image of them. As if they, though once bemused by this image, have exorcised it quickly and firmly, demanding their part in what must by that token be a changing USA, a new creation, partly theirs, whose dogged beginning in itself ensures that it must somehow grow.

The lady of the house brings coffee and chats to us before we leave. She's Mexican-born, like most of the others, but long a US citizen and speaks perfect English. The schoolgirl in the picture is her eldest daughter, she plans to be a doctor. 'When she first got the idea, one of the teachers advised her against it – she said it's hard for a Mexican. I guess she didn't mean any harm, but that's what she'd always tell her. So one day she answered: "Miss – you know something? I've never even been to Mexico." After that they saw she meant business.' She smiles. 'You have to laugh sometimes. That's what I've tried to teach them.'

Nearly midnight. On the way back the others talk and joke for a while, but then they're quiet. The highway flips by, a smooth neon dream, until the potholes and dim lighting announce that we're back in West Delano. But neither Anna nor Irene notice. They're asleep, Anna's head in Irene's lap.

Peter Mendoza, 18

MENDOZA, *Peter, 18.* b. *New Mexico, garbage worker, lives Chicano quarter, LA, with mother, younger brother, two sisters. Thick-set, short, slight moustache, faint limp. Looks very Indian. Family's only earner – spends $10 per week on 'Mary-Ann', his 650 cc Triumph.*

Couldn't get work in Albuquerque, not enough to keep us all – my dad never did anything regular – plastering houses. Plaster himself, then he'd plaster houses, adobe houses for Mexicans – eight months we've been here – mother I'm going to LA – had to pay off that bike, man, and my kid brother Joseph, I wanted him to stay in school, that way he could really be something. I quit school in eighth grade, that's why I got this bum job – can't hardly read, not like you, I read maybe one page in half an hour. Wasn't dumb. Just I didn't get on in school. Teachers bugged me –

place we lived was up in this canyon outside town. Adobe houses, just one feller had a well – pretty cold in winter, we'd have to get up and chop wood before school. Made us late and the teacher'd get mad, bawl us out – white teachers, they lived down there in Albuquerque. Seemed they didn't want to teach us. Used to say it was wasting their time, we were bad for the other kids. Joseph made out better than me. I just used to fight – folks got scared, kept outa my way. Joseph's smart – got thrown out. That's why he came here with me. He wants to quit school – I tell him to stay – if I got rich I'd like to go back to school, night school or something. Or go in the army, they teach you there. Only guys like me get sent to Vietnam – never did want to teach us. They said so –

up in the canyon we'd fight each other – us guys from one side of the mountain, we'd fight the other side. But when they got mean in Albuquerque we'd go down there and ride through town, put rocks through the windows. Cops never bugged us, they was chicken – white guys from Albuquerque, they'd bring picnics up in the canyon. If they gave us food we'd let em stay but if they didn't give us nothing we'd start some shooting – one time an army convoy came through, around twenty trucks, so we rolled rocks down – they came after us – 'we're coming after you, give up' – went down the arroyo behind them and watched them climbing up the hill – we used to go hunting. Looked real dry but up on top it was flat and green, there was flowers and deers. Real nice. I didn't go with other guys – went alone –

you seen a guy die? I never seen it. Seen a guy shot through the leg – I'd like to try it. Shooting a guy – we killed a dog once. Hung him up for about two hours – still alive – threw him in the canyon – came right back again – real dumb. So we ran him down in the car. Old Chevy. Messed her up.

You know that 650 Triumph? I got one, pretty near paid her off. Ten bucks a week. Mary-Ann, that's her name – started when I was still in school – teachers didn't like it – didn't like my clothes. They weren't too good, we didn't have money. Then I bought this leather jacket – teacher said: 'Why'd you buy that thing, why don't you buy some good clothes?' Made me real mad, I'd worked for the money – he said: 'You always make trouble, why don't you quit?' First I said no, I was learning to read. But he kept on at me. So I quit – why are people prejudiced, you reckon? Like if you took a black and a white guy and there was nobody else around, just them in the whole world, you reckon they'd ever think about it? – You been to Alaska? I took a trip to Alaska once, it was real nice up there, no one bugged you, you were the same. Not like in school.

I was glad to quit – couldn't get a job. Then I got this job in a gym, weightlifting, I was good at it. Then I lost it. They tried to rob me, started holding back my money. But I got my first check – made the down payment on Mary-Ann – 'Mary-Ann' cause of this girl I was going with, Mary, she was real wild. Then later I was going with another girl, Ann, she was quiet. So I called her Mary-Ann –

might go back to Albuquerque – used to ride in a club there. When you get in a club, a one per cent, means you're the top one per cent, you feel pretty good – guys get outa your way – best thing is doing eighty-five, ninety, in a speed zone, thirty-five-mile-an-hour zone. You have to weave, chu, chu, through the traffic, run red lights, you can get wiped out that way and the dudes in the cars get real mad, only they won't say nothin, they're scared – here it's real wild, they kill cops, then they have to keep quiet. But fighting – the girls like you when you've been in a few fights, the club broads, they'll ball with you. And you can take your girl on the back. I got a new sissy bar, that big aluminum bar at the back for the girl to lean on, leans right back and puts her legs up – always tell if she's the guy's wife or just his girl. Girl puts her legs up beside him on the top pegs. Wife keeps hers on the bottom pegs, wouldn't look right if she had her legs up.

I reckon I'll stay in LA – keep Joe in school, pay for his books – like it here? You sure ask some funny things. No. Never thought I would. Got fed up with the job the first day I was doing it – get up, go to work, come back, eat, go to bed – don't feel much. Only Saturdays and Sundays –

say, how'd you know we weren't going to kill you? When you gave us that ride on the Strip, weren't you scared? We don't usually get a ride. Guys slow down and look at us, then take off. Cause we look Mexican, I guess. You wanna be careful, LA's real tough. Guys get jumped, big guys – I'm ready for em, turn and duck, I keep my fist ready – if I'm travelling real far, I carry a knife. You feel okay then – don't like people walking behind me – laughing at me, cause I look Mexican or cause I limp. I don't know. Sometimes I hate them. Everybody. All of LA, I'd like to kill em. Don't talk, they don't want anything – if a feller's nice with you it only means he's trying something. They want your money, that's all they want. They don't want to know you. And they don't have nothing to show for it. I mean you can get a guy working for five bucks an hour and he's not happy. Another guy, maybe he's making nothing, but he's working in the mountains, he's happy.

You know what I'd like? I imagine things, like going back to Alaska – else I'd like to kill everybody and live all alone up a mountain with a bike and a girl. Start the whole thing all over again, like that Adam and Eve thing –

believe you? Why should I? Nobody'd ever believe a guy who says he's a writer – I don't mind. You couldn't get me for nothing I've said – I like talking – you coming back?

RE-VISIONS:
Los Angeles

Perhaps it's because we're nervous to leave that we dally in the diner by the Golden State Freeway, anticipating the city outside as a huge scale reproduction of the diner's own surrealism; it's stranger by far than in previous ones even deep in the Midwest or nearby in northern California, where the dream-like quality belongs to the places rather than people, who at least admit an identity by a remark or a mannerism. But here the dream includes the people. Their expressions are hard to distinguish and their looks elusive, uncertain, temporary like everything else, highways and the styles of buildings: the Italian-looking waitress, but is she, or is the dark hair a rinse, the Italian face no more than a mask? The fat man in a plain sports-shirt whose eyes are fixed in our direction but don't seem to focus on us or even on the double banana split lifted spoonful by spoonful into his automatic mouth as if by some hidden third hand; the family, parents, son and daughter, eating a meal whose ingredients, from spaghetti to pecan pie, are all equally disconnected. When they speak – about the food or cars on the freeway – their remarks seem interchangeable, as if they've picked them from a hat.

Back on the freeway the all new traffic is a glittering anaconda with the head a mile away controlling every swerve of the tail· *♪ day after day more people come to LA ♪ sssh! Don't you tell anybody the whole place shakin away* · hills receding in brown waves, palm trees, glittering suburban homes but the gas signs are bigger still, spreading their golden plastic wings over a twisted sea of steel, a whole valley of car-wrecks ushering you into the city and the sun like an overripe orange, or is it another diner sign behind the grey eye-stinging veil · *news from Vietland*

*today · those big babies of the sky the B-52 bombers pounded Viet
positions this morning no definite news as yet but it seems those
Viets took a pretty good beating ·* ♫ *Galveston oh Galveston* ♫ *I am
so afraid of dying ·* houses with balconies sunroofs swimming
pools even private overpass leading right to nice front drive,
but there's something strange about it. There isn't a person to
be seen ·* ♫ *while I clean my gun · in the USA the free enterprise
system has provided one car to every two persons whereas in the
communist Soviet Union there is only one car ·* palms little gardens everystyle architecture orange trees, but no one there.
Just the faces in the cars, like fittings. Otherwise nobody · *and
Californians of today are the best fed best clothed and apart from
professional troublemakers the world's most contented people ·* ♫
sssh! Don't you tell anybody the whole place shakin away ♫ *there
she goes ·* no one, though horns blare as soon as we slow to check
the signs · *Rabbi can you tell me what the Bible says about Communism? ·* no one · *descriptions have been issued · all three men
involved are Negro ·* ♫ *Galveston oh Galveston ·*

And the city does have the same code as the diner (the Golden
Platter, it was called) in the traffic and on the sidewalks and in
the huge, square-built buildings, forbidding either recognition
or recognizability: suspicion if you catch an eye, who d'you
think you're peering at mister, and a feeling that instant
destruction is the price of frailty, should you lose your way, say,
or find yourself in the wrong lane; or the fusing of your mind,
should you expose a nerve end of need or quirk or loneliness . . .

FOURTH WAY
AWARE SEEKERS
If you have
read Ouspensky's
4th way, started
self-work and
desire to work
on all three
lines in Far
East (not USA)
send self
or outline to
Zamoro, 124
Puako Beach
Drive, Kanela,

I get cases like
this in court
every day — there
was one kid, just
eighteen, his
parents had given
him everything
and then one day
he just disappeared.
One of our under-
covers picked him
up down on the
Strip, completely
high on LSD. In
court he couldn't

Fuck you, he says,
fuck you, fuck you,
moving his mouth
very carefully in
the contorted ring
of his face (a man
in his thirties,
well-dressed, brown,
driving a very new-
looking Ford), as if
he's afraid with the
windows closed and the
traffic blasting by
that maybe we won't
understand how he

Hawaii 96743.
Donations help.
Share water.
First of three
times.

open his eyes –
he'll never be the
same again. He said
a voice had called
him there and
there was a girl
he'd met but he couldn't
remember her name. He
said he could
communicate with her
and that she'd be
at the airport
when we sent him
back to Florida –
she wasn't, of
course. He took
one look at the
bailiff who came to
put him on the plane
and said he was an
angel who'd come down
to lead him home.

feels about our
having switched lanes,
early enough for him
hardly to brake but
not to prevent him
darting forward and
pinning us down askew
so that neither of us
can move, joy in his
eyes and he must be
screaming, mouths it
again and again and
again.

A Friday night. Larry and Jean, with whom we're staying – both of them are art teachers at a smallish college in LA – have invitations to a modern dance show in a fashionable downtown art gallery. As they don't feel like going, they offer us the tickets instead – it should be interesting, they add, the choreographer who's doing it is young and well thought of in hip circles. As is apparent as soon as we're there, sticking out like sore thumbs in our informal but ordinary dress. It seems to arouse a scepticism, if not a phobia, in our share of the everywhere glances ('Why can't you dress like other people?' Or perhaps they suspect we're undercovers trying to pull a double bluff): much the reception that many of them probably get beyond these four walls. We make it worse by forgetting the name of a girl who works there, whom Larry and Jean told us to contact; we can only remember her description, at which the see-through dress usherette hurries off and whispers to what looks like a Maoist bouncer, who eyes us for the rest of the evening. The girl's not here, says the usherette – and where did you buy those accents, anyway, her eyes add.

The audience has an exclusive flavour. Most of them seem to know each other, from the elegant forty-year-olds looking exactly like the Beatles to the reproduction Fidels, down to the beret and cut of the beard, even the studied tilt of the head, as if they're discussing a rice-growing project in the once-bourgeois heart of LA. Even being different colours fails to give us any sense of respectable idiosyncrasy. In fact there seems to be a rule that you can't hold hands unless you are. The cool is a bit ambivalent too – an air of common militancy over-shadows the quest for uniqueness and side glances of mutual appraisal make it all a bit like an inside-out society ball. Girls in granma's ankle-length dresses (they're selling on the Strip at three figures apiece) and one in orange plastic boots and a fur micro-skirt, who gets more than her share of looks. Outsize pink-tinted glasses bloom like iridescent poppies, a silver-haired youth sits Buddha-like in red and green silk pantaloons and a cascade of necklaces and every eighth or tenth person is some sort of photographer: one stock still in a corner, shooting sly from suede hip, others stooping, diving and leaping. The one with the gravest expression of all has been squatting, since we arrived, in front of the girl with orange boots, taking close-ups of her knees. Now and then she pats his head.

The choreographer emerges from one of the two entrances situated in opposite corners of the bare white gallery. A young-ish man with a Jesus-like face, very set, and a curly beard, wear-ing sneakers and a black shirt that hangs out over army denims. He raises a hand, a hush falls and the audience seat themselves on the floor. As he speaks he seems abstracted, only half aware of them, screened by the spell of his thoughts. 'Okay. This programme is a collection of dances I've been developing over the last two or three years. The first one's called "Satisfied Lovers".' He pauses and looks around. 'The stage really needs to be bigger than this, about two hundred feet ideally – never mind, let's begin.'

The audience settles down respectfully as he places three up-right chairs in the centre of the floor. Figures then begin to appear from the left-hand entrance and walk slowly across the room; their faces are expressionless, eyes held straight in front of them. They're dressed much as the audience, though perhaps more casually, and most of them look in their twenties, except one little girl of nine or ten, who seems to take it less seriously, looking round and giggling cheekily. Occasionally one or two of them pause stock still and the others walk by; then they move on again. Once or twice someone sits down, still staring straight ahead, then gets up and carries on. About fifteen people are taking part, re-emerging again from the first entrance. The audience are as quiet as mice, eyes glued on the performers. After five minutes or so, they cease to appear. Silence – it appears to be over, but no one's quite willing to commit himself. Then one brave soul starts to clap and the others follow suit as if the preceding interval was simply in appreciation of the performance's lingering flavour (one which is faintly reminiscent of the faces on the Golden State Freeway or perhaps a procession towards a gas chamber).

The choreographer reappears, hands clasped, eyes lowered. 'This next one's called "Beautiful Thoughts". I usually do it with a dog and it involves talking, ideas, as well as dance. You know how a dog reacts to a person, he's aware of what's going on, if you move back he comes forward, he knows how you're thinking. But unfortunately the dog couldn't come, so I'm using a typist instead. Judy' – enter a girl, who brings in a table, typewriter and chair as he talks. Then another table with a tape-recorder on it. This she places next to him. He nods 'Okay, let's go.' He switches on the tape-recorder, on which his own voice is recorded. 'I guess all life is a performance, everything, a man, a table, a dog, it's all like a performance' – he snaps it off as the typist raises a hand. She transcribes it. Then nods. Then he comes forward and does a quick movement, tumbling, rolling and springing up – he dances quite well – and goes back to the tape-recorder. Switches it on again. 'Much of the performance is on stage and much is in the mind of the audience, all life is like that, I think it's important. I'm interested in how we perform and what we find out, I mean what we learn from each other by it' – typist's hand. She smiles very hard all the time as if to suggest it's just like home and asks him to go back now and then, so that it becomes hard to tell whether the commentary, with its intervals of dance, is intended as a sequence or not. Meanwhile photographers leap and prance, multi-snapping his every

move. Once or twice someone laughs, not sceptically but knowingly. After five minutes it ends. Applause.

The next one, he announces, includes a pornographic movie –
artistically intended, he adds. They're going to project two
sequences on the screen at the same time: an extract from *Swan
Lake* on one side and a sex scene on the other – and meanwhile
he, on tape, will offer comparative reflections on them. A pro-
jector is set up and the movies and commentary begin. 'The
movement in dancing really starts with the back and the legs,
whereas in sex it's the pelvis.' And so on, essentially serious but
leavened with carefully timed little puns ('at this point the
dancer emerges', etc); and these get the evening's first real
laughter, some of it a bit unsure, along with the more conspicuous moments of the film's obscenity, very much in the
camera's eye, in the way the scenes are shot, rather than the
scenes themselves. But it goes down well; lots more clapping.
And gravity returns with the next performance, called *Foot*
('or maybe *Feet*, I'm not sure as yet'), which consists of his
walking round with the same little girl and commenting
as he does so on the properties of the human foot. 'The foot as an
instrument of walking is a pretty neglected object – people don't
talk about it much.' Pauses, one foot forward. 'See how easily
it takes my weight, around a hundred and fifty pounds, it's a
finely tuned instrument. And of course we learn a whole lot
about people from the different ways they walk' . . . and so on
for another few minutes, the audience high serious again. At one
point some new arrival has the temerity to make a noise; the
choreographer looks put out and the audience frown. Finally
he walks off abruptly.

Back again. 'This is the last piece. It doesn't have a name, but
I've been developing it some time, it's one of my original ones
and I guess it's changed, grown quite a bit.' He claps his hands.
The actors of the first piece stroll back, joined by more from the
audience. They stand in a casual group, fixed expressions, in the
centre of the floor. For three or four minutes they're motionless.
Then the lights flick on and off and they turn and face in different directions. One girl puts her hands on her head, but the
others remain as before. Cameras click feverishly, photographers

diving and twisting like eels for a more significant angle. The group breaks up. A long round of applause.

Afterwards, as they discuss it all, a girl standing next to us compares it to *The Rites of Spring*. 'They found that pretty way out when it was first performed', she says. But in fact no one seemed sceptical here. Except perhaps for the little girl who performed a couple of times and giggled quite often. And knowingly.

SENSITIVITY TRAINING
For Self-Discovery
Personal Growth
Loving Relationships.
First Group Encounter
Free. Call 651–5055
for reservations.
HUMANICS
438 S. San Vicente
Blvd., LA 48

And then there was a case the other day of a couple somewhere downtown who stripped naked one Sunday after-noon with their two children aged four and two – and then they started to take a walk. She was black and he was white and they said all they wanted was to show that black and white were the same and to protest for peace. They got around twenty blocks before the police picked them up. The children had to be taken into care and I think the parents were both committed . . .

a lone dove
flutters and
twists over the
zoop-by of the
freeway buffeted
lost in a vision
of concrete
        spins in a
panic of white
wings
            back-tracking
trapped nowhere
to fly
        nowhere
            dips snatched
            smashed
        pale feathers
over free way

The college Larry and Jean work at is the centre in LA for the Upward Bound program: as an anti-poverty project, its aim is to give high school pupils from low-income areas – in effect the ghettoes, black and Chicano – the training they need for college entrance. Run by staff and students from the college, along with teachers from the schools, it provides a summer school and regular courses on Saturdays, with transport to and from the campus and a meal afterwards.

At nine a.m. on a Saturday, even before entering the lecture block, it's pretty obvious that what's going on isn't the everyday routine of this private suburban college with its Spanish style buildings, well-endowed atmosphere and groups of regular students lounging quietly on the grass. The racket's deafening, with a crowd of teenagers, nearly all black, milling round the lobby and the entrance of the program office. The latter has a touch of the liberal ingenuousness suggested by the program's name – pictures of Rap Brown on the wall, Chicano protests against the jailing of school reform activists and 'Back to Black' and 'Black is Beautiful' – all like a slightly despairing attempt by prosperous white USA to wish away the gap between campus and ghetto by echoing the latter's voice in belated apology for not having heard it before. But the fair, sharp-eyed girl at the desk, who introduces herself as Phyllis, seems cool and sophisticated; she suggests we talk later over lunch and recommends a group-counselling class which is about to begin upstairs. She grins: 'Just follow the noise, you'll find it.'

She's right – a good share of it comes from the lecture hall at the top of the stairs, so much so that it seems unlikely that there's room for a visitor. But the volume's misleading. It's produced by just half a dozen students, two boys and four girls, all aged about sixteen, gathered round the teacher's desk. As it later turns out, they're from one of the biggest high schools in Watts, where pupils and parents, working through the Black Students' Union, recently staged a successful walk-out to press their demands for black studies and better and more black teachers; and where they're still campaigning for more local control over the school. They're almost all inexpensively but extremely carefully dressed: both the boys in pork-pie hats, one lean and laconic and smoking, the other shorter and more punchy; a couple of the girls with elaborate Afro hair-dos, another, who does most of the talking, in a flower petal hat and flower pattern trousers, and the fourth relatively plain and homely. Apart from her they all yell as they talk, even at the rare moments when no one else is doing so, in exuberance rather than emphasis, as if they've so much energy that they don't know what to do with it; non-stop banter, quick and sharp and sprinkled with obscenities whose fluent, integral character takes the obscenity out of them.

The girl in the flower petal hat sits on the teacher's desk kicking her legs occasionally while the others weave around, all except for the quiet girl and the more laconic of the boys, who has his feet up carefully on the desk in front of him. With the speed and the volume they put into everything, it's like landing in a theatre workshop; perhaps for a moment it is just slightly laid on for the unexplained white visitor – all six of them are black – maybe to knock him off the presumably liberal feet which have brought him. But this impression doesn't last, as the tempo never slows, even when the instructor appears: a middle-aged black school teacher, looking a bit staid in their presence, who raises his hand in a plea for quiet. They greet him with a hubbub of teasing familiarity ('Hi, mister, how're you doing?), the noise continues for a pointed moment and then they settle down at the desks – though the boy who's smoking keeps his feet up and doesn't put out his cigarette. The instructor ignores him. He's obviously used to the challenge in their style, with its refusal to be abashed in the middle-class setting of the campus, still less by him as the intermediary between its benevolence and themselves.

He glances at the girl in the flower petal hat. 'So, Jenny, you got yourself a scholarship for next year.'

She smiles proudly. 'Matter of a fact I got two –' but the smoker interrupts carefully, flicking his ash in studied time. 'So what the hell's that, man, we don't need no scholarships, you think that's a big favour or something?'

Jenny makes a fast recovery. 'What d'you know about favours, Earl – anybody ever give you one?' He makes as if to dive at her, momentary chaos, then they drop it and ignore each other studiously.

The instructor changes the subject. 'Okay, so what's the news today?'

The second boy flashes a grin round the room and takes the cue deftly in mock commentator's style. 'Today's big item comes from Vietnam, where the white cats are sending the black cats

to fight against the yellow cats' – looks round again with a snap
of his fingers.

Jenny: 'To keep what they stole from the red cats.'

Earl: 'RIGHT!'

Instructor: 'Okay, Eddie, okay, I just happened to mean
right here – '

Eddie: 'Happens right here, mister, blacker you are, quicker
you go.'

Instructor: 'I mean what are we going to do today? An
evaluation of the program, right?'

Earl: 'Aint that your job?'

Instructor (unruffled): 'And yours. You all want to write
something about it?'

Earl: 'I aint so sure.' (Looks around.) 'I don't dig writing too
much, I'm more of a talking cat' (drawing it out), 'don't have
no college education.' (To one of the girls with an Afro-cut):
'What you say, Clara?'

Clara: 'I go with that, let's talk about it, just any way we
want to talk.'

Instructor: 'Okay, but let's stick to the program. Any comments?'

Jenny: 'I got one. About the girls' rooms – the rooms right
here on campus that we use for summer school. How come they
don't allow boys to visit girls in their rooms?'

Instructor: 'Well, it was part of the agreement that when we
used the campus we'd accept the same rules as the regular
campus students. And that was a rule they voted themselves,
the regular girl students here – that they wouldn't have boys
in their rooms. They decided – '

Roars of laughter. 'Yeah?' 'Oh baby.' 'Man, those cats do
have problems,' and more such well-warranted banter flying
round like a volley-ball that the instructor just can't catch, until
the second girl with an Afro puts up her hand determinedly.

Instructor: 'Right, Andrea.'

She looks round scornfully at the others. 'How about you all
quit foolin? Mister, I want to ask you something. I don't see
no sense in discussing the program unless we discuss school too –
cause that's what really matters, the program's just something

extra. We can't make no use of it unless conditions are right at school. Anyways, most of the students there aren't even on the program. So I'd like to ask you somethin – you think the changes they've made in the schools – like the changes we had since the walk-out – you think they're good, you think they're enough?'

Instructor: 'Well, they've met most of the students' demands – we have black principals and teachers.'

Earl laughs sceptically, but the instructor has already been checked.

Jenny: 'You believe that? They look black, but they're not black. Being black is thinking black. Most of them's Negro, not black – '

Instructor: 'You mean they're token?'

Jenny: 'I mean they're Negro, same way as other folks mean when they call a guy a Negro. Or a nigger, aint no difference. Guys that look black but think white, like white folks have taught them to think, like they want us to think – "Yes, boss, thankya boss, that's pretty nice of ya, boss". Seems to me some of them's that way, they're just there to buy us off. Those folks think we're going to be happy just because they can find a few niggers who can play their game for them. Shiiitttt – '

Instructor: 'Okay, okay, we have a visitor – '

Earl: 'So? You want us to tell him yeah, we're gettin on pretty nice down there since they sent us a couple of blackmen?'

Instructor: 'Okay, what I mean is they changed the syllabus too, right? You have black studies now, Afro-American history, literature. Isn't that what you were asking for?'

Jenny: 'Sure, that's a part of it, but that's nothing special, is it? They should have been doing that all along, instead of just pretending black literature didn't exist. And they're still tellin us what we can and can't do – the teacher said so. Like Malcolm X, we can't discuss him in class. Those folks are just trickin us again. And now they banned the Black Students' Union. And that's why – cause they were the ones led the strike and they won't stand for just buying us off – '

Eddie: 'And the cops aint gone, they're right around the campus. And plain clothes guys right on the campus – you think they'd need cops there if they didn't know something's still wrong?

Instructor: 'So tell me this. The Black Students' Union – what do you think it's all about?'

Andrea: 'It's like they say – to make us aware of ourselves, proud of our own black history. When they taught us history before, it was like we didn't exist.'

Instructor: 'Right – but the Black Students' Union now, you know they're just power-driving. If something's wrong, it's the system needs changing and all the Union's doing now is making a noise and talking black, telling you to get naturals, Afro-cuts and all that. That won't change the system, will it?'

Jenny: 'So what will? Maybe you're right, I get tired of the BSU, they're so ape on being black. Black is beautiful, all that crap, I don't need no one to tell me that. Tell them white folks, don't tell me. But I still need a decent school. Like better books, better teachers – half of them don't teach you one thing. They're just reading out of some old book – and our school doesn't get the same money like the white schools, that's a fact. It's still a fact. So what's going to change all that? Don't seem like they're going to change it, so maybe the power-driving's the way, maybe the BSU is right – so's in the end we can change it ourselves.'

Eddie: 'That's right. That's why they keep the cops there – those guys know nothin aint changed. Our school, man, it always was like jail – no pictures, everything locked, the cops. I ain't forgotten what they told me – they said: "boy, you make trouble for us and we'll get you soon as you're out of the gate".'

Meanwhile the quietest girl, who hasn't yet spoken, has her hand up. Lacking the others' poise, she seems nervous. The instructor nods at her – maybe he's hoping she'll cool the debate, by now pretty much beyond his control. 'Mister, I want to say something about coming up here. When I told my mother where we came for this Upward Bound program, she said: "Is that right? I worked around there." When I was a kid she worked for some white folks, domestic work. And then she said: "It's nice up there, I always liked going up there." I guess that got me thinking about it. Even for domestic work I guess some place like this was nice – with clean streets and no cops in your way. And you know that's just about the reason why I like to come up here. Sometimes I don't even want to go back. So what's the difference? It's the same for me like it was for her. The program doesn't change where I'm living, it doesn't change our school, nothing. We get on back and it's the same. The program's foolin us, that's what it's doin.' She takes a breath, as if she herself is a bit surprised at how much she's said; and the others, quieter now. And the instructor. Then she goes on, as if it's been waiting so long to be said that, now she's had the nerve to start, it has its own momentum. 'It's down there that matters. How about my brother, he aint going to come. The program – you know what they should have, they should have some "Downward Bound program", not this Upward Bound one.' She begins to trail. 'It's foolin people.' Then she suddenly nods in my direction. 'Like him – he won't see nothing here, but he comes here to find out about us. If he wants to find out, he should come on down there. That's where it's real.' (One of the boys: 'You're talkin baby') 'But he comes here. It's foolin him too. And he'll go foolin other folks, tellin em it's nice for those kids – '

Instructor (embarrassed): 'Okay, okay.' (He hesitates, as if he hasn't an answer, but vaguely recalls some formula for which he's groping urgently). 'If that's how you feel, that's all right, but just power-driving won't get you places. That way nobody wins, things just keep on getting tougher – you've got to be constructive – '

Earl: 'Shittt!'

For a moment the instructor has exactly the expression of the court judge in Chicago after the outburst from one of the women about the prospects for her children: the same well-meaning hopelessness, even here in response to younger people who do seem to have a chance and from a man who must in some way share the experience from which they speak. But he keeps trying. 'That's no answer. If you feel that way, what d'you intend doing about it?'

Earl: 'Doing about it? If we're planning on doing something it don't make no sense talking about it – cause those cats aint going to give us nothing. We gotta take it, aint gonna warn them.'

Jenny: 'We have to fix it so's we can choose for ourselves, that's what we want. Not some big preacher or boss there in city hall or the school board telling us what we can do. They never even been to our school – '

Suddenly the bell rings. They jump up automatically and it's back to the same exuberant clatter as before the class began. As she goes by the one called Jenny swings her bag over her shoulder and drops a remark in my direction, mocking but challenging too, perhaps. 'Don't forget your invitation, mister.' They disappear down the corridor, swallowed up in the milling crowd. The instructor seems tired. He just nods goodbye and follows them out.

Over in the lunch canteen there's a blockage at the entrance, where they check identities before students get in for their free lunch. It appears that one boy is either masquerading as one or else had his name left off the check list. Phyllis and I get by without seeing the outcome, but it's a symbolic reminder of everything that was said in the class: of the question of just how much a programme like this can possibly mean in a world where it has to be re-stated that it's only for the few and also assumed that others may be here simply because they need a meal, in which case they must leave.

Phyllis isn't surprised at what I've heard. 'Some ways I already feel that what we're doing belongs to the past. Not that it hasn't succeeded in its own limited terms. Three-quarters of the program students have gone on to college since it began and they're not even high-risk students in college – their drop-out rate is below average. But there are only seven program centres in California and in LA alone the school population's increasing by something like 25,000 a year. And our intake's about a hundred. In fact it's less than that now, as they've been cutting our funds back. Partly because of Vietnam and partly hostility to the program – I guess you know how reactionary California can be. And these kids, the students, they know what this means. It strikes me they see things in a very un-American way. They've become very political. Just getting a break isn't what

they want. Maybe it was, but it isn't now. They want a change
for everyone and projects of this scale don't offer it. All we've
shown is that maybe it could have been done, if the will and the
circumstances existed. But they don't, even here. You wouldn't
believe the comments we get, even from the campus staff. "These
ghetto kids just use the campus for yelling complaints" –
"They've no gratitude" – "They're dangerous", etc – mostly
because they know they're militant and feel that our real job is
to wean them out of it. Anyway, it's now all scheduled to come
under state instead of federal control. And with Governor
Reagan, you know what that means.'

'The end of it?'

'Right – they've said as much, in their roundabout way of
course. So we'll be back to the status quo, or a patched up
version of it. And when there's trouble in the schools, they'll
just send the police in. Like in the past. Though there's one big
difference. These kids won't stand for it much more and these
days they know what they're doing. As you've seen.' She looks
around to where they're sitting, very much in blocs of their own,
separate from the regular students. 'And they say that California's the USA of ten years ahead. Those kids were right, though,
you don't get an honest picture of things here. Like I said, this
already feels like the past. Whatever the outcome's going to
be, it'll begin in Watts, not here. I'm convinced of that now.
You should go there. If you don't mind sticking your neck
out.'

A day or two later it's arranged and I'm walking towards a
cluster of buildings surrounded by a high wire fence and looking
less like a high school than an ageing military compound. In this
it matches the Watts around it, which gives a superficial impression of abandonment rather than anger, mostly separate
frame houses less cramped then I'd expected, even suggesting a
vanished comfort. A bit like a hugely enlarged version of the
black district in Ithaca; as if the common theme of ghettoes
isn't the rats and the fierceness of Harlem so much as the air of
having been used over and over and over again, until they're
finally ready for blacks as the eternal clientele of the second or

fifth hand side of the States, one through which other groups have passed in a hard but single generation.

Getting closer, I'm remembering Phyllis's warning: 'If you don't mind sticking your neck out.' Already, just stepping in here from the other LA seems so artificial and makes me feel so conspicuously white that my also being foreign doesn't promise the protection it usually affords. And right at the door the feeling's confirmed by a hard look, straight in the eyes, from a tall, graceful girl (the more disconcerting, as she knows, for her grace. And for my at least knowing she's right. Why am I here? So that for one absurd moment I feel like blurting out: they asked me.) But strangely enough it's about the first and last time this happens; so that maybe it's just a retort, from the quick intuition which does abound, to my hesitation at the door. A suggestion that she sees that I'm nervous and finds it naïve. She knows, I'm sure, that it's this suggestion which makes me ask her the way to the administration's office: an attempt to show her she's wrong. Which she isn't. She nods down the corridor. 'Right there.'

It's as they described it. A seemingly endless corridor without a picture on the walls, painted an indeterminate colour somewhere between green and brown, with its doors generally locked, to judge by the keys involved in opening them. In the office the atmosphere is outwardly cheery and competent. Then outside, with a break between classes, there's the same exuberant pandemonium as on the Upward Bound program. And as it spills over into the office, the teachers and secretaries suddenly seem strained; their interaction with the pupils suggests a constantly anxious effort to keep this flood of young energy from breaking out in all directions, now that the pupils have tasted power with the success of the recent walk-out and must be increasingly aware of the limits to what the authorities will concede to the school or the ghetto. Fortunately, with this avalanche of pupils' problems and requests, they hardly have time to do more with me than register who I am and leave me to my own devices. A handshake with a pleasant principal who, whether or not he's one of those to whom the pupils' strictures apply, is apparently tolerant enough to accept a casual observer on his presumably uneasy terrain. Then I'm given a list of classes with details of time and place and allowed to wander as I please.

It turns out that, despite Phyllis's words, I'm surprisingly ignored by the pupils, apart from that first look at the door. But why surprising? Why shouldn't I be? It suddenly comes home how hard it is in this land of turmoil not to see everything and anticipate everyone's reactions in terms of surface, group features, whether racial or otherwise. And it makes me a bit ashamed to have assumed that this would hold here, that attitudes wouldn't be more individual. The ease of being here is a rebuke. But it's more than that, given that I brought the assumption from a long while now in the USA and in that dominant part of it, middle-class, white or what you will, which formulates the preconceptions with which reality is described, in this case as black or racial; a suggestion of how fixed such assumptions are and how elusive understanding can be even in this open society overtly devoted, maybe over-devoted to it. (What then of how I've seen the rest? Too late for that though.) Because the vitality's here all right, but as something far more striking than just energy or resentment expressed in merely racial terms; something burning and coherent in precisely its apparent freedom from the racial finalities conventionally attributed to it, presumably in standard response to the outward symbols of Afro hair-styles and shades. So that they don't seem just young and innocent in avoiding ethnic clichés and the aggression these entail (with which June and I are over-familiar from adults of any colour in several corners of the world). Young, yes. But innocent, no. Sophisticated, rather, in their evident awareness of the clichés' inadequacy for confronting the surrounding world; a sensibility subtler by far than my own nervous preconceptions ever allowed me to expect.

With this nervousness receding I find myself enjoying the school, which is something I didn't anticipate; temporarily forgetting its issues for the simpler pleasure of just watching its vitality. An indulgence perhaps, given that I'm here to do more than window-shop on life. But it's one of the rather few times that I've managed to escape from a traveller's USA to its every-day counterpart, so that the faces, figures, noises, going-by and corner games, as a sequel to the earlier level, have a more than casual impact: illustrating remembered voices (Sara's, say, or Olga Green's), contrasting with others (Louis Forbes), faintly paralleling several (Saul and Judy, Chet and Anna, the Seattle group); or teasing the imagination by their sheer coexistence with others (Cap'n Charles Tawney or the Hendersons, in this same USA). Everything that's going on reiterates this country's tangy quality, which for me has come to lie – as if I were painting rather than writing – in the memorable uniqueness of its every human detail as the visual counterpart to its bigger human dramas. Dramas of which one is here, but from which I'm temporarily distracted by the brightness of these images in defiance of their gaunt and far from memorable surroundings.

The students' chic being one such image, all the more conspicuous for the expensive dowdiness which characterizes most of LA. The girl with a flaming orange rinse and square blue shades pushed up on her forehead who comes across to ask me the time, partly in curiosity and partly no doubt to be admired, which she is; a private answer, unique and she knows it, to the standard Capri pants and expensive wigs of that other LA. Or the stance of the tall boy at the corner who watches me briefly and casually in a way which precisely defies any particular interpretation, especially the one which might be expected. The noisy, rampaging gaiety, exchanges between boys and girls, girls being watched and each playing back with their own private game; no lull in it. The eager high-seriousness of one group when the door opens from a class which must have caught their imagination. The very adult quality of most of them, for all their bounce; the boys in their pork-pie hats, the girls very much young women, as if the changes of which they're a part, as much as the traditional Watts, have blurred the line between teenage and adulthood. The whole producing an effect almost exactly the opposite of the apathy or aggression which convention often imputes to black or any other youth. So that it's something of an effort to turn from the almost lulling effect of these random images to the question of what holds them together.

Whether I'm in the mood for it or not, though, the classes I attend tell a clear story. The first, on US Government, is taught by a stolid character apparently in his late fifties and a member of the old teaching guard. Since he's survived the walk-out, he must be one of its better examples, but although he seems well-intentioned it's hard to see how either he or the way he presents his theme – 'the potential conflict between freedom and security' – could catch his pupils' imagination. (Even its implicit irony for them as an all black class only arouses one muttered comment from a sceptic at the back: 'Like here we have the security, huh?') It sounds as if he's been giving the course, without any changes, for many a year. Keeping very much to the textbook of specific constitutional cases, he never arouses any discussion, though most of the class seem studious enough – just factual answers to factual questions when a particular student is asked. Their silence suggests that the hollowness of his conventional premise, that all Americans have always enjoyed a balance of freedom and security, makes them doubt the value of their being in the classroom at all. And when he does digress for a moment, he can't help preaching at them in laboriously pointed way, rather than opening a dialogue: 'If you feel your freedom's challenged, then you have to assert your rights, but you have to do it lawfully. Otherwise there's just anarchy – right?' Put this way, it gets no reaction, as if they regard what he's teaching and preaching as so intrinsically partial that it's not worth an argument.

He obviously wants to be friendly when he comes to talk to me after giving them something to write. But he does so as if my views are bound to be the same as his – or rather as if for a sane adult there could be no alternative. He seems to accept the changes in the school, at least in the syllabus, but not the way they occurred, under pressure. It's undermined discipline, he says. Yet he doesn't seem to admit the question of whether they could have been achieved by anything other than popular pressure; when I put it, he skirts over it. He also talks about his pupils as if they simply weren't in the classroom, either for me or for him. 'Of course their home life's a problem, it makes it hard for most of them to be strongly motivated. A lot of them come in here right off the streets.' The boy just in front of us can't but hear and his pen pauses, if briefly. Nothing more though. The only apparent retort to it all is the pointed defacing of the copy of the Bill of Rights on the wall. Under it someone, presumably the teacher, has written: 'Only neglect can destroy this document.' But it's not the last word. Has he noticed? Someone else has added: 'It sure did.'

The next class is far from smooth-running, obviously very new; but in spirit – and some of the same pupils are there – it's a generation younger. Taught by a man in his twenties, it's on Afro-American literature; they're covering the historical background. It's like a cooler, rationalised version of the corridor exchanges. Questions, answers and comments fly and they all seem so caught up in it that there isn't even a sign of the usual contingent of backbenchers that haunts the classrooms of the world: the cynics, if they existed, have apparently been swept off their feet and, whilst there are slower individuals, the striking thing about them is how eagerly they take part, their doggedness overcoming their difficulty in expressing themselves – pupils who give the impression that traditionally they'd have passed through school, certainly a ghetto one, with hardly a single question or comment. At the same time the questions they ask and the basic level of the introduction suggest how incredibly shut off from all this they must have been. The notion that traditional civilizations ever existed in Africa is clearly still a novelty, one that continually recurs with a note of half wonder in their questions: and the English-speaking black Caribbean seems to have been a closed book to them, despite its analogies and its considerable influence on the modern black USA. The same is particularly true of African independence movements, even the current ones like Frelimo; their very existence seems such news that one wonders if some guiding power, seeing a potential example in them, hasn't censored them from their horizons. Yet, for all the dizzy effect that these novelties might have, the atmosphere is rarely one of simple ethnic rhetoric. One girl finds it hard to accept that traditional

African slavery was any less cruel than the New World's, even though in suggesting this the teacher has offered an economic, not a moral, interpretation. ('But, Mr Johnson, you could spend all day talking about different people saying they did this or that – but don't you think they were all different, the whites and the blacks, I mean? Like you couldn't say that one was cruel and the other wasn't.') And the argument lasts a good while, with plenty of voices on either side. They seem to have realized, from learning how perverted truth has been, how little the effort would be worth if it merely swung in the opposite direction. When the bell goes – and for me too it seems a lot sooner than last time – they don't leap up and rush for the door as they appear to in most classes. The discussion goes on, first in the classroom and then in casual groups outside.

The teacher looks limp. 'This class keeps me busy. Still, it's worth it. How did you find it?'

'They seem very involved. And open-minded – I guess I expected them to be more dogmatic, prey to clichés. But they're not.'

'That's good, I'm glad.' He glances at me. 'I guess that's what many people expect. So maybe you learnt something too. I always do, every class. You want a coffee?'

Up in the staff-room he describes how it's been since the new courses began, mainly with fresh teachers, several of them, like himself, from well-known black colleges. 'It's pretty mind-blowing, what's happened. When I first came here the kids were miles away from you, they'd hardly respond at all. Everyone thought they were just passive. They believed they thought like the older people, you know the old proverb: "The black man has the least to live for and the most fear of dying." And the teachers taught accordingly. But in fact it was exactly this, the teachers' own attitudes, which made the kids hard to reach. Most of them would just read to the class. Or else they'd come in and write on the blackboard "Read this" or "Do exercise whatever-it-is". And if half the class was asleep – which they usually were, with the teaching so poor and irrelevant books about suburban, middle-class families – then they'd just let them sleep. It was less trouble that way. If a kid rebelled, he was dismissed – that was that, Then suddenly we had the walk-out. It was pretty indicative of a lot of teachers' attitudes that a third of them resigned. Some had to, but the others – they weren't all white, either – just couldn't accept the changes. Seems they didn't want live pupils.'

'So do you think the school's facilities and the chances it offers are now up to average?'

'Well, that's the big issue – not yet and it still looks a long way off. So many anomalies survive, yet the official line is hardening – from the city and state authorities. They feel they've already lost face and they don't want to lose any more – that's their way of defining it. If they took a closer look, maybe they'd see it differently. Lots of things aren't good enough still – the inadequate money and facilities we're given and the tokenism in everything. The community's very aware of it, including the pupils. Like in my course – I have to get official approval for all the literature I use and my suggestions are often rejected. They'll ask me questions like: "Mr Johnson, how does this book" – Baldwin, say – "how does this book contribute to the pupil's awareness of his duties as a citizen? To a respect for law and order, for example?" No kidding, that's typical, with reference to almost everything, even where it's irrelevant. So how do you negotiate between that type of attitude and the needs and demands of the kids – those guys are living in another world. And the kids are impatient, they won't take it much longer. It gets me down, standing between them and seeing how it'll probably end, with the kids getting trapped in a clash of forces. I mean if the black revolution in the schools comes to a full confrontation. It'll make it impossible to get through to them like we do now – as individuals – which I think has to continue, for change to achieve anything. I'm not for holding them back unless they look like busting their necks – after all, they got things moving and official attitudes aren't in touch with reality. But I'm afraid the resistance will destroy their openness or at least make it very hard to sustain. It's going that way. Among staff and parents and pupils. And of course with encouragement from the black movements.' He grins. 'Pretty soon they'll see me as a regular Uncle Tom. A lot of them, especially the bright ones, already feel that dialogue's useless – that things can only be improved in so far as they fight for more power, in school and out of it. And fight is the word, if necessary. You can't blame them. Experience proves it. I just hope there aren't too many bones to pick up.'

'Do you think I could meet some of them?'

'Sure – if you can take the hostility. Ask for Mr Lewis in the classroom over there – a lot of his class are BSU kids. Tell him I sent you.'

It's just above a milling courtyard where hundreds of students are taking a break. But not from Mr Lewis's class, which is more like a study group, its concentration the more intense for its contrast with the crowd below; though the crowd, in the last analysis, gives the concentration its meaning. They're only a handful, reading, talking and asking the occasional question, but their manner suggests they identify strongly both with their teacher and with each other. A bit older than the pupils in the previous classes, they seem very sharp and select. Like many a bright sixth form in its own sanctuary, perhaps, except in what they're reading, mostly Fanon and commentaries on him; and the single picture on the wall – a black man holding a gun high.

Mr Lewis is a cool, challenging man, like a mixture of Malcolm X and an urbane Harvard graduate. In terms of the logic of what he says, he shouldn't have much time to talk to me, but he does so volubly and rides the contradiction easily. Perhaps here at least my being foreign does give me a certain licence as he's more teasing than garrulous, more probing than aggressive towards me. The students too are perfectly restrained, though perhaps they take their cue from him. It seems that Mr Johnson's warning about their likely hostility was no more accurate than Phyllis's – they're much too concerned with their talking and reading to take any special notice of me; as if neither of them has quite realized, Mr Johnson even within the school, how far the new militancy is not a vulgarization but a rationalization of the previous one. And in having assumed that he was right, it seems I too need teaching twice that objectivity and not cliché is the order of the day.

This is apparently the lesson that Mr Lewis sets out to convey. 'So you came to find out what's going on? But suppose you do – the bare facts – what makes you think you'll understand them? For instance – how would you describe yourself? As a liberal, radical, or what?'

'I wouldn't – I'm outside the situation, so I'm hardly in any position to judge it. I guess I'm just a snooper. Who came of his own accord, though.'

He taps the desk thoughtfully, obviously enjoying his strategy of interviewing the interviewer. The pupils meanwhile go on working, just glancing up occasionally at odd points in the conversation to which they're half listening. 'Well, that's a fairly honest answer. I find that most white intellectuals wriggle like worms when you put that to them. "It depends what you mean", "if this", "if that". But whether you like to admit it or not, you obviously do come with a white liberal or radical outlook. And though those two are very different, it doesn't much matter which it is for the purpose of understanding us – all of us here in this room. Whichever it is, you have to drop it, drop everything, if you're to see how we see things. Begin again. Wash your mind out.' He taps one of the boys on the shoulder. 'Perry – tell this gentleman what you think about white liberals.' He smiles. 'If I understand him correctly, you needn't be afraid of hurting his feelings. You don't have to quote me either.'

Perry: 'I won't quote anybody. But I'd say a white liberal is more dangerous than a Klansman. They're travelling salesmen – "Buy a tomorrow, it's going to be lovely". They look at us without seeing us even, they're so full of telling us not to rock the boat, that crap. Only thing worse is a black liberal – he should know better.' He goes back to his reading.

CH: 'And what about white radicals like the Students for a Democratic Society? After all, their views of things are closer to yours than the average liberal's – how do you stand in relation to them?'

Lewis: 'In a similar position, maybe. But not in the same one, though other people, like Cleaver, think so. Certainly as far as I'm concerned black nationalists can't stand with them. What the radicals are saying is that they want to subvert the society so as to alter the way it works, while the liberal just wants to improve it. But we're not concerned with any of that, we're concerned with survival. Survival. Can you understand that? Time's shown that white society won't concede us anything basic and that we ourselves can't change it as Martin Luther King hoped. So that society's no longer our problem, as it is for white revolutionaries. We just want to get away from it. By weakening it, they make that easier and that far we coincide. But our goal is power, black power, outside the society, which is the only place we can get it. Which means local power in the black communities. And that's what we're waiting for, all of us here.'

CH: 'But LA isn't exactly a likely place to concede it, is it?'

Lewis: 'It certainly isn't. But that's not the question. Nowhere in this society would give its black community power. You see, you're just thinking liberal, that because white New York is more liberal, black prospects are better than here. But even there they're still limited – so it's black attitudes, not the white ones, that matter, and in this respect LA's better placed.' (He nods at the window.) 'Look out there. Then think back over driving down here, what you saw. Think about it.'

CH: 'Well?'

Lewis: 'Did you see any white people? D'you see any now?'

CH: 'No – '

Lewis: 'And you're in the heart of LA. It's a black city. Black and Chicano. Drive fifty blocks from here and you'll hardly see a white face outside a squad car. And in this it's like most American cities, increasingly so. White people don't live here, they live in the suburbs. They're doing it for us – blacks don't have to take the city. We just have to hold it – see what I mean? Most blacks know this now.'

CH: 'So suppose you do have power – as you already have a community. Its being black doesn't say how it works. Is it just going to be a black USA? Or socialist? And segregated?'

Lewis (laughing): 'There you go, real white thinking. You're a good specimen for the kids. Rationalize, calculate, plan – it bears no relation to the realities. You've already forgotten what I said. Survival. That belongs to the present. There are plenty of differing views about what the black community should become, economically and socially – lots of black power people are the only straight-thinking integrationists I know, for instance. But we're all agreed on the first step – to create the conditions for the functioning of the black community as a community: which means power, right now. That's what you can never grasp. You ever saw a black kid handling a car for the first time? A white kid's going to take it apart and put it all together again before he even starts to drive it. But a black kid jumps in and goes. It's the difference between talk and action. You're embedded in talk, plans. We're ready for action, we've no other choice. We'll plan again when we can and have to.'

CH: 'But your black and white kids are pretty simple stereotypes, aren't they? For instance, it doesn't strike me that the black one would apply to your pupils.'

Lewis: 'No, they're not stereotypes, because I'm not talking of character – I'm talking of rational responses to two very different situations. They show the difference, that's why I used them. The black kid's never had a car, this one probably isn't his, and if it is the cops will soon get him. He's got nothing to gain by taking it apart and little to lose by smashing it. So he makes the most of it. Right in the present. And that's where we stand. Suppose we start debating step two – then we lose step one, which we're all agreed on. It has to be power first and just getting it is a full-time concern. Just that alone is a big step forward, for American blacks to conceive of power as a possibility, let alone a necessity. You know in 1965, when we had the riots here, the blacks were so brainwashed that when they were driving cars full of loot they actually waited at the stop lights! That's how far we had to go before conceiving of more than anger. But things move fast. Blacks now know what power means. And they know it's possible. Including everyone in this room.'

CH: 'You mean in terms of the school or beyond it?'

Lewis: 'Both, because the school reflects what's happening in the community. Which means that next time there's trouble here they won't just walk out again. They'll take the teachers they object to and put them on the sidewalk. Why not? The

BSU certainly see it that way, as a part of the whole set-up. That's partly why they've moved off campus to concentrate on the community. And they're learning what power entails, its psychology and its tactics. They're not performing any more, that initial phase is finished. That's why you don't see so many of them now with Castro jackets or Black Power buttons. Because if they advertise themselves, if they stick their necks out, the cops will pick them off like flies when the showdown begins. If you want to use a gun in a city, you don't go waving it around beforehand.'

Then, for almost the first time except when a pupil's come up with questions, he pauses, watching them for a moment. If it's them he's referring to, he's right; few of them sport black power symbols. And aside from his interpretation, their confidence wouldn't seem to require them. They look as if they've long since moved beyond the air of boisterous liberation which still reigns in the corridors and the courtyard right below.

Lewis: 'They're secretive even with me these days. I guess they've worked it out for themselves, half the time I don't know what they're up to. But the next time anything happens, they'll be ready for it all right.'

It's their naturalness which makes what he says at once faintly unearthly yet doubly real. The fact that their manner is so much that of any intelligent teenagers: and that at the same time it leaves no doubt as to their seriousness. As he says, there's no performance to it; but for the two teachers' comments, it could be quite hard to tell whether they are studying Fanon with reference to the streets of Watts or for a public examination. Is Lewis justified in speaking for them as he has? In their pre-occupation, they themselves give little away. But as he's described it, and credibly, this in itself is an affirmation. Certainly they've raised no objection to anything he's said, all in their hearing. And their unostentatiousness already gives them a quality of freedom in a way so un-American, because it's not institutionalized, that it feels as if the revolution with which they're concerned has already occurred on their own, private level. Ironic: that their very spontaneity, this quality of having been saved from the social contortions around them, should mark them off as that much closer to the eye of whatever storm may be coming. Some of them seventeen or eighteen; but certainly no more than that.

One girl in particular, whose looks are as striking as they're natural, is an incarnation of this air of freedom. Sitting with her back to us, she gets up every now and then to check something at the desk behind her, so that her face is held forward at different angles in successive moments, not very far from where we're talking. She wears very little makeup, just her eyes slightly pencilled. Her hair, which isn't straightened at all as generations of Negro hair have been straightened all over the New World, is also worn naturally short and so describes the round of her head; and while this round isn't perfect and her head is rather big for her slight figure, it's hard to believe she'd have looked this way had she been born a few years earlier, before this freedom of mind existed. If she had escaped the traditional, obligatory contradiction of her own particular beauty, it would only have been at home in private, informal moments. And she's that much more authentic in that her face isn't classically Negro: brown-skinned, big eyes and a rather pixie-like oval shape, not stunning except in its uniqueness but as soon as this is glimpsed very hard to look away from. Not because of the negritude of the style she's adopted, this being slight and incidental, but because of the freshness of her seeming freedom from any image, from being anything other than herself, unrepeatable.

A face that haunts me (remember how often I mentioned it?) not just after leaving Watts but for many of the several weeks and thousands of miles still ahead, so that much which occurs in them recedes behind it in recollection, its telling superfluous to the point which the impact of this face represents in an experience of this kind. Which I should continue, rather, if I could, with some foreknowledge of her future, so independent and yet so close to the unpredictable heart of things, or from the future of anyone like her, youngish and with a touch of new vision – to know what lies ahead for all.